Cumbrian Communities and their Railways No. 4

Whitehaven

The Railways and Waggonways
of a Unique Cumberland Port

Howard Quayle

Other publications by the Cumbrian Railways Association in their 'Cumbrian Communities' Series:

- No. 1   Grange-over-Sands *(L R Gilpin)*
- No. 2   Ravenglass *(P van Zeller)*
- No. 3   Dalton-in-Furness *(E R Battye)*

Text © Howard Quayle and the Cumbrian Railways Association

Maps © Alan Johnstone and the Cumbrian Railways Association

Photographs © as credited

**Published by the Cumbrian Railways Association,
104 Durley Avenue, Pinner, Middlesex. HA5 1JH**

**The Association is a Registered Charity No. 1025436
www.cumbrianrailwaysassociation.org.uk**

Membership Secretary, 36 Clevelands Avenue, Barrow-in-Furness, Cumbria LA14 5SL

Design and layout by Michael Peascod

Printed by Lambert Print & Design, Settle, North Yorkshire. BD24 9AA

ISBN 0-9540232-5-0

All rights reserved. No part of this publication may be reproduced, stored in a retrieval system or transmitted in any form or by any means, electronic, mechanical, photocopying, recoding or otherwise without prior permission in writing from the publisher.

The Cumbrian Railways Association is the local railway history group for Cumbria and North Lancashire. With a membership of around 400 it is a registered charity with the aim of promoting interest in and knowledge of the railways of this area, and the part they played in its development over the last 150 years.

Contents

	Introduction	5
1	Early Whitehaven: *The Pre-Industrial Period*	7
2	Whitehaven: *The Town and Industry Develop*	9
3	Early Waggonways: *The Howgill Colliery*	13
4	Early Waggonways: *The Whingill Colliery*	21
5	The Coming of the Railway: *The Whitehaven Junction Railway*	29
6	Towards the South: *The Whitehaven & Furness Junction Railway*	33
7	Ore from the Iron Moor: *The Whitehaven, Cleator & Egremont Railway*	39
8	Consolidation of the Railways: *Its Effect on Whitehaven*	43
9	Industrial Railways: *The Harbour*	49
10	Industrial Railways: *The Inclines and Other Lines*	57
11	The Main Lines: *From Consolidation into the Twentieth Century*	73
12	The Main Lines: *From Grouping to Nationalisation and Beyond*	83
13	Whitehaven: *Into the Twenty-First Century*	95
	Postscript - The Cumbrian Coast Line and Whitehaven Today Dr Paul Salveson	96
	Chronology of the Railways and Town of Whitehaven	97
	Acknowledgements	99
	Bibliography	100
	Index	101

Front cover:
  A coloured postcard showing the view of Whitehaven from Bransty Hill. In the right foreground is part of the carriage sheds at Bransty station. This area of the town is dominated by the Grand Hotel, which in part also acted as offices for the Whitehaven & Furness Junction Railway. In the middle distance is the town itself, with its usual pall of smoke from industrial and domestic activity alike. Beyond lies the ridge of the Howgill Colliery, with Wellington Pit at its northern end. (Alan Johnstone collection)

Mathias Read's famous painting 'Bird's Eye View of Whitehaven 1738'. On the hillside above the town, in the middle distance, the relatively new Parker Waggonway can be seen gradually descending, from left to right, to the harbour staithes. The junction with the more steeply-graded Saltom Waggonway (opened in 1735) can just be seen as the Parker route approaches the harbour. Note the 'byeway' of the Saltom route, climbing away from the staithe before being turned to run parallel to a wall and rejoin the waggonway. In the town itself, St Nicholas and Holy Trinity churches are clearly visible, as well as Whitehaven Castle (far left). Across the Irish Sea is the Isle of Man (right of centre).
(From a photograph supplied by The Beacon, Whitehaven)

Introduction

Today's visitor to Whitehaven sees a planned town of 18th century houses, a pedestrian promenade running the length of the old port, colourful sailing craft moored in the South Harbour, and, to the north, the distinctive hills of south-west Scotland. He or she may have arrived by rail, from either the Carlisle or Barrow directions, at Bransty's modest but still staffed station, having enjoyed a journey over what is undoubtedly one of Britain's most scenic coastal routes.

A walk alongside the South Harbour towards the Old Quay, however, reveals another side of Whitehaven, as the monumental chimney of Wellington Pit, known locally as 'The Candlestick' comes into view. Coal, mined locally since the 13th century, was the fuel on which Whitehaven's prosperity was founded, but few traces of this industry now remain, although less than a quarter of a century has elapsed since the last Whitehaven coal mine was in production and since coal was being shipped by sea to Ireland from the harbour.

Railways or waggonways have always played a significant role in the transport of coal, with Whitehaven being among the earliest of the pioneers, a crude wooden track being recorded in the Ginns as early as 1683. Later lines, such as the Whitehaven Junction and the Whitehaven & Furness Junction Railways, while undoubtedly having been built to transport the mineral wealth of the area, were instrumental in providing new and faster transport links to the rest of the country, and played a role in lessening the isolation of this corner of north-west England.

Specific books on Whitehaven's harbour, coal mining and chemical industries, and architecture have been published at various times over the years, but this is the first publication to focus on the area's railways and industrial waggonways. I hope that it provides a worthy addition to already published works on the town of which Norman Nicholson, the Cumberland playwright and poet, once wrote: *Whitehaven is unquestionably the capital of industrial Cumberland. Few mining towns have a more exciting history; none have greater character.* He was right.

Howard Quayle, Bury St. Edmunds.   October 2007

Guard's view from the rear cab of a Carlisle-bound DMU as it leaves Bransty on 4 May 1973. In the foreground, the fresh ballasting in front of the catch-points indicates the diagonal flat crossing of the Parton Waggonway, which had been removed a number of years previously. On the left, the Furness line runs through Platforms 2 and 3 into Whitehaven Tunnel, while the London & North Western Railway's single platform is in the centre. A rake of loaded coal wagons awaits collection alongside the LNWR line.   (CRA Photo Library ref. MON038C)

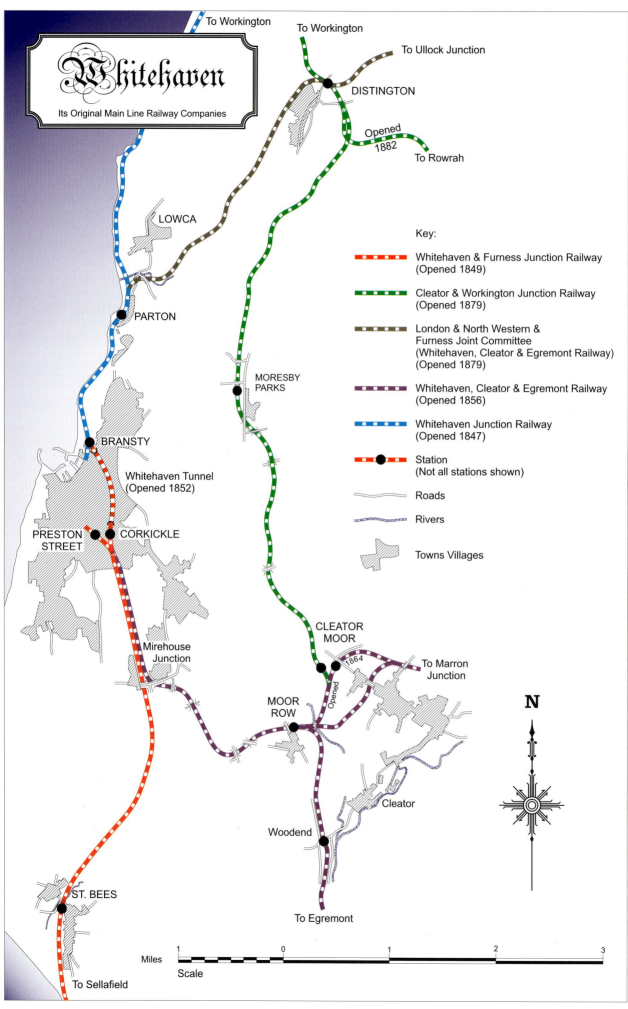

Early Whitehaven:
The Pre-Industrial Period

AN EXCELLENT description of the location and site of Whitehaven is given in the 1828-9 edition of Pigot & Co.'s 'National Commercial Directory' for Cumberland, Lancashire, and Westmorland:

Whitehaven, the principal sea port in Cumberland ... in the ward of Allerdale above Derwent, is 320 miles from London, 41 from Carlisle, 35 from Penrith, 15 from Cockermouth and Maryport, 8 from Workington, and 6 from Egremont. The town is seated in a remarkable creek, overlooked by high ground on three sides. From the south, the town makes the best appearance, commanding a view of the interior of the streets, the harbour, and the castle belonging to the Earl of Lonsdale ... In 1556, the town is said to have had only six houses, subsequently being supported by the fostering hand of the Lowthers.

However, the origins of Whitehaven pre-date this description by almost two thousand years. While it is generally accepted that the name 'Whitehaven' has Scandinavian roots, the first settlements in the area were established before the period of Danish occupation, and were probably made south of the existing town, around present-day St Bees. According to the historian R G Collingwood, writing in 1928 in 'Cumberland and Westmorland Antiquarian and Archaeological Society Transactions', the physical western end of Hadrian's Wall may have been at Bowness-on-Solway, but an extended line of defence continued down the Irish Sea coast. Collingwood contended that this chain of signal stations and so-called 'mile forts' extended as far as St Bees Head, and that this was the actual western end of Hadrian's great barrier.

This great mass of red sandstone, with its two headlands, North Head and South Head, rising precipitously to a height of more than 300 feet above the sea, has long provided shelter from the prevailing west winds to settlements in its lee, and it is possible that some form of settlement to service the Roman fortification would have existed by the 2nd century AD. What is more definite was the establishment of a Benedictine nunnery, around 650, dedicated to the Irish St Bega, who was allegedly shipwrecked on the neighbouring coastline.

At some date before 900, the Danes, having first sacked Carlisle, destroyed the nunnery as they continued to settle in Cumberland, and the name 'Whitehaven' most probably originated around this period. 'The Place Names of Cumberland', published by the English Place Names Society, states that the Scandinavian name for the small harbour, north of Saltom Bay, was '*hvithofudhafri*', which translates as '*hvit*' (white) – '*hofud*' (headland) – '*hafri*' (harbour or haven), and that *Whit-toft-haven is a creek ... at the north end ... of a rising hill ... washed with the flood on the west side ... where there is a great rock or quarry*. This appears an apt description of the topography of the site of the future settlement.

Even today, north-west Cumbria, facing out to the Solway Firth and the Irish Sea, is relatively isolated from the rest of the United Kingdom. A thousand years earlier, the Norman Conquest in 1066 had no initial impact on what had by then become an outpost of the Kingdom of Scotland. Within fifty years, however, Norman influence had extended its tentacles to all corners of the kingdom, when Henry I (1100-1135) created the baronies of Allerdale, Wigton, Levington, Greystoke and Coupland.

Coupland was given to the Norman baron, William Meschin, who founded the Priory of St Bees in 1120 in the settlement of Kirkby Becoc: this suggests that a village had grown up around the original nunnery ('Kirkby Becoc' translates as 'St Bega's Church'), and that the establishment of the priory was continuing this monastic tradition. In his book, 'Whitehaven: A Short History', Daniel Hay writes: *the establishment of the Priory saw the inauguration of ... record keeping, which enables us to form a fair idea of what Whitehaven ... between the Conquest and the Reformation was like. It formed part of a scattered rural community which raised* [animals] *and maintained one or two minor industries*. These records make it clear that Whitehaven's boundaries extended from the mouth of the Pow Beck (or Poe River), along its eastern bank (now in culvert) to roughly the proximity of the present 'Focus Store' in Preston Street (close to Coach Road). From there the boundary moved eastwards across to the tiny Midgey Ghyll and along the front line of Whitehaven Castle, continuing along the present High Street and Wellington Row to the mouth of Bransty Beck. It is interesting that, more than 700 years later, John Wood's 1830 plan of the town showed its boundaries to be virtually unchanged.

There is evidence that coal – the 'Black Gold' of Whitehaven – was being mined in the area as early as the late 13th century, probably around Greenbank in the Manor of Arrowthwaite, about 1½ miles south of the town, but these coal seams are likely to have been worked only spasmodically. Additionally, the seams dipped to the west, which meant that these early miners would quickly have encountered water, limiting the depth of any shaft or the length of an adit. In any case, demand appeared to have been fairly limited, with most used as fuel for the salt pans along the coast. Oliver Wood, in his scholarly work 'West Cumberland Coal 1600-1982/3', notes that coal was required by immigrant German miners smelting copper near Keswick in the mid-16th century: *They used both coal and charcoal ... and were complaining that their operations were seriously handicapped by a lack of fuel*. However, early supplies came from the Workington area, where the harbour exported coal to Dublin and the Irish coastal towns for a number of years, although these shipments had declined by the end of the 17th century.

The decline of the Workington coal industry was mirrored by the rise of Whitehaven as an important mining centre. The dissolution of the monasteries, under Henry VIII in 1538, resulted in the transfer of the lands of St Bees Priory, first to Sir William Leigh, and then, in 1553, to the Chaloner family, who knew of the existence of the coal seams under their property but made little effort to exploit them.

After 1553, title to the estates changed on several occasions, but the most significant came in 1630, when title was transferred to Sir John Lowther (1581-1637) for £2,450. Sir John appointed his second son, Sir Christopher Lowther (1611-1644) as steward of the Whitehaven estate. The two Lowthers quickly moved to exploit the coal reserves, records showing that commercial sales were taking place as early as 1632, with 2,400 tons being sold in 1636.

Sir Christopher was the first creator of the Lowther family fortunes in the Whitehaven area. Apart from converting the mouth of the Pow Beck into a harbour by building a pier in 1634 (the basis of the later commodious harbour), he bought much land in and around the present town, and expanded trade with Dublin, not just in coal, but also in fish, tanned hides, tallow and other commodities. The relatively small ships then available were a constraint on the coal export trade, although a primitive mining industry, again using adits and again experiencing drainage problems, had been established roughly along the line of the Low Road running from the Ginns district of Whitehaven towards St Bees.

Chapter One

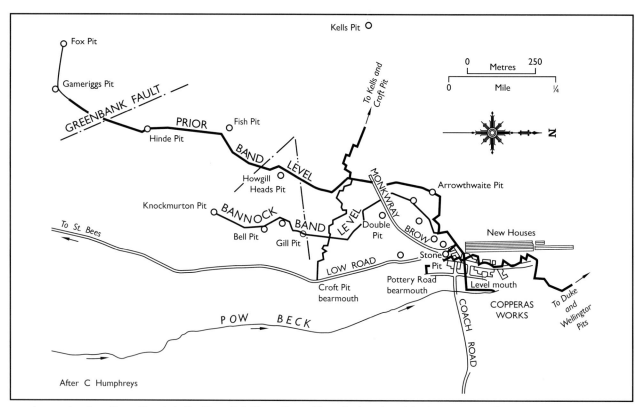

A map showing pits and levels in the Howgill Colliery. Stone Pit, at the junction of the Low Road (to St Bees) and Coach Road, acted as the drainage sump for the Prior Band and Bannock Band Levels. Note that the sump discharged into the Pow Beck, using the level constructed by Sir John Lowther in 1663. Coal was being extracted at Arrowthwaite as early as 1272.
(Original from 'Old Lakeland' by J D Marshall, redrawn by Alan Johnstone)

After the death of Sir Christopher in 1644, his two-year old son, Sir John Lowther, succeeded to the baronetcy. Initially in the care of a guardian, Sir John gained day-to-day control of the estates in 1660, after which, according to Wood, *this man of considerable energy and foresight ... quickly* [acquired] *coal-bearing land which he worked systematically and skilfully.* Sir John was far-sighted in many ways, not least of which was his appreciation of the economies of scale which single ownership of the coalfields would bring to this Whitehaven industry: a contemporary publication noted that *Where people have but the Coals of a smal* [sic] *compass, they can work it to little or no advantage: the Colliery can be but wrought in part: the best of the Coals are drown'd & lost.*

Sir John understood the technicalities of draining shafts by means of levels, and using engines to draw water from coal seams below level. After initially driving a main adit, in 1663, into the Bannock Band, about 100 ft. above the Main Band (again in the Ginns area), his technical knowledge allowed him to drive vertical shafts, ranging in depth from 60 ft. to 180 ft., into the Bannock Band, the coal being drawn to the surface by jackrolls (hand-worked windlasses). Sir John eventually combined the separate shafts into a single system, gravity-drained via levels, between 1680 and 1705 (the year before his death), and named this complex the Howgill colliery.

Sir John's last engineering achievement was his working of the lower Main Band seam, which, like the other seams, dipped in a westerly direction, creating a severe drainage problem as it was followed downwards. The solution was to build an underground level, below the limit of free drainage, discharging into a sump at the foot of a pit shaft, from where the water was raised mechanically by a chain pump operated by a 'cog and rung' gin: it is likely that this is how the locality, the 'Ginns', got its name. The sump was constructed in Stone Pit (located at the foot of the present-day Monkwray Brow junction leading up to Kells), historically important as the site where atmospheric pumping was first attempted in north-west England, in 1717.

Until late in the 17th century, coal handling was relatively crude, being loaded into 'corves' (circular baskets made from hazel rods) at the coal face, and then tipped into carts, or bagged for pack-horse transport, at the mouth of the shaft, for transport to Whitehaven Harbour. This mode of operation may have been adequate for an annual 2400-ton output, but towards the end of the century, production from the pits was averaging 20,000 tons per annum, 96% of which was shipped from the harbour, mainly to Dublin.

The proposed solution for speeding-up transport between pithead and harbour was made in 1682 by John Gale, Sir John Lowther's colliery manager. Gale proposed *making a Causey* [causeway] *... which ... he presently Sett on 14 Carts ... each 4 bags apeece & for their more ready dispatch had Slings fastened to them, so that they had nothing to doe but let down the Tackle and hoyse them up Immediately.* This will be described more fully in Chapter 3, but briefly, a 'causeway' in this context was a roadway of parallel timbers, upon which the wheels of a waggon could run, thus preventing their sinking into soft ground. The 'causeway' was constructed in 1683, and ran from Woodagreen Pit (sunk in 1679 near the Ginns) to the harbour. Although a 'first' for the Cumberland coalfield, it was not in any sense a pioneer causeway, as examples of this transport mode had already been constructed on Tyneside between 1605 and 1608.

Sir John died in 1706, having achieved much in his lifetime. M Davies-Shiel and J D Marshall, in their book 'Industrial Archaeology of the Lake Counties', noted that *By the end of Sir John's* [life], *Whitehaven was established as a port of consequence. In 1693, when St. Nicholas Church was rebuilt, the population of the town* [was] *2,222, and by 1702, it had reached nearly 3000.* By comparison, the population of Carlisle in 1698 was only 996. At the end of the 17th century, output from the Whitehaven coalfield was 40,000 tons per annum and increasing.

It now lay to the next generation of this energetic dynasty to make their mark on both the urban and the industrial landscape of West Cumberland.

Whitehaven:
The Town and Industry Develop

2

AFTER GAINING CONTROL of his estates in 1660, Sir John Lowther began the process of what can best be described as 'controlled expansion' of the town of Whitehaven, pushing north from the old settlement. By the time of Sir John's death in 1706, the whole area was commercially confident, with coal output increasing and with a flourishing base of mining-support industries. Increased demand for coal meant increasing trade with Ireland, resulting in an increase in vessels based in the port (the town's fleet rose from 32 ships in 1676 to 77 thirty years later), and gave rise to Whitehaven's shipbuilding industry.

To sell his coal in Ireland, Lowther was in competition with the colliery owners of Ayrshire, Flintshire, Pembrokeshire and Lancashire, but by 1675 he had driven most of his rivals out of the Dublin market, mainly through competitive pricing. William Gilpin, Lowther's chief steward, seems to have been responsible for monitoring the Irish coal market, noting, in January 1695, that Scottish competition was the most to be feared, although the quality was much lower than that of Cumberland coal. The Irish market was critical for the Whitehaven collieries: in 1695, 93.3% of production was exported to Ireland, and in 1705 (the year before Sir John's death) the situation was virtually unchanged, with 33,426 tons mined and 85.4% exported across the Irish Sea.

Merchant trade in Whitehaven was also expanding. In the 1670s, the first cargo of tobacco was imported from Virginia, this American colony, together with Maryland, becoming the main sources for the town's tobacco trade. It is difficult now to imagine that Whitehaven once had a thriving trade in the importation of tobacco, although, at the beginning of the eighteenth century, it was one of the few ports in the country allowed to handle the commodity. This trade was substantial, 16% of tobacco consumed in England and Wales being imported through the Cumberland town.

As well as being sold in the domestic market, tobacco could be bartered for other goods, and this gave rise to a thriving trade between Whitehaven and the Baltic countries (for imported timber, hemp and tar) and, more controversially, those West African settlements where the slave trade flourished.

Against this background, it was not surprising that a fine new town developed at Whitehaven. Dr William Rollinson, in his book 'A History of Cumberland and Westmorland', opined that while *Sir Nikolaus Pevsner has called Whitehaven 'the earliest post-medieval planned town in England', it is also arguably the first planned town of the Industrial Revolution.*

Once more, it was the dynamism of the Lowthers which lay behind the new model town. Sir John Lowther had been succeeded by his second son James, who was responsible, in 1708, for incorporating the Town and Harbour Trustees through an Act of Parliament. Taking effect on 25 March 1709, this Act was of major importance to the history of Whitehaven, as it formed the basis for all subsequent developments of both town and harbour. The Act also specified the harbour works to be undertaken, which can be summarised as completing and finishing *the New Mole ... and to make a Counter Mole and Head on the North East side of the Harbour, to strengthen and repair the Pier with a new Bulwark ... and to cleanse and deepen the said Harbour.* Additionally, the Act defined the duties on commodities handled through the harbour, coal exports attracting $\frac{1}{2}$d per ton: imports attracted varying rates of duty, such as 3d per hogshead of tobacco and 1d per barrel of herrings.

The Trustees numbered seven, and were headed by James Lowther. The Act also provided for fourteen other positions on the Board, drawn from the local merchant classes. The first members included familiar local names such as Peter Senhouse, Thomas Lutwidge, and Robert Biglands. The Board of Trustees was responsible for the development of the town and harbour until 1894, when Whitehaven was incorporated as a borough. Having succeeded to the baronetcy in 1731, Sir James performed eminent public service, as a Cumberland MP, Vice-Admiral of the county, and alderman of Carlisle.

The basis of the new town was the grid-iron layout, best shown in Mathias Reed's remarkable 1738 painting 'Bird's-Eye View of Whitehaven', which can still be seen at Holker Hall – today the estate is the property of the Cavendish family, but at that time it belonged to Sir William Lowther. Dr R W Brunskill, in his book 'Traditional Buildings of Cumbria', emphasises that: *Although Whitehaven was a planned town in the sense that its street layout was determined and maintained by the Lowthers, the houses ... were built by individual owners to traditional designs.* There has always been some speculation that Sir John's scheme for a planned town was not his own, but was developed through a possible relationship with his contemporary, Sir Christopher Wren.

The first elements of the grid developed under Sir John's stewardship, with the building of the north-to-south King Street paralleling the line of the harbour, followed by the east-to-west Lowther Street, the town's main thoroughfare, which ran from the harbour to The Flatt, the home of the Lowther family. Purchased by Sir John in 1675 and extended twenty years later, The Flatt (or Flatt Hall) was totally rebuilt in 1769/1770 as a castellated mansion by a later Lowther, Sir James, now Earl of Lonsdale, and became known as Whitehaven Castle. The building of Duke Street created a central square, bounded to the west by Church Street and to the east by Queen Street, in which the new St Nicholas' Church was built in 1693, replacing an earlier smaller chapel. A third church on the site, in red sandstone, was erected in 1883, but was demolished, apart from its tower, after a fire in 1971. The north-east end of Queen Street rises up to a hill, on which sits Whitehaven's most beautiful church, St James's, built in 1752/1753 to the design of Carlisle Spedding. (Spedding was chief steward of the Lowther estates in the Whitehaven area and a highly talented mining engineer, whose work will be covered more fully in later chapters.) The interior of the church, with its galleries on three sides supported on Tuscan columns, was described by Pevsner as the finest Georgian church interior in the county of Cumberland.

Eighteenth-century domestic architecture was (and happily continues to be) well-represented in Whitehaven. Pevsner described No. 14 Scotch Street (now solicitors' offices) as the finest house in Whitehaven, with its classically proportioned doorway five steps above street level in order to avoid flooding. Pevsner dates the house as mid-18th century: it certainly appears on John Howard's 1790 map, and scrutiny of Matthias Read's famous painting suggests the existence of a house on this site in 1738. At the easternmost end of Duke Street, the elegant Somerset House was built in 1750 by Samuel Martin, a Whitehaven merchant who traded with the American colonies. Its most noteworthy feature is its Gothic porch, once again reached by a pair of matching stairways. A Georgian theatre, modelled on the Theatre Royal in Bath, was opened in 1769 in Roper Street, and, although the interior was modernised in 1909, it still, according to Pevsner, retained *the mood of Georgian theatres in small towns.* Sadly, this building was demolished around 1970.

9

Chapter Two

While Whitehaven cannot rival the larger planned towns from the same period, such as Bath and Edinburgh, its architectural significance lies in its successful integration of what can best be termed a 'Cumbrian vernacular' style into the Grecian characteristics of the Georgian era. This provides probably the finest example of the regional adaptation of a building style in the whole North-West of England.

Sir James Lowther's dynamism in town planning was equalled by his skill and foresight in making Whitehaven Colliery one of the leading coal-mining complexes in the country. Oliver Wood describes him as *a shrewd, clear-minded business man continually in pursuit of money ...* [using] *twentieth-century methods against eighteenth-century competitors*. Nonetheless, he could not have succeeded as an entrepreneur, especially in view of his long stays in London as a Cumberland MP, if he had not been well supported by a long line of able land agents resident in the county, beginning with the previously-mentioned William Gilpin (born in 1657), who had succeeded Thomas Tickell as chief steward to Sir John Lowther in 1693.

It was, however, the innovative Spedding family who most successfully promoted the Lowther interests and who overcame the challenges posed by deep mining in the eighteenth century. The first of this family to settle in Cumberland, Edward Spedding came from Scotland in the 1680s, taking office as chief steward to the Lowthers. His son, John Spedding (1685 to 1758), entered the service of the Lowther family in 1700, working alongside John Gale, Sir John's colliery manager. Whatever the reason, it had become clear that Gale had lost his employer's confidence, and he was dismissed in 1707, soon after Sir John's death, with John Spedding now taking sole charge of the Lowther collieries. Here output was continually rising, and more than 35,000 tons were shipped from the port in the year ending in March 1708. In 1722, Richard Gilpin succeeded his father as chief steward, but like Gale, he eventually lost the support of the Lowthers, and in 1730 was succeeded by John Spedding in this role. In his book 'Old Lakeland', Dr J D Marshall described Spedding as *an immensely able and dedicated man, somewhat obsessed with the complexities of his task, slow to make up his mind, and rather a worrier.*

Described by Wood as the greatest of all the Whitehaven mining engineers, Carlisle Spedding, John Spedding's younger brother, was also recruited into the Lowther enterprises in 1710 at the age of fifteen. While the younger Spedding was learning his mining skills, John was spending more time on assessing potential solutions to drainage at deep level, and was instrumental in negotiating a licence for the use of Thomas Newcomen's steam pumping engine, at a cost of £182 per annum. This was ordered in November 1715 and fully commissioned in March 1717 under the supervision of the famous inventor's partner John Calley, extracting water from the shallow shaft at Stone Pit, which had been sunk into the Prior Band in 1701. Little documentation exists on Calley, who died near Leeds nine months after the pumping engine was commissioned, although Marshall concluded that his contributions to engineering and economic development were just as significant as those of Newcomen himself.

When John Spedding became Sir James Lowther's chief steward in 1730, Carlisle Spedding replaced him as manager of the Lowther collieries, in which role he undertook his most noteworthy project, the sinking of Saltom Pit, which involved not only pumping from the unprecedented depth of 456 ft., but was the first instance of undersea working from the coast near Whitehaven.

The historic nature of this now half-forgotten mine, whose pithead stood only 20 ft. above the Irish Sea, should not be underestimated. Davies-Shiel and Marshall commented that this *monument to Carlisle Spedding ... is indicative of the progress of local and national mining technology in a broad sense*. Sinking began in March 1730, with the first coal mined in February 1732. During the sinking of the shaft, Spedding discovered a powerful methane 'blower' (gas escaping through a crack), which he piped to the pithead and offered to the Town and Harbour Trustees for town lighting: the offer was not taken up. Further experiments during construction resulted in Spedding's 'steel mill', a device which allowed underground illumination through a shower of sparks, and which would therefore not ignite firedamp. The importance of this device is reflected in the fact that it was not superseded until the invention of the Davy lamp in 1815, almost a century later.

Additionally, deep-level mining brought problems of ventilation not experienced in the relatively shallow Howgill pits, where the inter-connection of adits, levels and shafts provided an adequate air current. Spedding solved this problem with a ventilation system known as 'coursing the air', a system of sheets and boards, installed to force incoming air down one side of the underground roadways, and by a return route along another side. This method was linked to the oval-shaped split shaft, another Spedding invention, the landward half of which was used for drawing-up the coal by means of a horse gin, and the seaward half for steam-powered pumping, using what Davies-Shiel and Marshall described as an unusually large version of the Newcomen engine, drawing water from the full depth of 456 ft. using four pumps with cisterns, each capable of lifting water through 114 ft.

However, the problem with Saltom Pit was its location close to the Irish Sea shore, at the foot of (and hemmed in by) steep cliffs. A three-storey staithe was already in use at Whitehaven harbour, construction work having started in 1732, on land along the West Wharf, and being completed the following year. The term 'staithe' (or 'staith') generally referred to wooden jetties and the associated coal chutes for loading vessels, but (as in the case of Whitehaven) also covered storage bays which allowed for stockpiling when bad weather prevented sailings to Dublin. However, pack-horses carrying only 2 cwt. of coal up a steep cliff path were not seen as an economic or safe form of transport from pit to port, and Spedding constructed a small staithe and quay at Saltom. This appears to have been unattractive to the coal exporters, with only 861 tons being exported in 1733 and a paltry 22 tons in 1735.

The answer lay in the construction of a waggonway (later known as the Saltom waggonway) to the Whitehaven staithe, and this was completed in 1735. However, lifting Saltom coal through a height of 638 ft. was a relatively inefficient process, involving no fewer than three transhipments between coal face and the cliff-top waggonway. Filled corves were first raised up the Saltom shaft, before being transferred onto sledges or wheeled frames (known as 'trams') and pushed into a tunnel leading into the existing shaft of the adjoining Ravenhill Pit. From there, the corves were lifted 182 ft. to the pit top, before final transhipment to wagons bound for the harbour. It is possible that this process may have been rationalised at some stage, as a tramway is clearly marked on an 1864 map of the site, sixteen years after the pit was abandoned. Such a tramway would perhaps have allowed corves to be tipped into chaldron wagons on the Saltom site for lifting up the Ravenhill shaft, at the top of which turntables would have allowed direct access to the waggonway. However, there is no firm evidence for this modified method of operation.

The Whitehaven coal workings were divided by the St Bees valley. Saltom Pit was part of the Howgill Colliery which lay to the south and west, while to the north and east lay the Whingill Colliery. Initially worked by William Christian between 1678 and 1690, the colliery resumed production in 1714, the first pit sunk being on the top of Harras Moor, nearly 500 ft. above sea level. By this time, the Whingill complex was in the hands of the Lowthers, and the sinking of the pits was the responsibility of the young Carlisle Spedding – a tremendous responsibility for a 19-year old youth. It is also clear that Spedding gained much experience about level drainage while

The Town and Industry Develop

This type of Newcomen engine was installed in 1717, draining the shaft at Stone Pit, and was the first application of atmospheric pumping in north-west England. (Drawing from 'Old Lakeland' by J D Marshall, redrawn by Alan Johnstone)

working on the Whingill side, driving a watercourse eastwards under Harras Moor, commencing from Bransty Beck at the bottom of Wheelbarrow Brow. This watercourse, about 1½ miles long, took many years to construct: a letter written by Spedding in 1750 noted that: *We have just Thirld* [tunnelled] *our level to Whingill Colliery which we have been 12 years in driving.*

Bearing in mind the existence and commercial benefits of the Woodagreen causeway, it is surprising that it took so long to begin the construction of a waggonway from Whingill to Whitehaven harbour. In 1716, packhorses at the colliery were 'very numerous', and while carts were more economic, transport costs remained relatively high. Although a waggonway had been under consideration since 1738, construction did not begin until 1754, under Carlisle Spedding's direction, with the first traffic passing over it the following summer. Spedding's untimely death in August 1755, in an underground explosion, prevented the completion of the waggonway onto the quays for nearly half a century, the coal being discharged into the Bransty Row staithes, before being carted across the road to the vessels.

Carlisle Spedding's death brought to an end one of the most innovative periods in Whitehaven's mining history. Wood remarked that Spedding *had shown courage, skill,* [and] *inventiveness ... Mining methods at Whitehaven in his time were the most advanced in the kingdom.* While the waggonways in the district undoubtedly had an earlier genesis, there is little doubt that Spedding was a great influence on their technical development, and on their extension.

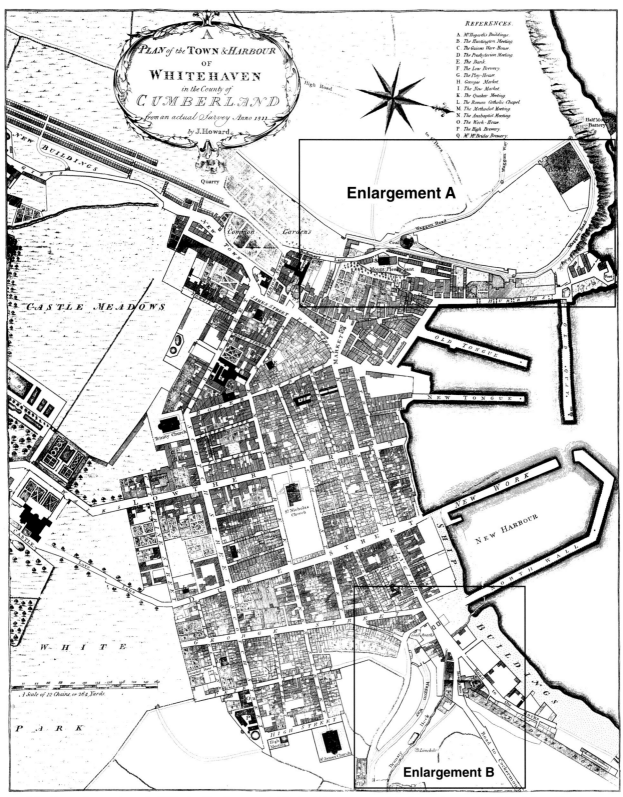

John Howard's map drawn in 1790, showing the truncated Parker Waggonway and the line and turntables of the Saltom Waggonway (top right). Route of the Whingill Waggonway, and pier abutments for Bransty Arch are shown bottom right. The two rectangles indicate enlarged sections of this map which are shown on pages 14 (A) and 15 (B). (Courtesy Michael Moon)

Early Waggonways:
The Howgill Colliery

3

THE WOODAGREEN causeway of 1683 has already been mentioned in Chapter 1, but waggonways in West Cumberland pre-dated even this early route. In 1568, Elizabeth I granted a charter to the Company of Mines Royal to mine *gold, silver, copper, and quicksilver* in a number of areas of England and Wales, one of which was the present Lake District. As most of the expertise in mining these minerals existed in the German-speaking areas (mainly Austria), it was logical to recruit miners from these countries. According to Dr M J T Lewis, in his book 'Early Wooden Railways', the Germans *set up a smelting house at Keswick, and worked copper ... in the Newlands Valley just west of Derwentwater ... to the north of Skiddaw ... and at Grasmere.* Interestingly, although production from these mines began to decline around 1580, Lewis points out that most of the Germans based in West Cumberland never returned home, meaning that the technical expertise they brought with them remained in the area.

Chapter 1 notes the contact of these miners with the West Cumberland coal merchants at Workington, during the early years of the Mines Royal charter. Of more 'railway' importance was the use of waggons for handling underground traffic at the three Cumberland sites, the vehicle being the 'Leitnagel Hund' (literally 'vehicle with guide-pin') – a wheeled mining tub, running on two parallel planks, placed close together but not quite touching. An iron bar fixed to the wagon extended into the slot thus formed (in the manner of the 'Scalextric' model car system!), thereby allowing the vehicle to be guided when pushed. Lewis is sceptical about the influence of the 'leitnagel Hund' on later waggonway development in Britain, pointing out that *whereas the Hund was designed for pushing by manpower in restricted galleries underground ... the English waggonway developed in the North* [was designed] *to carry large quantities of coal overland by horse-power.* Nevertheless, there remains the intriguing possibility that the 1683 Woodagreen causeway partially used German ideas, in utilising timber planks (baulks) on which a wagon could run, but without wooden strips at the extremities to guide the wagons. The system has all the characteristics of the 'leitnagel' system, without the iron bar, and Lewis points out that this type of construction was almost unique in England and Wales.

There is a common belief that all waggonway systems in the North of England were based on Tyneside technology, but there is no evidence that this was the case before the 1720s, when the engineer of an obscure Sheffield waggonway was noted to have visited Newcastle to learn about construction methods. Indeed, in Whitehaven, the reverse seems to have applied, John Gale (the Lowther agent) stating that *our case* [for building a Tyneside-type waggonway] *is different from theirs ... their Waggons are only Used to a Staith ...* [ours] *must go to the Ship Side, which a Waggon was most incapable off.* Additionally, Thomas Tickell's records make it clear that carts would be used on the causeway, noting that: *The Carts generally carry 4 loads apiece ... some 8 carriages ye day & some six according to their abilityes* [used the causeway]. This appears to have eliminated around thirty packhorse movements down to the harbour each day.

The Woodagreen causeway ran from Woodagreen Pit along Preston Street to the harbour. It appears to have been a level route, unconnected with the later and gravity-operated Parker waggonway, which ran at a higher level. Although the causeway was highly successful, however, its technology became obsolescent almost as soon as it opened, since, in the 1680s, Sir John Lowther established staithes at the harbour, allowing coal stocks to be kept in bulk storage. At a stroke, the problem involved with the use of waggons was eliminated.

However, of greater importance than the erection of staithes was the introduction of the flanged wheel. It is difficult to say when the flanged wheel was first used on an English waggonway, but Lewis suggested a date sometime in last quarter of the 17th century. This development was quickly followed by the replacement of wooden wheels by cast-iron, with the Coalbrookdale (Shropshire) ironworks recorded as producing cast-iron wheels for wagons as early as 1729.

This had important ramifications for new waggonways (as opposed to causeways) in West Cumberland, with the combination of flanged cast-iron wheels on wooden rails providing guidance for the wooden wagons: the forerunner of the modern railway was now recognisable. At Whitehaven,

The high ridge on the far side of Whitehaven Harbour marks the Howgill side of the Whitehaven Colliery, and well illustrates its height above the town. In the Queen's Dock lies one of the lighters carrying phosphate rock from the larger vessel anchored offshore; lorries were loaded with the rock from the Marchon silo seen to the left of the vessel. The Cumberland Motor Services Leyland bus, pictured on 20 July 1972 and almost new from the National Bus factory at Lillyhall, Workington, is seen ascending Bransty Brow.

(Peter Robinson ref. 132b12)

Chapter Three

In July 1960, an unidentified 0-4-0ST (possibly an Andrew Barclay) moves a coal train along the West Strand. The large house in the centre was known as the 'Staith House', and remains of the coal staithes can be seen above the Ford Popular on the left. The wagons included ex-North Eastern Railway 10-ton vehicles, which by this time were limited to internal use within the Harbour area. The 'Wellington Candlestick' can be seen at the top of the photograph.

(Peter Robinson ref. 007a01)

although the Saltom waggonway is generally regarded as being the first of its kind, Wood noted that Corporal and Swinburn pits, in the Ginns area of the Howgill Colliery, were connected to Sir James Lowther's new and more sophisticated staithes *by a railway or wagon-way constructed between 1732 and 1733*. The site of Swinburn Pit, and its proximity to Arrowthwaite, suggests that this was the first section of the Parker waggonway, and perhaps provides the answer to Lewis's statement that although the Parker waggonway was *usually considered the first at Whitehaven ...* [it was only] *opened on 4 August 1738*. The waggonway descended gradually along part of the route of the present 'Brows' footpath, until it crossed Rosemary Lane near Mount Pleasant; it then continued past Duke Pit, in the direction of the staithe.

The operations of the waggonway and staithes are well described by Joshua Dixon in 'An Account of the Coal Mines near Whitehaven', published in 1801, but based on Dixon's work with Dr William Brownrigg (1711-1800), who had been a close friend of Carlisle Spedding. Dixon writes: *Frames of wood are placed, in an exact parallel line, along the road leading from the pits: which has an uninterrupted declivity, though in some parts it is scarce perceptible. The loaden wagon is carried upon these frames down the inclined plane ...* [only] *by its own weight. The occasional assistance of one man is necessary, to prevent the wagon from acquiring too great a velocity ... . This is performed by two levers, connected with the first pair of wheels, the friction of which regulates their motion ... .*

In the Howgill Colliery, the wagons proceed in this manner, until they arrive at a covered gallery made of wood ... elevated about 37 ft. above the quays. From this gallery, [coal is discharged] *by means of spouts. Five of these are fixed, at ... 45 degrees,* [and] *5 vessels ... may be loaded at one tide, under them. The bottom of the wagon being opened, the coals run ... down the spouts to the ships. When there are no vessels ready to receive the coals, they are dropped, through holes left in the gallery, into the magazine ... 25 feet below the waggonway.*

This fascinating and highly detailed account of the waggonway's operation provides details of the ruling grade, con*tinuing: The waggonway ... has a descent ... of about $1/8$th of an inch in each yard*. This suggests that the gradient between pit and port was approximately 1 in 288, although it is likely to have been somewhat steeper, given the amount of axle-friction generated by 18th century waggon construction. More statistics emerged from Dixon's account, when he pointed out that the staithe's magazine held 6500 tons of coal, equivalent to the contents of 3000 waggons, which means that a wagon typically held 2 tons $3\frac{1}{2}$ cwt.

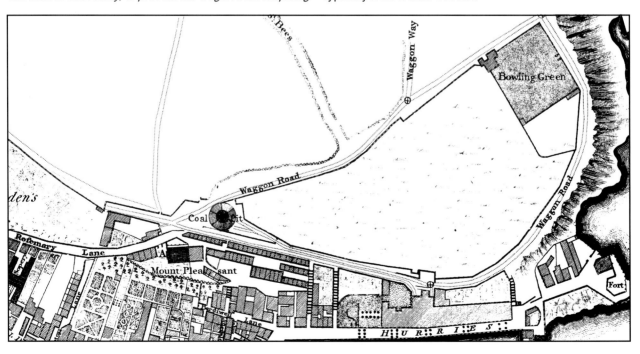

Waggonways - The Howgill Colliery

The completion of the Parker waggonway in August 1738 probably involved no more than an extension of the shallow incline in a south-westerly direction to Parker Pit, near the top of Monkwray Brow. It is unlikely to have been in operation long after 1781, as most of the Howgill pits it served had closed by this time. John Howard's map of Whitehaven, dated 1811 but apparently drawn in 1790, clearly shows the waggonway extending only 80 yards south of Duke Pit, its end being marked by a wall across the 'trackbed', although the course of the dismantled waggonway can clearly be seen beyond this point. John Linton, in his 1852 'Handbook of the Whitehaven and Furness Railway', makes the assertion that this was the first 'railway' in England to be laid with iron rails, but this is unlikely to have been true, as other accounts support 1800 or thereabouts as the date of the first rebuilding of the Whitehaven waggonways with such rails.

The Saltom waggonway, already mentioned in Chapter 2, was opened on 15 November 1735, transporting Saltom Pit's coal from the top of the Ravenhill shaft to Whitehaven harbour, a distance of slightly less than one mile. A contemporary account mentions a gauge of *4 ft. 10 inches asunder,* surprisingly close to standard gauge, and probably the same as used on the Parker waggonway, given the physical connections between the two systems. The falling gradient towards the harbour is likely to have been somewhat steeper than on the Parker waggonway, as there was no natural descent running from south to north.

The building of the Saltom waggonway introduced two engineering features not previously seen in West Cumberland: the double-track route and the turnrail (or turntable). All early waggonways were single-track, and even after 1730, Lewis commented that single track was probably the norm. On a double-track waggonway, the 'main way' handled loaded wagons, while the 'bye way' was used for returning empties to the pit. It became clear that the Saltom waggonway was more sophisticated than its predecessors, when, on the opening day, John Spedding wrote: *We led Coals & carry'd the wagns* [wagons] *round the Stage in the Steath* [staithe] *& the Empty Waggons the Backway.* This 'backway' appears to have been a one-way system, allowing empty waggons to be moved away from the staithe and slightly uphill towards the Bowling Green, whence the backway ran south-east to a point adjoining the 'main' Saltom waggonway.

Joshua Dixon provided the evidence that the Saltom waggonway was double-tracked, writing that, after the discharge of the coals down the hurries, *a horse waits for each wagon, to draw it up the hill, a little to the south-east of the Bowling Green,* [where] *the main and bye waggonways lie adjoining each other.* The main line descended gradually towards the harbour before swinging east along what is now Harbour View and passing on the south side of Duke Pit. It appears that waggons had to reverse here, in order to join the last section of the Parker waggonway down to the staithe, and this headshunt may well be the reason for the retention of the previously-mentioned 80-yard section of the line near Rosemary Lane.

Lewis also refers to the 'bye way' of the Howgill line, when mentioning the use of turnrails (or turntables) on this waggonway. As the wooden rails were normally about six feet long, it was not too difficult to build a curved section of track, and this could be improved by the use of slightly curved rails or by the use of shorter sections. However, when the curvature was too sharp on the Saltom waggonway, such as the point above Half Moon Battery, where the bye way had to be turned back towards the main way, Spedding built turntables. While turntables were recorded on Tyneside in 1726, their use on the Saltom waggonway was probably the first instance in West Cumberland. Howard's 1790 map also shows a turntable on the staithe itself, where it performed the more conventional role of aligning the waggon with the hurries.

Carlisle Spedding, after his death in 1755, was succeeded by his son James (1720 to 1788) as the Whitehaven Collieries manager. James proceeded to sink new pits, the most important of which was Croft Pit, which opened in 1774 and did not cease production until 1903. The Saltom waggonway was extended south, by 1,400 yards and on an incline, to serve Croft, although information is sparse on when it actually opened. However, when the success of the original waggonway is considered, it cannot have been long after the pit's opening. The Saltom waggonway was again extended south-east for a further half-mile, to Wilson Pit, sometime before 1788.

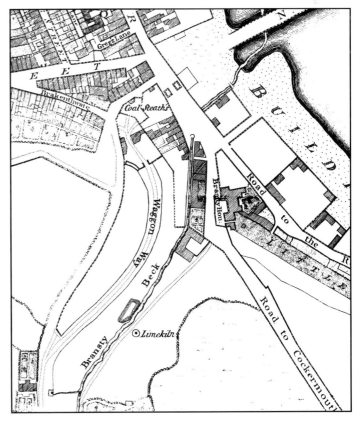

Enlarged sections from map on page 12

Left - In John Howard's 1790 map, the Saltom waggonway can be seen descending from the Howgill Colliery, the 'main way' using a turnrail to run south-east towards Duke Pit and the connection with the truncated Parker waggonway. The 'backway', allowing the empty wagons to be returned to the main Saltom waggonway, runs uphill towards the Bowling Green. A connection between the two parallel routes approaching the hurries appears to have been omitted.

Right - The same map shows the lower section of the Whingill waggonway, curving behind what is now Wellington Row on the final approach to Bransty Row staithes. The central siding in the triple fan served the 'town' staith, the right hand siding servicing the 'harbour' staith. Note the isolated support piers, in Tangier Street, of the unfinished Bransty Arch, which was finally opened in 1803.

Chapter Three

The head of the Croft extension from Ravenhill in more modern times. On 2 September 1967, NCB 'Austerity' 0-6-0ST Weasel *propels internal-user chauldron wagons, loaded with stone, onto the spoil siding for dumping over the cliffs and onto the Irish Sea shore.*

(Peter Robinson ref. 083e17)

Around 1800, wooden rails were being replaced by cast iron rails, with evidence that these were already in use in Workington by that year. Almost all the Whitehaven Colliery underground waggonways had been converted to iron rails by 1811, and in 1813 a local commentator wrote: *the waggonways, which were before of wood, were laid with cast iron.* Bertram Baxter, in his book 'Stone Blocks and Iron Rails', indicates a rebuilding date of around 1810 for the Saltom waggonway.

In 1811, John Peile, the viewer at Whingill Colliery, was appointed as the Earl of Lonsdale's Colliery Agent (Sir William Lowther having been ennobled in 1807), and in many respects was to prove as innovative as Carlisle Spedding had been in the previous century. One of his earliest experiments was in the field of steam locomotive haulage.

In 1812, Blenkinsop and Murray's steam locomotive was in use on the Middleton Railway in Leeds, rapidly followed by Hedley's engine, at Wylam on the Tyne, the following year. John Peile was known to have an interest in steam locomotion, and by March 1815 had written to John Buddle of Wallsend, regarding the latter's experiments with the 'Union Moving Steam Wagon'. It appears that Peile visited Buddle on Tyneside, and that he observed a locomotive, built by Phineas Crowther of Tyneside's Ouseburn foundry, working on the Lambton Railway.

By November 1816, Peile had ordered, through John Buddle, one of Crowther's locomotives, an eight-wheeled geared locomotive, with two vertical cylinders, and built to 'Chapman's Patent Design'. Crowther supplied the majority of the working parts for the locomotive, the remainder being manufactured in Whitehaven by Taylor Swainson, a Whitehaven colliery engineer. Swainson appears to have been responsible for the final assembly of this locomotive, which was known locally as the 'Iron Horse'.

The locomotive was trialled between Croft and Ravenhill Junction in 1817, possibly with the aim of eliminating rope and horse haulage on the incline. However, the locomotive broke up the brittle cast-iron rails, despite the reduced axle-loading of an eight-wheeled design. John Buddle, as an engineering consultant, visited the waggonway to see what could be done, but by July 1818, the experiment had been abandoned, and the waggonway reverted to its original operating mode. Interestingly, the locomotive was modified to serve as a stationary winding and pumping engine at a limestone quarry near Distington, being noted there in 1877, though nothing is known of its subsequent fate.

Ten years later, the Ravenhill Junction-Croft section of the Saltom waggonway was substantially rebuilt, the new 1,400-yard-long incline allowing twelve loaded waggons to be coupled together as a 'train' and to descend by gravity. After emptying, these wagons were coupled to a rope, to be drawn back to Croft Pit by a stationary steam engine. No doubt this was to handle the increased traffic after Piele's deepening of Croft Pit down from the main coal band to the six-quarters seam, driving seaward from there until reaching the main band once more. An amusing story relates to the 'communications system' for the working of this incline: apparently, the winding-house operator was provided with a telescope to observe signals from the waggon-attacher at the foot of the bank. When fog drifted in from the Irish Sea, the telescope was replaced by a messenger running between the two points!

Equally as innovative as Peile's experiments with steam traction was his construction of the first Howgill Incline in 1813, linking the head of the Saltom waggonway, at cliff-top level, with the staithes below. Although a technical marvel, however, its origins were politico-economic, as Brian Scott-Hindson described in his book 'Whitehaven Harbour': *Peile encountered difficulties with recalcitrant* [waggon] *leaders who were employed to convey coal on the waggonways from the pits to the Harbour staithes. Strikes by the leaders resulted in stockpiles of coals at the pits, but a shortage at the Harbour. In 1813 … Peile built the Howgill Inclined Plane, which was designed to displace 40 men and horses.*

Two contemporary accounts provide an idea of the scale and complexity of this incline. One noted that *on the Howgill side, a self-acting inclined plane was constructed, 290 yards long with a perpendicular altitude of 115 feet.* Another wrote that: *From the point where the declivity commences, a regularly inclined plane has been cut, down which three waggons in a string roll at a time. The loaded waggons pull up three empty ones in their descent, but this counterpoise does not sufficiently reduce their speed, and they are therefore made to give motion* to a device which forced air into a cylinder, the increasing pressure acting as a brake.

John Wood's 1830 map of Whitehaven shows the incline terminating at a turntable on the staithes, in exactly the same position as shown on John Howard's 1790 map. This suggests that this turntable was perhaps the most significant 'traffic centre' on the staithes, and that it was the most important factor in determining the bottom position of the Howgill Incline.

The Howgill staithes were extensively rebuilt in 1838-1839, again under Peile's supervision, the main change being the construction of four new iron loading spouts (hurries). The 1865 Ordnance Survey (25 inches to 1 mile) map shows that the base of the incline had been moved a few yards to the north-west, on a slightly curving alignment, to run onto a turntable from which it was possible to access all four spouts, although the layout

Waggonways - The Howgill Colliery

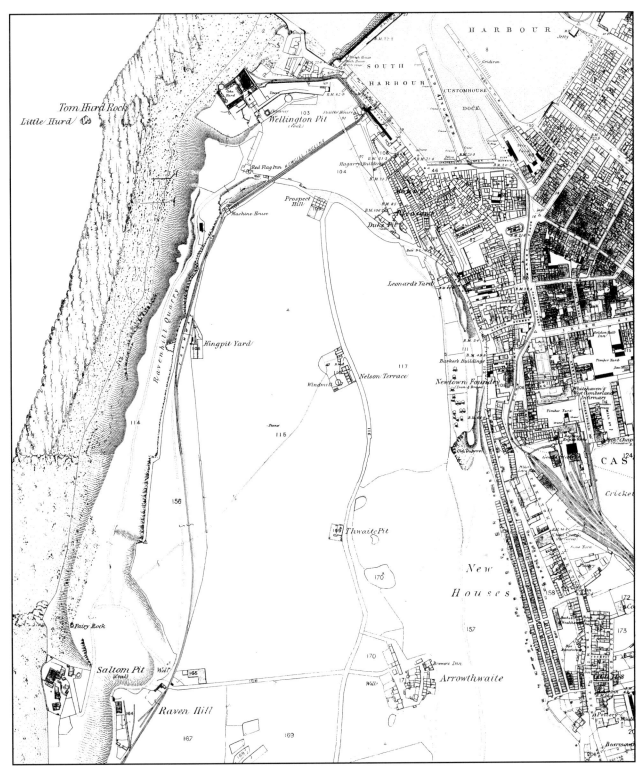

Much of the Saltom Waggonway is shown on this map, including the sidings at Ravenhill serving the shaft down to Saltom Pit. The Howgill Incline and staithes are clearly marked. The course of the abandoned 1824 Whaite Field Quarry Incline can be seen to the north of the Red Flag Inn; the earthworks were severed when construction of Wellington Pit began in 1838. The WFJR's 1854 tramway, running through Market Place to the Old Tongue can also be seen.
(Reproduced from the 1865 25 inch Ordnance Survey Map sheet 67.2., Cumbria Record Office, Whitehaven, with the kind permission of the Ordnance Survey)

Chapter Three

Wellington Pit, the greatest of Whitehaven's mines, sunk by John Peile between 1838 and 1845, looking north over the New West Pier and its lighthouse. Note the castellated buildings designed by Sidney Smirke, a renowned architect of the period. On the right stands the great monumental chimney known locally as the 'Candlestick', which still survives today. The building in the foreground, the Red Flag Inn, was allegedly once the home of Jonathan Swift, author of 'Gulliver's Travels'. (Sankey ref. E68)

suggests that the Howgill pits may have mainly used the most south-easterly pair, the other two being used by chauldrons (waggons) from perhaps the greatest of Whitehaven's mines, Wellington Pit, which Peile sunk between 1838 and 1845, and which was probably the 'raison d'etre' for the reconstructed staithes. By 1845, Peile had driven out levels nearly 3,000 feet from the shoreline, in order to intercept the Main Band of coal.

The sinking of Wellington Pit eventually accounted for more than half the coal traffic passing over the Howgill staithes. The 1865 map clearly shows both the 'main way' and the 'bye way', running parallel between the pit yard and the north-westernmost arm of the staithes; separation of tracks would clearly have been needed for such high traffic levels. Wood provides some useful statistics, pointing out that, by 1847, the Howgill staithes were handling 63,136 waggons per annum, equivalent to around 150,000 tons. This meant that around 175 waggons were being handled daily across the staithes, with 100 originating from Wellington Pit and the remainder coming down the Howgill Incline as 75 out-and-back workings.

The Howgill side also had a little-known tramway not connected in any way to coal mining. The Whaite Field Quarry Incline had its provenance in John Rennie's 1814 scheme to extend the New Pier of the harbour by 250 yards in a north-east direction, at a cost of £96,115. The plans were accepted in November 1815 by the Town and Harbour Trustees. Clearly much stone was to be required during construction, and Scott-Hindson provided details of how this was to be handled: *A new quarry was to be opened ... at Whaite Field, some distance from the bowling green* [the later site of Wellington Pit]. *An inclined plane was to be built on arches, from the New Pier to the bowling green,* [with] *a double track railway of ... five hundred yards*.

A remarkable nineteenth-century photograph of Wellington Pit, taken from the sea, showing the crenellated walls and tower at the western end of the site.

(Peter Robinson Collection ref. 105d17)

Waggonways - The Howgill Colliery

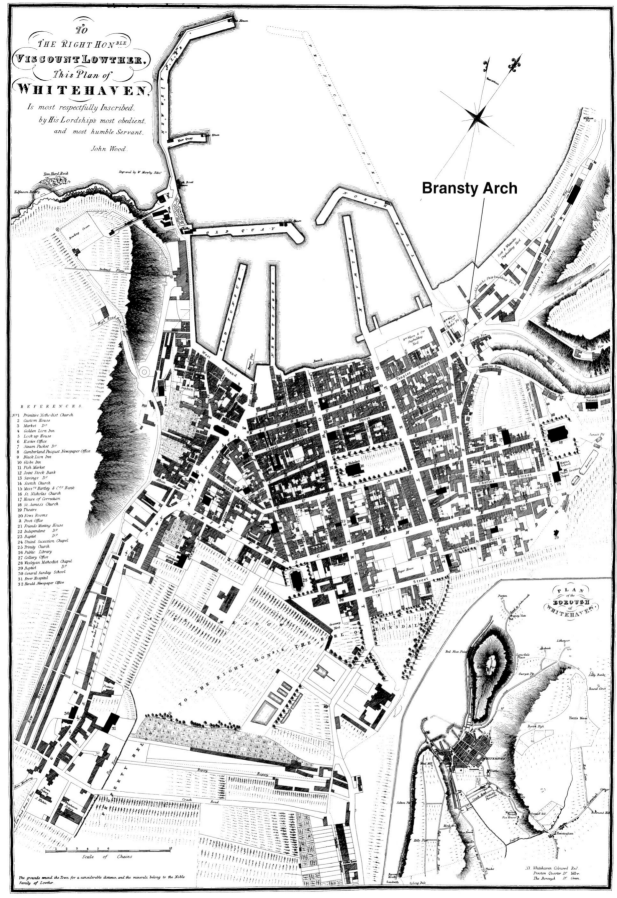

John Wood's map drawn in 1830, showing (top left) the 1813 Howgill Incline and the 1824 Whaite Field Quarry Incline. Note that, while the Whingill Waggonway has been lifted, the Bransty Arch survives (centre right). The first section of the Parton Waggonway, opened in 1806, can be seen running north towards William Pit from the North Wall of the harbour.   (Courtesy Michael Moon)

19

Chapter Three

The Croft extension on 25 April 1966. An Andrew Barclay 0-4-0ST (Works No. 1660, built 1920) approaches Ladysmith Washery through stone retaining walls dating from the 1838 incline rebuilding. The covered hopper wagons to the right of the locomotive's chimney are on the Marchon rail system, having just arrived from Corkickle Brake head. (Peter Robinson ref. 050g29)

A year later, the Trustees were told to begin work as soon as possible, but a reduction in the harbour's traffic and revenue caused work to be suspended in September 1817, at which time construction of the incline's arches was well-advanced. Work did not re-commence until May 1824, with John Rennie's son, Sir John Rennie, being appointed engineer-in charge. John Peile was now told to complete the inclined plane, and to begin quarrying operations at Whaite Field. At the foot of, and west of, the incline, a limekiln was constructed, the burnt limestone most probably being used as a cement during the pier construction. In general, progress was slow, and the New West Pier (as it was now called) was not completed until the autumn of 1830, its length having reached 359 yards.

It is clear that the inclined plane had a working life of around six years, and may have survived longer as a closed line, in case stone had been needed for a new lighthouse at the end of the New West Pier. The incline is shown on John Wood's 1830 map, terminating at a point between the fort and the West Strand buildings, on the connection between the Old Quay and the New Quay. However, no extension of the line is shown onto the New West Pier, which might have been a logical method of transporting the stone blocks to the actual construction site.

The 1865 OS map reveals that, despite the sinking of Wellington Pit after 1838, the course of the inclined plane was not completely obliterated, with a cutting and a bridge still visible on the lower section, and the upper section appearing to terminate near the Red Flag Inn. Intriguingly, despite the description of the incline as five hundred yards long, the 1830 map only shows it as six chains (132 yards). Projecting a distance of five hundred yards south west from the West Strand extends to the site of 'Ravenhill Quarry', which suggests that this was the source of the New West Quay's building material and the upper terminus of the Whaite Field Quarry Incline. Equally intriguingly, the 1865 map shows the course of the incline heading in the direction of the 'Machine House' at the top of the Howgill Incline, raising the prospect that the two inclines shared a common winding method and that about 250 yards of the Saltom Waggonway could have been used by stone traffic in order to gain access to Ravenhill Quarry.

Most of the 1813 Howgill Incline still survives, running under the small road leading from the site of Wellington Pit towards Duke Pit fan house; the upper section of the incline can be accessed from Harbour View. The walls of the incline are lined with dressed sandstone, indicative of the high level of harmonious architectural appreciation which existed in the Georgian era.

The remains of the incline up the Croft extension from Ravenhill Junction, running in a shallow cutting between stone retaining walls, can still be visited; the width of the cutting suggests that the incline was single-track with a mid-point passing loop. Stone retaining walls, as with the Howgill Incline, suggest Georgian building practice and lead to the conclusion that these date from the 1828 rebuilding.

Early Waggonways:
The Whingill Colliery

MENTION OF Whingill Colliery has already been made in Chapter 2, noting the relatively lengthy gestation period of this waggonway. Described by local historian Norman Gray as *the most elusive of Whitehaven's waggonways* in his paper 'The Waggonways and Inclines of Whitehaven' (published in 2004 in 'Cumbrian Railways'), the Whingill system was in many ways more substantial than the Saltom or Parker Waggonways. Not only was it steeply graded, descending from 500 feet on Harras Moor down to sea level, but it was also longer than the Saltom system – around two miles, with the branches adding a further half mile or so.

There also seems to have been problems during construction, Carlisle Spedding writing in 1754 that *we shall begin the Laying of Timber in a week's time. We are covering the way about 8 or 9 inches thick with flat Stones and Rubbish, for 'tis all been clay and* [would] *not support the Waggons.*

The waggonway must have been completed in the late spring of 1754, as there was correspondence in June and July between Spedding and William Brown (a Tyneside mine and waggonway owner) on the subject of gradients. Spedding was clearly worried about checking the speed of waggons descending the main way, asking Brown about *your Several ways of Managing the Runs and waggons in them, our way falls about 2½ or near 3 foot in Ten Yards in some places.* This indicates that the steepest gradients were between 1 in 12 and 1 in 10, indicating that care would have been needed to control the waggons on the falling grade.

Spedding had obviously considered a crude method of slowing the waggons (*Ruffen the Railes with Ashes, Small coales, and suchlike*), and Brown confirmed that he used a similar technique on Tyneside, together with an improved type of brake, concluding that there would be *no Deficulty ... in getting your* [waggon] *Down, Tho your way be Streight, as your greatest Descint is no more than 3 foot in Ten yards.*

The same correspondence makes it clear that Spedding considered the use of check rails to increase friction on the long descent from Harras Moor, but these would have been 18th century check rails, fitted to the **outside** edge of the curve, fastened tightly to the wooden rail, and protruding 4 or 5 inches above the rail head. However, the local topography generally ruled against bends in the route *which both lessen the Decent & create more friction by Rubbing against Check Rails*. As the Whingill and Howgill waggonway systems were not connected, the gauge on the former may have been 4 feet 2 inches, as this was also mentioned in the Spedding-Brown correspondence.

Despite the fact that virtually no trace of the Whingill Waggonway now remains, Gray's researches have established the route of the line. Davy Pit, half a mile west of Moresby Parks, was the most probable starting point of the waggonway, which then followed the present course of Victoria Road; George Pit was linked by a siding to the main way.

Probably during the course of construction, Spedding linked Harras Pit and Lady Pit with the main way by means of a half-mile-long branch which then ran north-east, connecting with the main way just below George Pit siding. The connection was not direct, but by means of a turnrail (turntable) whereby the waggon was turned to join the main waggonway in a south-westerly direction. This meant that any runaway waggons on the Harras Pit branch would not collide head-on with those descending the main way. Part of this branch now lies to the east of the present-day A595 road (commonly called the 'Loop Road') as it runs high above the east side of the town, on the course of the former private driveway from the Bransty turnpike to the rear of Whitehaven Castle in Flatt Walks.

Passing under this driveway, the gradient of the Whingill Waggonway became distinctly steeper as it passed Solway View and Hilton Terrace, before curving to the west, away from Wellington Row, to terminate on the staithes at Bransty Row (the site of the former Cumberland Motor Services bus garage, and now a night club known appropriately as 'The Bransty Arch').

In his 1961 article, entitled 'Early Railways in Cumberland' and published in the Journal of the Railway & Canal Historical Society, Bertram Baxter refers to the Whingill route as the 'Branstey [sic] Wagonway', and that it ran to James Pit, north-east of St James' Church. This is somewhat confusing, as James Pit did not become operational until 1800. It seems likely that the James Pit section of the waggonway was, in fact, a 150-yard-long siding off the main Whingill Waggonway. The 'Branstey' name may well have its origins in the waggonway's quayside connection with the early nineteenth-century waggonway from William Pit, in the Bransty area. Baxter confirmed that, at the time his article was published, no traces of the 'Branstey Wagonway' remained, except for *about fifty yards ... at the rear of a row of houses situated on the west side of Wellington Street* [sic], *opposite High Street.*

These houses, actually in Wellington Row, are private, and there is no public access to the rear of the properties. However, by kind permission of the owner, the author was able to obtain access to the rear of one of the houses, from where the curving course of the waggonway, running high above the 'New Road' to Cockermouth, was clearly visible. At the lower end of the Wellington Row terrace, a small portion of sandstone retaining wall marks the site of the entrance to a yard serving the Bransty Row staithes.

A good description of the underground railways in James Pit is given in the remarkable 'Railways In England: 1826 and 1827' by C von Oeynhausen and H von Dechen, being a detailed record of the observations of two Prussian mining engineers during a visit to England. The authors noted that the gauge was 2 ft. 1 in., and that the 'waggons' were actually cast-iron rail-mounted frames on which a wicker basket, holding 11 cwt. of coal, was placed; wheel diameter was 19 in. The authors also recorded that *one horse draws ten ... wagons coupled together, laden with 110 cwt of coal, which is a very good load for mine haulage.*

Technologically, the Whingill Waggonway was more advanced than the Saltom system, especially in its use of pointwork and protection for runaway wagons. Indeed, the Whingill Waggonway may well have been the first application for points (switches) in Great Britain. Spedding wrote, in 1755, that, to prevent accidents with runaways, *the Bottom of the Run* [will] *have a Branch laid, and a switch Rail to be Shutt by an Old Man ... with an Iron Rod thro' a Conduit fixt to a small Leaver, he may Shut the Switch Rail and turn the* [runaway] *into the* [rising gradient] *Branch ...* [Running] *against a Battery of Earth and Turf* [it] *will take no harm ...* [running back down the branch], *another Switch Rail will turn the Waggon ... into another Branch, where it will rest till brot* [brought] *into the Main Way below the first mentioned Branch.*

Mention of an 'Old Man' as an early signalman was not quite as amusing as would be thought today. Bearing in mind that an 1800 manpower survey in the Howgill Colliery revealed septuagenarians and octogenarians still at work in the pits after sixty or seventy years' labour, this suggests that 'old men' were eminently employable!

It is not clear whether the sophisticated trackwork mentioned above was actually constructed, although Howard's 1790 map shows what appears to be a short siding

Chapter Four

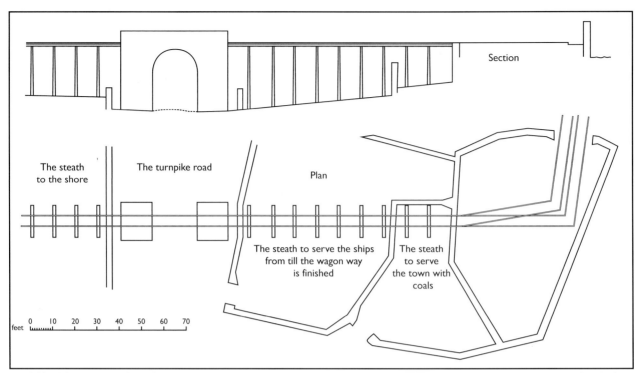

This side elevation of the Bransty Arch shows that the Whingill waggonway was carried on 20 feet high wooden geers (trestles) each side of the masonry arch. The geers to the left of the arch were unlikely to have been constructed: when the Arch opened in 1803, it is likely that a masonry ramp descended to the North Wall.
(Original from 'Early Wooden Railways' by M J T Lewis, redrawn by Alan Johnstone)

abutting the upper end of Wellington Row, where it adjoins Hilton Terrace. Approximately half way down the steepest section of the waggonway, and well clear of the staithes area, this would have been the most logical place for an emergency siding for runaway waggons.

The Bransty Row staithes were not intended to be the terminus of the waggonway, Spedding having grandiose plans to bridge Tangier Street at Bransty Row with a monumental arch, to reach new staithes and hurries on the North Wall of the New Harbour. Lewis, in 'Early Wooden Railways', showed the plan and section of the so-called 'Bransty Arch'. The elevation revealed a solid masonry arch, 27 feet high and with a 20 feet span, flanked by arched pedestrian ways. Howard's 1790 map shows three sidings discharging at the Bransty Row staithes, one of which would have continued over the arch and been supported by timber trestle supports on each side of the structure. It is clear that Spedding started work on the arch, as the 1790 map shows isolated supporting piers on each side of Tangier Street, but Spedding's death in 1755 meant continuing use of the Bransty Row facility to discharge coal into horse-drawn carts for the final 250 yards to the quayside.

Interestingly, the 1790 map also appears to show that the staithes were constructed as planned by Spedding, the line of the waggonway passing first over a small *steath to serve the town with coals*, then a much larger *steath to serve the ships from till the wagon way is finished*. Gray has calculated that the staithes were 30 ft. high, 150 ft. in breadth, and 100 ft. deep.

In his book 'Staith to Conveyor', Terry Powell includes a plan (possibly by John Smeaton) of the lower part of the Whingill Waggonway as it existed in 1786. As well as confirming that the waggonway had a main way and a bye way, the plan surveyed an ingenious alternative route between the staithes and the North Wall. This zigzag route involved the building of turnrails on the site of Bransty Row staithes, allowing the reversed waggons to descend by gravity into the valley of the small Bransty Beck and on to the 'New Road' to Cockermouth. The rising gradient

A view of the Bransty Arch (demolished in 1927), taken from the corner of Brackenthwaite and looking towards Bransty Row. The first building seen through the arch is the Grand Hotel, while the façade of Bransty Station is in the background. The charabanc Lady Margaret (left) was operated by Whitehaven Motor Services Ltd.

(Sankey ref. 6129)

Waggonways - The Whingill Colliery

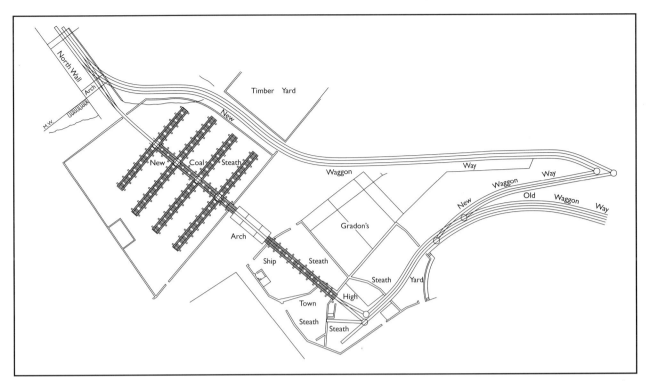

A 1786 plan, showing an ingenious alternative zig-zag route between the staithes at the lower end of the Whingill waggonway and the North Wall. Note that the plan shows the zig-zag to have both a main way and a bye way, and that its design would have allowed wagons descending the Whingill waggonway to complete their journey by gravity. The plan also shows the Bransty Arch, as eventually opened in 1803. (Original from 'Staith to Conveyor' by Terry Powell, and based on a plan in the Cumbria Record Office, Whitehaven. Redrawn by Alan Johnstone)

would have checked their speed as the waggons ran onto further turnrails, allowing a further reversal onto the final descending section of the waggonway towards the quayside. There is no evidence that this pre-Bransty Arch route was ever built. It is likely that completion of the arch was a more cost-effective option of gaining access to the North Wall.

The Bransty Arch was finally opened on 9 August 1803, although there is some confusion about the extent of its use. Both Wood and Lewis suggest that it was used by waggons, and Scott-Hindson goes further, stating that *when the Bransty Arch was ... brought into operation ... a staithe was built near the North East Wall* [for the] *coals from the Whingill Colliery*. This would certainly have been in line with Spedding's original drafted plans.

However, Gray's paper describes the line as *descending* [from the arch] *and* [running] *along the North Wall of Whitehaven Harbour*, and there is evidence for this. Scott-Hindson's book includes a Victorian view of the arch, which appears to show a ramp descending towards the harbour, while Wood's 1830 map shows the Howgill-side staithes but no structures on the North Wall. Most convincing of all, Ackermann's 1834 print 'Whitehaven from Bransty Hill' clearly shows this ramp in its entirety; it seems to have been about 100 yards long. Some of the ramp was probably removed during the 1870s, when the north wall of the harbour was pulled down during the construction of the Queen's Dock, although photographs opposite and on the front and rear covers provide evidence that the section adjacent to the arch survived until this structure was itself demolished.

C.F Dendy Marshall, in his book 'A History of British Railways down to the year 1830', published in 1938, claimed that the arch was never used, but this is unlikely to have been true, since James Pit was still in full production (although linked to William Pit sometime after 1812). Moreover, Wood records that North Pit, on the Harras Road, was still operational in 1806. Records made in 1799, of production costs at Lady, George, and Davy Pits, give no indication that these were on the point of closure. Traffic from all of these pits is therefore likely to have been carried over the Bransty Arch. The waggonway had probably been closed by 1830, as it is not marked on John Wood's map. However, Oliver Wood noted that both North and Wreay Pits, in the Whingill Colliery, were still in active production in 1847, and for some time thereafter, and North Pit's proximity to Harras Moor supports the possibility of continuing operation over the waggonway as late as the mid-19th century.

Sadly, the dignified Bransty Arch was demolished in March 1927, having become a notorious bottleneck in Whitehaven, and part of the site, opposite the CMS garage, was occupied by a new bus station.

While the Whingill Waggonway appears to have been relatively well documented, the same cannot be said for the second line to serve this side of Whitehaven, the Parton Waggonway, and indeed, the only research on this line appears to have been made by Norman Gray. Mention has already been made of the connection between the quayside line of the Whingill and a waggonway from William Pit, approximately 650 yards long. The latter is clearly marked on Wood's map of 1830, cutting through the shipbuilding yards of Brocklebank and Scott & Whiteside and passing the 'gas house', the site of the later gasworks, before curving round into William Pit. In fact, this first section of the waggonway dated from 1806, when William Pit first became operational, and may have been laid with wooden rails. However, as the first use of iron rails at Whitehaven was noted around 1800 and all local waggonways had abandoned wood by 1813, an 'iron road' is more probable.

The sinking of William Pit was a significant event in Whitehaven's industrial history. Its genesis lay in Sir James Lowther's 1781 purchase of fifty acres of land at Bransty, for which he paid Lord Egremont £26,000. This completed Lowther ownership of land around Whitehaven Harbour, and allowed the sinking of a major new shaft on the north side of the harbour, giving access to new undersea reserves. Sinking was begun in 1802, marking the beginning of John Bateman's second period in office as the General Manager of the Whitehaven Colliery.

The previous chapter has already mentioned John Rennie's 1814 plan to extend the New Pier, using stone from Whaite Field Quarry. Rennie also planned to quarry stone in the vicinity of Redness Point, a cliff around 600 yards north of William Pit, and to bring it by rail to the North Wall of the harbour. This was to be done by effectively extending the

23

Chapter Four

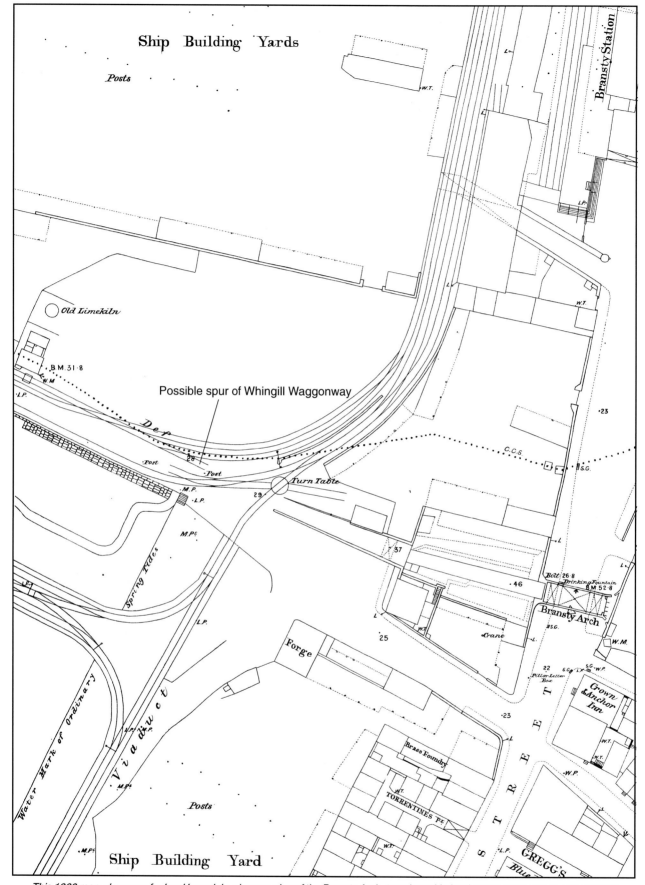

This 1860 map, drawn up for Lord Lonsdale, shows a plan of the Bransty Arch, together with the descent ramp running towards the North Wall of the harbour. It appears that the Whingill Waggonway descended at a slight angle when compared to the line taken across the arch. Interestingly, it seems that a length of the Whingill waggonway may be shown running onto the North Wall in a north-westerly direction as indicated on the map. This line is also shown linked in to the Parton waggonway, reopening the issue about whether both waggonways were the same gauge, although by this time, the Whingill system had been closed for 30 years and any surviving quayside sections may have been re-gauged.   (From a plan in the Cumbria Record Office, Whitehaven)

existing William Pit line in a north-westerly direction. From the North Wall, the stones were to be lowered into specially constructed boats, to be taken across the harbour to the New Pier construction site. As with the Whaite Field Quarry Incline, initial work was started on the Bransty Quarries extension, for, at the time of the suspension of work in September 1817, *the breast wall needed to be completed 'to the height required for the railway', and the structure secured against the sea*. When preliminary work on the New Pier restarted in the summer of 1823, John Peile was instructed to *finish the Iron Railway through William Pit Yard to the Quarries*, and iron rails were purchased from the Dowlais Iron Co. in Cardiff for this purpose. It is likely that this stone traffic continued to use the waggonway until the summer of 1830.

Bransty Quarries were served by an interesting rail-mounted crane, fully described by von Oeynhausen and von Dechen, who noted that *the frame on which the crane rests lies wholly over the running wheels, and is necessarily wider than the gauge of the line: it is 7 ft. and just as long*. The crane could be moved by rail between faces, after which *the crane is raised by four screws so high that the wheels rise off the rails*, thereby preventing track damage. The crane appears to have been moved by means of a crank axle linked to a drum and to a pinion wheel. In view of its width and its specialised mode of operation, use of the crane was probably restricted to this particular quarry.

In April 1833, plans were approved to extend the North Wall of the harbour, and once again the waggonway was used to transport stone from the Bransty Quarries. Work appears to have been completed, but a severe storm in January 1836, in which a number of vessels were destroyed, suggested that the design of the New Pier was not deflecting the seas correctly from the newly-completed pier at the North Wall, and further rebuilding of the North Wall took place between 1836 and 1841. It is likely that stone traffic over the waggonway continued during this period.

In 1827, John Peile began the Parton Drift, as the first stage of extracting a large area of inland coal. It is unclear whether the waggonway from the Bransty Quarries was extended northwards at this time, but it would not have been later than 1836, when the Countess Pit at Parton (which utilised the Parton Pit shaft to bring coal to the surface) was opened. A plan in the Whitehaven Records Office, and dated 1835, shows this waggonway. This extension was around 1,500 yards long, giving the Parton Waggonway a total length of around 1½ miles between the pit yard and the North Wall at the harbour. A 120-yard-long tunnel took the waggonway through the Redness Point outcrop. The 1865 Ordnance Survey map (25 inches to 1 mile) shows the waggonway to have been single track with passing loops. It was probably horse-worked, as it was level for much of its distance. In his book 'Parton: Part One', D Bradbury noted that the tramway used stone blocks instead of timber sleepers, and that its gauge was about 118 cm. This equates to around 3 feet 10 inches, an unusual gauge, although it may have actually been 4 feet, as used on the Dinorwic Slate Quarries system in North Wales.

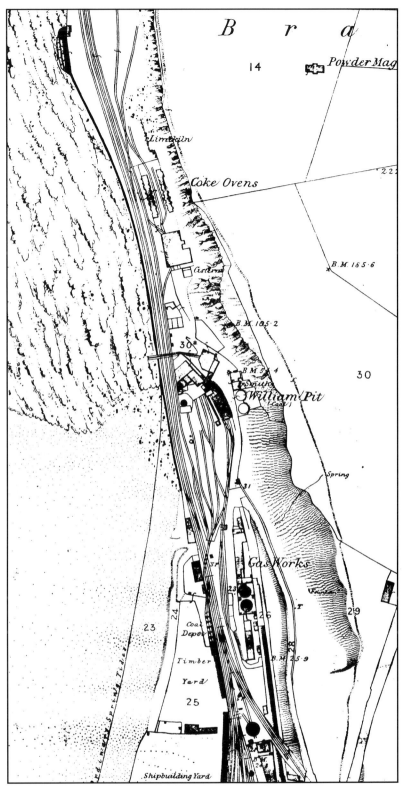

The southern section of the Parton waggonway can be seen on this map. After crossing the WJR diagonally just north of the gasworks, the 3 ft. 10 in. (possibly 4 ft.) gauge waggonway served William Pit, beyond which the single line ran north towards Redness Point. By this date, the quarry here appears to be served by a standard-gauge siding, linked directly to the WJR.

(Reproduced from the 1865 25 inch Ordnance Survey Map sheet 67.2, Cumbria Record Office, Whitehaven, with the kind permission of the Ordnance Survey)

Chapter Four

The northern section of the Parton waggonway is shown here. Note the tunnel through Redness Point, and the three passing loops between the north portal and the coal depot at Countess Pit sidings (almost certainly closed by this date).
(Reproduced from the 1865 25 inch Ordnance Survey Map sheet 67.2, Cumbria Record Office, Whitehaven, with the kind permission of the Ordnance Survey)

William Pit in the mid-1930s, with the upcast winding gear in the centre. The wagons passed through the screens and dry grading plant (on the left) to be loaded. The LNWR line from Bransty lies to the left of the ornate railings.
(Peter Robinson Collection ref. 183f28)

The sidings at Parton Pit appear to have been quite extensive. Five sidings entered the complex, with three running under what appeared to be an overhead gantry, possibly for direct discharge from underground mining tubs into the waggons. One of the three curved round almost in a semi-circle to terminate beneath the gantry.

The opening of the Harrington-Bransty section of the Whitehaven Junction Railway (covered more fully in Chapter 5) on 15 February 1847 meant that the new railway ran between the Parton Waggonway and the sea. In consequence, the waggonway had to cross the WJR on the level. This was covered by an agreement, dated 8 February 1845, between the WJR and the Earl of Lonsdale *as to waggonways and accommodation works*. The agreement contained no clauses about the regulation of waggonway traffic over the flat crossing, presumably because signalling rules and installations were then still in their infancy, although it is understood that colliery waggonway traffic enjoyed precedence over WJR services.

Countess Pit was highly profitable, and in 1859 was still the fourth largest pit in the Whitehaven Collieries in terms of manpower. However, the Parton Drift was closed in 1863, and Parton coal traffic is unlikely to have used the waggonway after this date, the route being totally abandoned from just north of Redness Point to the Countess Pit sidings.

The surviving section of the Parton waggonway (probably in rebuilt form) continued to see extensive industrial use, and this will be covered in Chapter 10.

Running on former Whitehaven Junction Railway metals, on 21 July 1979 a Class 108/2 curves above the shore of Tanyard Bay with the 13-05 Whitehaven-Carlisle. On the right can be seen the Parton Pit coal staithes, served by the Parton waggonway, while the centre-left skyline shows the chimneys of the Harrington collieries.

(Tom Heavyside ref. 501/27A)

Redness Point, north of Whitehaven, on 11 July 1988. A class 142 unit in Greater Manchester PTE livery forms the 16-59 Whitehaven - Carlisle where West Cumbria's industrial past merges into seashore.

(Dave McAlone ref. P02)

Parton's down outer distant and Bransty's up distant are on show at Tanyard Bay between Parton and Whitehaven on 10 June 1988. 31 460 heads the Workington - Huddersfield TPO which included parcels for Preston.

(Dave McAlone ref. P06)

Parton on 30 August 2003. Direct Rail Services' 20901 with its lights ablaze leads three sister locomotives (37 229, 33 025 & 33 207) and 6C43, the 09-25 SO Sellafield - Kingmoor tanks round 'Windy Corner'. The 102 tonne tankers are for nitric acid and caustic soda for the Sellafield reprocessing plant. The extra locomotives are simply moving to DRS Kingmoor for fuelling. In the background three of Whitehaven's lighthouses can be identified and further on - some four miles from this location - the lighthouse on St Bees Head can just be made out.

(Dave McAlone ref. P12)

The Coming of the Railway:
The Whitehaven Junction Railway

THE TOWN of Whitehaven was still of considerable importance during the first quarter of the nineteenth century and coal was still the primary industry upon which Whitehaven's prosperity depended, although shipbuilding was to remain an important factor throughout the century, together with pottery making.

The harbour was seeing development around this period. Earlier proposals for enlargement had come from John Smeaton (1768), Captain Huddart (1814), John Rennie (1814), and William Chapman (1821). Despite some initial work on Rennie's scheme to construct the New Pier, it was not until 1823, when Rennie was joined by John Whidbey, that serious steps were taken to enlarge and improve Whitehaven Harbour. In their report of May 1823, they stated: *The principal object we have in view is to obtain as much water as possible at low-water at the proposed pier-head, and also to make the water smooth within it, so that ships may enter with ease and safety ... at all states of the tide.* Work on the New Pier commenced in 1824, but construction was slow, only 116 yards having been built by 1826. The New Pier was not completed until 1831, and was immediately criticised by the shipmasters, who complained to the Harbour Trustees that it was now difficult to approach the harbour when the wind was blowing from south-south-east through to south-west. In an ominous portent of what was to come (on 23 January 1836, a number of vessels were destroyed in a storm), the masters added that *any farther extension of the pier would* [create] *danger and difficulty to vessels entering or sailing from the port.*

Certainly the town of Whitehaven was sufficiently important for a main line railway to be discussed as early as 1805. On 1 December of that year, Sir William Lowther (who was to be created Earl of Lonsdale on 7 April 1807) wrote to the Mayor of Carlisle about improving communications between the Border City and the Cumberland port. Lowther proposed the general improvement of the roads, adding that *if it were thought that a Navigable Canal or Railway (the latter of which ... might be thought most eligible) would give greater facilities to Trade, I should be glad to ... Promote it.* As a result of this initiative, the Whitehaven Town & Harbour Commissioners formed a committee to investigate the proposals, but there is no record as to the outcome of their deliberations.

With or without a railway, economic pressures were beginning to exert themselves. Production in the Whitehaven Collieries remained relatively constant, rising marginally from 193,404 tons in 1816 to 202,511 tons in 1832, but the profitability of the Lowther-controlled industry declined from £51,575 12s 6d to £27,318 14s 3½d in the same period. The reasons for this were numerous, but were mainly due to the reduced price per ton paid by the Whitehaven ship-owners, lower tonnages shipped, and the increasing costs of developing the seams within the colliery.

From 1831 onwards, John Peile kept detailed records of tonnages moved from the Whitehaven, Workington, Maryport, and Harrington Collieries. In that year, Whitehaven produced 190,907 tons, far more than the Maryport Collieries' 61,877 tons. By 1840, however, the production gap was closing: 219,789 tons from the Whitehaven pits and 111,058 tons from the Maryport coalfield.

Two main factors lay behind the rise of Maryport, the first being improvements to the harbour. An 1815 account described the port as *very small, and ill-suited to the wealth and commercial importance of the place ... [some ship-owners] have deserted the port.* The harbour was controlled by the impecunious Senhouse family, but in 1833, the Maryport Harbour Acts were repealed, and Senhouse family control was replaced by elected trustees. Improvements to the harbour were commenced immediately, resulting in the opening of a new two-acre dock in January 1837.

The second factor was the incorporation of the Maryport and Carlisle Railway, the first public railway wholly within the county of Cumberland. The opening of the first section of the Newcastle and Carlisle Railway, in March 1835, was seen as the first step in improved cross-country communications between Newcastle and Whitehaven, and there is some evidence that the Lowthers were keen to support the westernmost leg of this enterprise. Josias Jessop's 1825 survey of the N&CR spoke of the line forming *part of a communication between the German Ocean and the Irish Sea.* The original company formed in 1836 to push a railway south-westwards from Carlisle initially envisaged Whitehaven as its terminus, but George Stephenson's survey of the route covered only a railway as far as Maryport, mainly on cost grounds.

The M&CR was incorporated by Act of Parliament on 12 July 1837, and was opened in stages, the first in July 1840 with the section from the South Quay in Maryport to Arkleby Colliery. The line was open throughout on 10 February 1845, the M&CR immediately introducing a horse-drawn coach to carry passengers on to Whitehaven.

There was also another Whitehaven connection with the M&CR. Professor Jack Simmons, in his book 'The Maryport & Carlisle Railway', writes that: *The first locomotive owned by the company ... was also the first to be built by Messrs Tulk and Ley of Whitehaven,* [arriving] *at Maryport by raft* [because] *the journey ... by the steep road would have been a formidable undertaking.* Tulk and Ley operated the Lowca Foundry between 1840 and 1854, as predecessors of Fletcher, Jennings & Co., constructing seventeen locomotives, of which no fewer than seven were for the M&CR. The first, a 2-2-2 named *Ellen* was delivered in 1840, and the last, a 4-2-0 with 7 ft. driving wheels, in 1854, although this was almost certainly delivered over Whitehaven Junction Railway metals.

The incorporation of the M&CR coincided with the promotion of various schemes to complete a West Coast trunk railway from London to Glasgow, in particular the section from Lancaster to Carlisle. These schemes have been well-covered in other publications, but one could have resulted in Whitehaven's becoming an important town on a main railway route to Scotland. Clearly driven by West Cumberland interests, who saw such a trunk line as a means of eliminating the area's relative isolation, the committee of the proposed Whitehaven, Workington and Maryport Railway asked George Stephenson, in June 1837, to survey a coastal route from the proposed terminus of the Lancaster & Preston Junction Railway in the city of Lancaster to Whitehaven. From Poulton-le-Sands (later Morecambe), this spectacular line would have crossed both Morecambe Bay and the Duddon Estuary on lengthy embankments, and would have tunnelled beneath Lindal Moor.

Stephenson's positive feasibility study for a 'Grand Caledonian Junction Railway' resulted in proposals for a much lengthier scheme than a local line connecting Maryport and Whitehaven. There appears to have been much localised support for this, as instanced by the existence of 'the Whitehaven Committee of the Grand Caledonian Junction Railway', which published its own observations of Stephenson's report dated 16 August 1837. The observations began: *The Whitehaven Railway Committee was appointed ... for the purpose of concerting measures for bringing forward the Newcastle, Carlisle, and Maryport Line* [sic] *from Maryport* [to] *Whitehaven, or for promoting the great national undertaking of the Grand Caledonian Junction Railway.* In addition to the existing coal traffic, which now had a potential rail outlet, Whitehaven was also seen as a future packet port, the committee noting that *steam vessels to Dublin, Belfast, and the Isle of Man would add greatly to the number of railway passengers*.

The committee of the so-called 'Caledonian, West Cumberland, and Furness Railway' was established in February 1838, appointing John Hague and John Rastrick as engineers to provide a more detailed survey based on Stephenson's earlier proposals. Both Hague and Rastrick confirmed the practicability of the Cumbrian Coast scheme, but government intervention in this strategically important issue resulted in a Parliamentary Commission to examine all alternatives. In May 1840, the Commisioners chose the more direct but more steeply-graded Shap route. Whitehaven was denied its place on the West Coast main line and, with it, an opportunity to break out of its hinterland. John Hague perhaps foretold the future when he wrote: *If [this railway is not built], West Cumberland will forever remain in the back settlements*.

As a result of this decision, Whitehaven had to wait for several more years to become connected to the M&CR. Indeed, the Town and Harbour Trustees appeared not to be overly concerned about the situation, when, in the autumn of 1839, with the M&CR under construction and the debate about the West Coast route in full flight, they were asked to give their opinion on an extension of the M&CR to Whitehaven. Scott-Hindson notes that *on 3 December 1839, the Trustees voted 'not to give an Answer'*! This was despite the fact that, by 1837, Maryport had overtaken Whitehaven in respect of tonnage of coal exports through its new dock.

The Whitehaven connection south from Maryport was not long in coming, however. In his book 'A Regional History of the Railways of Great Britain: The Lake Counties', David Joy notes the commissioning, in 1843, of a detailed report from George Stephenson (who undoubtedly had surveyed the route several years before) and one F Forster. The two surveyors estimated the cost of the Maryport-Whitehaven line at around £80,000, concluding that: *If [the line] is not made ... Maryport Harbour will be so improved as to seriously affect the trade of Whitehaven*.

The impact of the M&CR was dramatic, Wood noting that *as early as March 1844, the coal traffic at Maryport ... [had] nearly trebled since the construction of the ... railway*. There is no doubt that the rise of Maryport as Cumberland's leading port was almost entirely the work of the railway: 140,473 tons of coal were shipped through Maryport in 1842, rising to 213,152 tons in 1846. (For the same years, Whitehaven handled 205,518 and 220,870 tons respectively). In 1842, in his annual report on the Whitehaven collieries, John Peile forecast the benefits of the railway in reducing transport costs, commenting that *the promoters of the Maryport & Carlisle Rail Way* [have] *the avowed object in view to injure Whitehaven, in which they have been successful*.

Just as with the waggonways in the previous century, it was the Lowthers, in the shape of William, 2nd Earl of Lonsdale (after 1844) who were at the forefront of the push to establish the rail link southward from Maryport, and who were behind the incorporation of the Whitehaven Junction Railway (with a capital of £100,000) on 4 July 1844. Given his association with the scheme over several years, and his business dealings with the 2nd Earl, it was not surprising that George Stephenson was appointed as Engineer.

Construction progress of the WJR along the coastal plain presented no difficulties, and the first 5$^{1}/_{2}$ miles from Maryport to Workington were opened on 19 January 1846, the intermediate station of Flimby also being brought into use on the same date. The southward extension from Workington to Harrington (2$^{1}/_{4}$ miles) was opened on 18 May the same year, and the final section – the 4$^{3}/_{4}$ miles from Harrington to the Whitehaven (Bransty) terminus – became operational in 1847, opening for goods traffic on 15 February and for passengers on 19 March; the same opening dates also applied to the intermediate station at Parton. Originally, this last section was scheduled for opening before the end of 1846, but this was delayed due to storm damage to the sea wall at Redness Point, additional stone requiring cutting at Bransty Quarry for repairs. According to H G Lewin, in his book 'The Railway Mania and its Aftermath, 1845–1852' (published in 1936), the WJR was initially worked by the Maryport & Carlisle *as each section ... became available*, but Lewin was not regarded as totally reliable, and Simmons confirmed that he was unable to find any good evidence to confirm this statement, noting that both companies had their separate Officers. However, more recent research by P J Ashton, published in 'Cumbrian Railways', has revealed that M&CR locomotives were certainly operating the Maryport-Harrington section at the time of the opening of the Workington-Harrington section in May 1846, though Ashton discovered no evidence of such workings south of Harrington.

The Fletcher, Jennings Works Register records the delivery of two locomotives to the WJR in 1847: No. 1 *Lowther* and No. 2 *Whitehaven* (Works Nos. 6 and 7). These were 0-4-2 outside-framed tender locomotives, with 4 ft. 6 in. driving wheels. As the WJR was only 12$^{1}/_{2}$ miles long, two locomotives may well have been sufficient for most of the traffic, with M&CR locomotives being hired as necessary: in any case, any motive power problems disappeared after 1854, when the establishment of a Joint Committee of the WJR and the Whitehaven & Furness Junction Railway placed the rolling stock of the two companies under a single consolidated control (see Chapter 6).

The crest of the Whitehaven Junction Railway, depicting the Bransty Arch in front of the train. It is not clear whether the locomotive was one of the Maryport & Carlisle 0-4-2 tender locomotives or whether it was an invention of the artist.

(Peter Robinson Collection ex-Harry Fancy ref. CA1335)

Opening of the combined M&CR/WJR route reduced the Carlisle-Whitehaven journey time to 2 hours 10 minutes, whereas previously, the coach trip had taken six hours. Whilst the Maryport-Workington section had been relatively easy to construct, it was a different story south of Harrington where steep cliffs, rising to 150 feet, dictated a sinuous course along a wall just above the Irish Sea. Landslides were common along this stretch, as was storm damage. As early as 1852, a severe storm washed away part of the line between Parton and Whitehaven. Damage to this section of line has continued periodically up to the present day.

South of Parton station, beyond Redness Point, a siding from the WJR crossed the Parton Waggonway on the level, a trailing connection near the coke ovens just over 200 yards north of William Pit giving access to the Redness Point stone quarries. Opposite the gas works, however, the waggonway itself curved towards the south-west to cross the WJR on the level. The agreement between the Earl of Lonsdale and the railway company regarding the terms and maintenance of the flat crossing is mentioned in Chapter 4, although, given Lonsdale's involvement in both undertakings, it can scarcely have been less than amicable! The agreement was signed by both John Dixon ('Engineer of the Whitehaven Junction Railway Company') and John Peile ('Colliery Viewer and Agent of The Earl of Lonsdale'). At this stage of the line's construction, Dixon had been appointed by Stephenson as Resident Engineer.

An extension from a junction alongside the Bransty terminus to Whitehaven Harbour was authorised on 22 July 1848, construction beginning the same year. This ran to the North Wall, allowing the loading and unloading of vessels using the North Harbour. In conjunction with this new standard-gauge link, the Harbour Trustees agreed to strengthen the south-west side of the Wall, and to deepen the adjoining section of the harbour. On 28 July 1856, the Harbour branch was extended onto the Bulwark separating the North Harbour and the Inner Harbour (this extension being primarily for the benefit of the Whitehaven, Cleator & Egremont Railway's iron ore traffic).

Increasing traffic levels led the WJR Board to consider doubling of the line. Towards the end of 1859, a contract was let to double the Harrington-Workington section, and by mid-1860, two lines of rails extended over the full Harrington-Flimby route. Within 12 months, the whole of the WJR had been doubled, work being completed in the summer of 1861. The final stages of this scheme included the replacement of the original wooden single-track viaduct at Harrington with the double-tracked structure which did not require replacement until 2004. The longevity of the double-track viaduct owed much to the report of Captain Tyler, of the Board of Trade, who noted extensive rotten timber on the single-line structure in his December 1860 inspection. He advised the WJR to rebuild the structure with *materials of a less perishable nature*, believing that the company could well afford this with healthy weekly receipts of £53 per mile.

Running on former Whitehaven Junction metals adjacent to William Pit, an unidentified former LNWR Class 2F 0-6-0 (also known as a 'Cauliflower' or 18 in. goods) approaches Bransty around 1930. The 12D shedplate on the smokebox indicates that the locomotive was shedded at Workington. The chimney in the background served the bee-hive coke ovens before they became unused.
(CRA Photo Library ref. PA0905)

The 1865 25 inch to 1 mile OS map shows the single-track Parton Waggonway running behind the shipbuilding yards, curving north-west along the north side of the North Wall, and curving again before terminating on the North Jetty. Between the junction at Bransty and the North Jetty, this section had three passing loops. By comparison, the WJR Harbour branch made a single-line connection with the WJR main line, but, running immediately east of the waggonway, became double-tracked for the full distance behind the shipbuilding yards before terminating on the south side of North Wall, with a single-line connection to the Jetty and the Bulwark lines.

The completion of the WJR in 1847 connected the West Cumberland town to the growing national rail network, but all traffic had to be worked north, via Carlisle. It was again George Stephenson, through his close friendship with the Earl of Lonsdale, who pressed for the continuation of the railway southwards from the town in order to develop the mineral wealth of the area. Lonsdale, with his local mining interests, saw the commercial benefits of such a line, and proceeded to set up a committee to promote what was to become the Whitehaven & Furness Junction Railway. The next step in a Cumbrian Coast through route was under way.

Running on former Whitehaven & Furness Junction Railway metals, Class 40 1-Co-Co-1 No. 40 099 enters the passing loop at St Bees with an ICI sodium carbonate tank train from Northwich to Corkickle, the tanks being destined for the Marchon Products site via the Corkickle Brake. The main station buildings, constructed of sandstone, can be seen on the extreme left.
(Tom Heavyside ref. 503/2A)

The north portal of Whitehaven Tunnel on 21 July 1979, with Class 40 1-Co-Co-1 No. 40 084 emerging with empty flat wagons bound for the British Steel works at Workington. Note the survival of a short section of the platform canopy above the first vehicle, together with the banner repeater for Bransty No. 2 Down Home signal, giving the driver advance warning of this signal's aspect.
(Tom Heavyside ref. 501/22A)

Towards the South:
The Whitehaven & Furness Junction Railway

IT WAS NOT just the mineral wealth of the area, to the south and east of Whitehaven, which lay behind the promotion of the Whitehaven & Furness Junction Railway. Ease of access to Whitehaven Harbour was an important factor, but Lonsdale's committee must also have been influenced by contemporary events nearly forty miles to the south.

On 23 May 1844, the Furness Railway was incorporated as *a Railway from Rampside and Barrow to Dalton, Lindale [sic], and Kirkby Ireleth, in the County Palatine of Lancaster*. Little more than twelve months later, on 21 July 1845, the Whitehaven & Furness Junction Railway was authorised to build *a Railway from Whitehaven in the County of Cumberland, to a ... Junction with the Furness Railway in the Parish of Dalton in the County Palatine of Lancaster* with a capital of £350,000.

The railway's Whitehaven terminus was to be at Newtown (known locally as 'Preston Street', which became its official name in 1860), from where it was to run south to St Bees, then along the coast to Seascale before bridging the Mite and Esk estuaries on substantial viaducts. After rounding the great mass of Black Combe (1,970 ft.), the course of the line was originally routed east across the Duddon Estuary, from Borwick Rails to Dunnerholme, to join the Furness Railway about one mile north of the later (April 1851) halt at Ireleth Gate (later Askam-in-Furness).

The Duddon Crossing, by lengthy embankment and viaduct, was undoubtedly a revival of George Stephenson's plans for his earlier 'Grand Caledonian Junction Railway', although the May 1840 decision of the Parliamentary Commissioners in favour of the Shap route meant that a Cumbrian Coast through line could no longer be considered a main-line Anglo-Scottish corridor. In 1846, the W&FJR, with the aim of connecting with the West Coast route, promoted its Lancashire Extension Railway, commencing at Dalton and passing through Ulverston before linking up with a projected branch of the 'little' North Western Railway near Carnforth. This included the obtaining of running powers over the four-mile section of the FR between the junction at Dunnerholme and Dalton, thus providing a through route for the Whitehaven company not just to the main West Coast route to London but also to the industrial cities of the West Riding of Yorkshire. However, this scheme was dropped on a Parliamentary technicality, and was never revived in this form.

Construction of the W&FJR began, from the Whitehaven end, in the autumn of 1847, James Dees being appointed Engineer, with Messrs Fell, Joplin, Rigg & Brotherton as the main contractors. However, even before construction began, two more Acts were passed, which were to influence the future direction of the company. The first came on 27 July 1846, authorising the Furness Railway to *extend* [its] *line to Broughton and to Ulverstone*, and this probably influenced the deliberations of the W&FJR board – dominated by Lord Lonsdale – when seeking an alternative to the now-too-expensive 1¼-mile-long Duddon crossing. As a result, an Act of 14 August 1848 allowed the Whitehaven company to *deviate or extend their Line of Railway from Silecroft to Foxfield, and to abandon a Portion of ... Line between Silecroft and Ireleth*. The course of the line was now changed to run along the north shore of the Duddon, passing Under Hill (site of a station which closed as early as 1 January 1860) and crossing the Duddon on a substantial timber viaduct, 370 yards long, before making a junction with the FR's Broughton extension about a mile south of the terminus.

The second important Act was passed on 3 August 1846, authorising the W&FJR to *construct an extension ... to a Point of Junction with the Whitehaven Junction Railway*. It was this Act which authorised the construction of Whitehaven Tunnel, to run beneath the grounds of Whitehaven Castle. Lord Lonsdale, despite his domination of the WJR and the W&FJR Boards, did not want a railway within sight of his residence, insisting on a clause in the Act stating that a cutting should not be substituted for a tunnel without his consent. Despite this, it appears that the previously-mentioned August 1848 Act included powers for a surface line, to be built on arches, running from the Preston Street terminus to the WJR near Bransty. This would presumably have resulted in much property demolition, and the scheme appears also to have been opposed by the Town & Harbour Commissioners, being eventually dropped.

The construction of the W&FJR seems to have been relatively uneventful, the first section from Preston Street opened to traffic being the 16¼ miles to Ravenglass, which opened on 19 July 1849 with a connecting coach service to Broughton-in-Furness. The next 4¾ miles, to Bootle, was opened the following year, again connecting with the Broughton coach. There have been some differences about the precise opening date of this section: the papers of W B Kendall, a civil engineer with the Furness Railway between 1867 and 1883, and one of its earliest historians, include a W&FJR timetable, indicating a Bootle opening date *on or after 1st June 1850*, while W McGowan Gradon's book on the Furness Railway reproduces a timetable headed *This railway will be OPENED to BOOTLE ... on Monday next, the 1st of July 1850*. However, local newspapers, including 'The Whitehaven Herald' and 'The Cumberland Pacquet' carried accounts of a fire which damaged the wooden Esk Viaduct, south of Ravenglass, on 28 June, thus delaying the opening of the Ravenglass-Bootle section until 8 July 1850.

In the Down (southbound) direction, there were four through trains between Whitehaven (Preston Street) and Bootle, with an evening train running only as far as St Bees. The first departure, at 8-45 am, was a mixed working, 'Mineral & 3rd Class', which took 2 hours 5 minutes for the 21 miles! The 2-45 pm working was almost as slow, but the fastest working of the day was the 9-30 am ex-Preston Street, which ran to Bootle in 1 hour 15 minutes. This connected with the 6-10 am departure from Carlisle, which covered the 39½ miles to Bransty in 2 hours 10 minutes, arriving at 8-20 am and allowing passengers a leisurely walk between the two unconnected termini. A similar pattern of services existed in the opposite direction.

Single fares between Whitehaven and Bootle were not particularly cheap - 4s 5d for a first-class single, and 1s 9d for a third-class - while the connecting coach to Broughton cost 4s 6d inside, and 3s 3d outside. Interestingly, 1st and 2nd class season tickets were available between Preston Street and St Bees, but not to any additional destinations.

The final section of the W&FJR through to Broughton-in-Furness was opened on 1 November 1850, joining the Furness Railway's extension from Kirkby-in-Furness which had been open since February 1848. At a celebratory dinner in Broughton, the Earl of Lonsdale made an interesting speech regarding proposed schemes for connecting the W&FJR with the Lancaster & Carlisle line. Lonsdale referred to a *proposed route from the Furness line via Windermere,* [and another] *proposed to cross the sands and join the L&C line. I am of the opinion that the shortest line would be the best and, opening out as it would do, the most direct communication with the manufacturing districts of Yorkshire and the South*. This reference is interesting on two counts. The first is the reference to the Furness & Windermere project, originally mooted in 1845 and revived in 1850, to link Ulverston and Newby Bridge with Birthwaite (Windermere), thence via the Kendal & Windermere Railway to the L & C line. Lonsdale must have known that this roundabout scheme was dead by the time he made his speech at Broughton, since the Earl of Burlington (the Furness Railway Chairman) noted, on 31 October 1850, that the K&W directors *had given way*, following a meeting with three of the FR directors.

The second is Lonsdale's open endorsement of the proposed Ulverstone & Lancaster Railway, which had already been fully surveyed by Messrs McClean and Stileman by the time of the Broughton dinner. Indeed, McClean had been one of the FR officials who had persuaded the Kendal & Windermere to 'give way', and Burlington was the Vice-Chairman of the U&LR scheme! Lonsdale also added that there was capital available to complete the cross-bay route, although it was not clear whether he saw the W&FJR's backers as the source of this capital. Lonsdale was clearly planning for the future, since, later in his speech, he was forecasting that, within three to five years and following completion of the U&LR, Whitehaven would become the *Government Mail Packet Station for the important commercial town of Belfast*.

Despite the completion of the W&FJR line, there was no change in service frequency, with four departures south from Preston Street deemed sufficient. Indeed, the 2-30 pm departure from Whitehaven only ran as far as Drigg. Schedules were slow, apparently the result of extended halts at the smaller stations to allow passengers, railway employees and locals to enjoy the delights of the traditional Cumberland sport of cock-fighting! The fastest train of the day, the 10-30 am ex-Whitehaven, took 2 hours 15 minutes to cover the 35¼ miles to Broughton-in-Furness, where it made a 15-minute connection into the Furness Railway's 1-00 pm departure to Piel Pier, reached at 1-55 pm. Arrival at Fleetwood, for onward rail connections to Liverpool and Manchester, was at 4-00 pm.

While Lonsdale may still have harboured visions of Stephenson's 'Grand Caledonian Junction Railway', the reality was more sobering. Joy writes: *the W&FJR ... was a long and straggling single line, encountering ... few settlements or* [traffic] *sources,* [and the abandonment of] *the direct route across the Duddon estuary in favour of ... a reversal at remote Broughton ... [created] what was to be a permanent legacy of inconvenience and delay.*

As the main line was being extended southwards in 1850, work began on the construction of Whitehaven Tunnel. The tunnel itself curved gently to the north-west. During its construction, difficulties were encountered with old coal workings, almost certainly associated with James Pit. The 'Whitehaven Herald' of 18 September 1852 noted that freight was now using the tunnel. For the purpose of opening to passengers, the mandatory inspection was made by Captain Wynne, from the Railway Commissioners, on 24 September 1852, and the single-line tunnel opened to all traffic on 30 September. Joy notes wryly that *its 1,333-yard*-[length] *created the apparent contradiction that the longest railway tunnel in England's most mountainous county was almost at sea-level.*

Despite the opening of the tunnel, with its direct link to the Whitehaven Junction Railway and its branch to the North Wall of the harbour, the W&FJR decided to build its own line into the port, this being authorised on 4 August 1853. Taking the form of a tramway, this 600-yard-long single line was opened on 27 January 1854, emerging from the goods yard at Preston Street, and running through James Street and Market Place before curving left in front of the Customs House, erected in 1811. A single line served the Customs House Quay, but not directly, being accessed from a headshunt on the Old (or Sugar) Tongue, built between 1733 and 1735 to service West Indies trade.

Other sources have indicated that this tramway allowed access to the WJR's North Wall branch, providing a continuous (though tortuous) link between Preston Street and Bransty. However, this cannot have been the case, as the 1865 OS map clearly shows no connection, and that the sea wall between the New (or Lime) Tongue was yet to be constructed. (Authorisation was only included in the 1871 Whitehaven Dock and Railway Act, covered in more detail in Chapter 9.) Some confusion may have arisen because of the extension of the WJR's North Wall branch onto the Bulwark and the Jetty, which was opened on 28 July 1856. A more likely explanation, however, involved an 1850 W&FJR plan to construct a street tramway from Newtown (Preston Street), through the Market Place, along Strand Street and Tangier Street to Bransty. The plan was vetoed both by householders along the route, and by farmers using the Market Place. A revised line, routed via Newtown, Irish Street, Scotch Street, George Street, and Tangier Street was also rejected.

Much of the rationale behind the construction of the tramway was to handle future traffic from the iron ore mines of the Cleator area. Current production required the use of 500 to 600 horse-drawn wagons each day between the mines and the harbour, along poor roads, and with the planned construction of a railway serving the Cleator ore-field, a continuous line of rails between pits and port was forecast to reduce transit times between mines and ironworks. The

Whitehaven & Furness Junction Railway goods advice note, dated 21 January 1860.

(Michael Andrews Collection)

tramway, however, could not be used on Whitehaven market days between 7-00 am and 3-00 pm, and the 1853 Act authorising the tramway prohibited the use of locomotives between Preston Street goods yard and the quayside, only horse-traction being allowed.

For the first ten years of the W&FJR's existence, its financial position remained poor, mainly due to its isolation from good communications to the South. The August 1848 Act had stipulated that the junction with the Furness Railway was to curve south-east towards Foxfield, but when constructed, it faced towards Broughton. The Commissioners of Railways had noted this during their inspection, but decided not to enforce the original stipulation. However, this involved two miles of unnecessary running, as well as the Broughton reversal. The situation was not remedied until the opening of the direct Foxfield curve between the W&FJR and the FR on 1 August 1858, when a new station, together with sidings, engine shed and turntable, were built at Foxfield jointly by the two companies for the exchange of traffic. The opening of a second 'Expedition Curve', further south between Park (later Goldmire) and Dalton Junctions, took place on 1 July 1858, allowing through running without reversal between Whitehaven and Carnforth, the Ulverstone and Lancaster Railway having been opened throughout in 1857.

Historical information on Whitehaven & Furness Junction Railway locomotives is extremely scanty, and the accuracy of the better-known sources is now regarded as somewhat debatable. However, correspondence from E Craven, a reputable locomotive historian, published in 'The Cumbrian Railways Circular' in April 1978, is more definitive than most.

Craven concluded that the W&FJR's first two locomotives were large long-boilered 2-4-0s, built by Robert Stephenson & Co. These had 6 ft. driving wheels and outside cylinders which curiously drove the rear pair of coupled wheels. Evidence to support this was reported in the 'Ulverston Advertiser' of 12 July 1849, which described the arrival of the first locomotive from Newcastle (where the Stephenson works were located) and its subsequent manoeuvrings through the streets of Whitehaven, between Bransty and Preston Street stations. During these operations, the locomotive ran away, causing one fatality. The second locomotive arrived on 18 August, but was also soon involved in a fatality, the 'Whitehaven Herald' of 20 October noting: *The No. 2 engine got out of control and crashed into the schoolmaster's house at Preston Street, killing a child.*

The W&FJR soon regarded these locomotives as too heavy for the permanent way, too expensive to run, and too large for the traffic on offer, and in 1851 replaced them with two 'light tanks' from E B Wilson of Leeds. These 2-2-2T locomotives had 5 ft. 3 in. driving wheels, and were described by Gradon as *dwarfs*, although they were probably ideal for the company's relatively level route. The Stephenson locomotives appear to have lain out of use until their sale to the Stockton & Darlington Railway in February 1854, although doubtless they were used to replace the 2-2-2Ts in the event of a locomotive problem.

Craven noted that the W&FJR had five locomotives on its books in April 1853, and speculated about possible identities of the fifth locomotive. The most likely was Messrs Tulk & Ley's No. 8, which was built for the Cockermouth & Workington Railway in 1846. This 0-4-2 locomotive, with 4 ft. 9 in. driving wheels, was the C&WR's No. 1, and carried the name *Derwent*, but was sold in 1853, possibly to the W&FJR since a contemporary historian noted that *Derwent* was *running on the Whitehaven line*. A further, though unlikely, possibility was that the fifth locomotive had been purchased for use in the W&FJR's construction, and was then taken into capital stock. The 'Cumberland Paquet', in describing the line's opening on 21 July 1849, refers to *the locomotive ... which has been ... employed in conveying the earth required for the embankment over the Meadows near this town*. This is likely to have been a second-hand locomotive sourced from the Grand Junction Railway.

By 1853, neither the Whitehaven Junction Railway nor the Whitehaven & Furness Junction Railway were in good shape financially. Repairs to the notoriously exposed sea wall between Parton and Whitehaven had cost the WJR around £11,000, reducing profits by £4,000. As a result, the dividend for the year as a whole was only 2¼%. With the Ulverstone & Lancaster still under construction, traffic on the W&FJR remained low, and the company paid no dividend at all. Despite the opening of the W&FJR's tunnel, the company's trains continued to terminate at Preston Street, largely due to inadequate facilities at Bransty.

Lonsdale's chairmanship of both companies undoubtedly facilitated the agreement, signed on 31 December 1853, by which the locomotives and rolling stock of the WJR and the W&FJR were to operate under the control of a Joint Committee, whose board members were drawn from both companies. The main purpose of this agreement was the rationalisation of locomotives, rolling stock, and associated management. It would appear that the agreement was renewable initially on a three-year basis, as the Whitehaven Record Office holds a further three-year agreement for joint working, starting on 1 January 1857. This document was endorsed as having been renewed for one year, on 29 February 1860, and thereafter the agreement was renewable on a six-monthly basis, unless notice for termination was given by either party. James Sebastian Yeats and James Dees were appointed Secretary and Manager, and Resident Engineer respectively. Neither appointment was a success, Lonsdale accusing Dees of incurring unnecessary expense in locomotive hiring, while Yeats was suspected of 'financial

Purchase order from the Joint Locomotive Department of the Whitehaven Junction and Whitehaven & Furness Junction Railways, dated 7 September 1857. The word 'Junction' was sometimes dropped in references to the W&FJR, as instanced also by John Linton's 'A Handbook of the Whitehaven & Furness Railway', published in 1852.

(Michael Andrews Collection)

Chapter Six

irregularities' with station accounts and subsequently dismissed. However, the outcome of this management crisis was significant, as, in 1856, William Meikle was appointed as Joint Locomotive Superintendent, replacing Dees, and Henry Cook as Joint Secretary and Traffic Manager. Cook later transferred to the Furness Railway as Secretary and Assistant Traffic Manager when the W&FJR amalgamated with the FR, being appointed to these positions on 1 May 1866. He enjoyed a long and distinguished career with the Barrow company until retiring as Secretary in 1895, having earlier relinquished the Assistant Traffic Manager's role.

Benefits were immediate, with staff and rolling stock of both companies being pooled under the Committee's control. A Joint Committee renumbering and renaming was introduced, together with an olive green livery. The three locomotives provided by the W&FJR (the Wilson 2-2-2Ts, plus the probable Tulk & Ley 0-4-2) have already been mentioned. The other four in the Joint Committee's stock were WJR locomotives: the two Tulk & Ley 0-4-2 engines (see Chapter 5) delivered new for the opening of the line in 1846, plus two 2-4-0 locomotives, with 5 ft. 6 in. driving wheels, delivered from R & W Hawthorn in July 1847, and with works numbers 600 and 601. Originally named *Lonsdale* and *Maryport*, they were later renamed *Phoenix* and *Petrel*.

This Joint Committee had a life of more than ten years, until, on 1 July 1866, the WJR passed to the London & North Western Railway and the W&FJR to the Furness Railway. It should be stressed that, during this period the Committee existed purely for locomotive and stock pooling purposes, with both the WJR and the W&FJR operating as separate concerns, each with its own Board of Directors. At a meeting in Whitehaven on 30 June 1866, between the Furness and the London & North Western companies, it was recorded that *the joint working of the Loco Dept of the Whitehaven & Furness and Whitehaven Junction lines be continued for a month, subject thereafter to a month's notice from either Company to determine*. This was done undoubtedly to ensure the smooth continuation of motive power and rolling stock operation over the absorption period. After dissolution of the Joint Committee, it is likely that ex-W&FJR locomotives and stock were maintained at Preston Street shed, but that facilities for ex-WJR motive power had to be moved. A Minute of the LNWR's Locomotive & Engineering Committee noted that it was agreed to close the Whitehaven Joint Repair Shops on 30 November 1866, after which date, the LNWR and the FR would carry out repairs to their own stock. This date is likely to have marked the formal dissolution of the Joint Locomotive Committee.

Following the provision of additional facilities at Bransty, the Joint Committee concentrated all passenger facilities at Bransty from 3 December 1855, with Preston Street

The Preston Street branch and Coach Road crossing. On 21 July 1979, Class 25 Bo-Bo No. 25 149 heads towards the goods depot with a short train of tank wagons and CovHops, probably destined for the Albright & Wilson (Marchon) plant. Note that the Furness Railway signal (also shown on page 44) is still operational.
(Tom Heavyside ref. 502/25A)

Whitehaven & Furness Junction Railway architecture. The derelict Stationmaster's House at Corkickle in the early 1960s, at the junction of the Preston Street branch and the WFJR main line through Whitehaven Tunnel. The building is shown on the 1865 Ordnance Survey 25 inches to 1 mile map, making it possible that the house was built when Corkickle station was opened in December 1855.

(Allan Beck Collection ref. 1544)

Preston Street Goods Depot, probably taken in early BR days, looking north-west from Coach Road level-crossing. The original Whitehaven terminus of the WFJR, Preston Street became goods-only from December 1855, handling both WFJR and WJR traffic. The passenger terminus would have been much smaller than the large buildings shown here, erected later by the FR. The signalbox (left) appears not to be controlling the layout at this date. *(CRA Photo Library ref. PA0226)*

remaining as a goods station. This was not without its operating problems, as northbound passenger trains had to halt opposite William Pit before reversing into Bransty's terminal platforms. In the opposite direction, freight traffic originating from the North had to set-back for 900 yards into Preston Street depot. To compensate those passengers living in the vicinity of Preston Street, the W&FJR opened a new, single-platform station at Corkickle, adjacent to the south portal of Whitehaven Tunnel, also on 3 December 1855, although the Bransty reversal was not eliminated until 24 December 1874 when the Furness Railway opened its new platforms on the through lines.

Somewhat curiously, the W&FJR's offices were housed in the 80-bedroomed Lonsdale Hotel, erected between 1846 and 1847 by Lord Lonsdale. Alan W Routledge, in his book 'Whitehaven: History & Guide', stated that *the hotel had just been completed when it was taken over by the* [W&FJR], *who numbered ... Lonsdale among its principal shareholders.* It appears that the railway company's offices only occupied part of the building, as the 'Cumberland Pacquet' of 11 November 1856 advertised an extraordinary General Meeting of W&FJR shareholders at 'Ballard's Railway Hotel, Bransty Station' – undoubtedly the Lonsdale Hotel. It seems to have changed its name once more within a few years, as the 1865 OS map shows it as the 'Bransty Hotel'. The building probably ceased to house railway offices when Bransty was enlarged in 1874, and thereafter resumed its business as the 'Grand Hotel', a role it maintained until its destruction in a fire on 21 January 1940. Today the site is occupied by the Tesco supermarket.

Following the organisational tidying-up of locomotives and rolling stock resulting from the WJR/W&FJR Joint Committee, the stage was set for the next entrant on the Whitehaven railway scene. This time, the main rationale was exploitation of the local iron deposits, which extended for nine miles, from south of Egremont to Lamplugh. The result was the authorisation of the Whitehaven, Cleator & Egremont Railway.

Looking south, with Corkickle No. 1 box behind the camera. The double-track WC&ER climbs at 1 in 52 towards Moor Row, while the single-track W&FJR descends gradually towards St Bees via the valley of the Pow Beck. The building to the right of the overbridge is almost certainly Mire House, from which the nearby junction took its name. (CRA Photo Library ref. PA0355)

A busy scene at Moor Row around 1900, as FR D1 Class 0-6-0 No. 30 awaits departure with a stopping passenger train, probably for Egremont. The carriage on the left belongs almost certainly to the LNWR, as the lettering on the rear panelling says 'Whitehaven District No. 10'. An FR cattle truck can be seen on the extreme right. (CRA Photo Library ref. KER071)

Ore from the Iron Moor:
The Whitehaven, Cleator & Egremont Railway

JY LANCASTER AND D R Wattleworth, in their book 'The Iron & Steel Industry of West Cumberland: An Historical Survey', described the special qualities of the local haematite iron ore in some detail, stating that haematite *has a high iron content compared with most indigenous iron ores and is particularly free from ... phosphorus. It is this latter feature which made it unique among British ore deposits, and particularly suitable for the production of pig iron acceptable for conversion into steel by the Bessemer process"*.

As early as the 12th century, iron ore was being mined at Egremont, but no substantial production was recorded until the mid-18th century. Again, as with coal mining, transporting the raw material posed considerable difficulties, with carts or pack horses the only means of supplying the blast furnaces at Little Clifton (between Workington and Cockermouth, just south of the confluence of the Derwent and the Marron) and Barepot (at Workington itself). However, most of the ore was carted to Whitehaven Harbour, for shipment to furnaces in South Wales and Scotland, and at Newcastle and Chester, although, as with coal in the 17th century, logistics could be a nightmare, with 'buffer stores' (such as existed at Hensingham) having to be opened in order to hold ore which could not be immediately shipped. Apart from the inconvenience of double handling, transport costs were substantially increased.

1841 saw the opening of the Whitehaven Hematite Iron Company's blast furnace at Cleator Moor by Thomas Ainsworth, who was already mining ore in the area, and by the mid-1850s pig-iron production from the site had reached more than 300 tons per week. Iron ore mining also intensified during this period: 100,000 tons were shipped out through Whitehaven Harbour in 1850, doubling to 200,000 tons in 1856, the year in which the Whitehaven, Cleator & Egremont Railway was opened. Ainsworth appears to have been an innovative businessman, having introduced a large screw-driven steamship on the Cardiff-Liverpool-Whitehaven route, mainly for ore traffic, as early as 1852. A few years later, he wished to introduce a larger vessel of over 400 tons for this traffic, but insisted that the Harbour should be deepened for this purpose. The Harbour Trustees refused, on the grounds that the Harbour had already been deepened as far as possible, indicating that the port was already inadequate for the larger steam driven vessels then being built.

It was clear that the Whitehaven & Furness Junction Railway recognised the potential importance of the area's ore deposits, as James Dees, the company's Resident Engineer, had proposed a branch line to Cleator from Nethertown, three miles south of St Bees, in February 1851. Almost certainly because of financial reasons, the company made no effort to promote this link, and it was not until 1853 that plans were drawn up for a railway to Egremont and to Frizington, but this time starting from a junction with the W&FJR at Mirehouse, just over one mile south of Corkickle station. The second Earl of Lonsdale was one of the promoters of this scheme to link the Cumberland port with the two inland towns, but the main impetus came from Anthony Benn Steward, a Whitehaven solicitor and later High Sheriff of Cumberland, who became Chairman of the Whitehaven, Cleator & Egremont company. John Linton, who became Company Secretary, is perhaps better known for his 'Handbook of the Whitehaven & Furness Junction Railway', with its superb engravings, which was published in 1852.

The Whitehaven, Cleator & Egremont Railway was incorporated on 16 June 1854, to make *a Railway from the Whitehaven and Furness Junction Railway, near Whitehaven, to Egremont ... with a Branch therefrom to Frizington in the same County*. The initial share capital was £50,000.

Joy gives a concise description of the route of the line, writing that the WC&ER left the Whitehaven & Furness Junction line at Mirehouse Junction, after which, by means of sharp curves, and gradients as steep as 1 in 52, it climbed for two miles to reach Moor Row in the Keekle Valley. Here the main line continued southwards for a further 2½ miles through Woodend to the historic market town of Egremont, a 2¼ mile branch diverging at Moor Row to serve Cleator Moor before terminating one mile south of Frizington.

The exact date when construction commenced is unclear, but is most likely to have been in the final months of 1854. On 24 July 1855, the 'Cumberland Pacquet' reported on the WC&ER's progress, noting that *a single line only is being laid down but the embankment is being made sufficiently wide to* [allow] *a double line*. (The following month, the WC&ER board decided to double the Mirehouse Junction-Moor Row section, at a cost of £20,000.) The newspaper also noted that three quarters of a mile of the Egremont branch was already in place from the junction at Moor Row.

There appears to have been some confusion over what improvements the Harbour Trustees had planned for the port, to accommodate the increased iron ore traffic, and in what specific locations, Steward (the WC&ER Chairman) noting in August 1855 that *the accommodation for the iron ore* [at Whitehaven Harbour] *has not been provided as we were led to expect*. The expectations appear to have been the construction of additional jetties in the South Harbour, already served by the W&FJR tramway from Preston Street and opened nineteen months earlier. In consequence, the Chairman warned the Trustees that the harbour would lose business, as iron ore would be conveyed *by the railway to the East Coast and to Scotland*.

By December 1855, construction of the WC&ER was complete, and 100 mineral wagons had been delivered for use on the line. The first freight train ran on 11 January 1856, the 'Cumberland Pacquet' noting that the train, from the Parkside mine at Frizington, had run direct to Scotland *over the Whitehaven Junction Railway and other railways*. This first working, of 70 tons, appears to have been something of an experiment, perhaps to monitor braking capability on the steep gradients down from Moor Row, as the following day saw a second train depart for Newcastle with 124 tons behind the locomotive. Freight services over the Egremont branch commenced on 30 April 1856.

On 18 August 1856, Captain Tyler, of the Board of Trade, inspected the WC&ER, with the objective of an opening for passenger services. Tyler was highly critical of several aspects of WC&ER operation, particularly in respect of its exchange facilities with the W&FJR. The WC&ER's separate single line, which ran from the physical junction at Corkickle as far as Mirehouse, was constructed on W&FJR land, parallel with the latter company's line to the South, and Tyler felt that the W&FJR should be responsible for all notifications regarding the opening of this section. The Inspector also felt that the siding accommodation at Corkickle was insufficient for the exchange of both passenger and freight traffic, particularly as Corkickle was a single-platform station at the mouth of a long single-line tunnel, and he was also not satisfied that adequate working agreements existed between the two railway companies.

39

Chapter Seven

Perhaps more damning was the situation regarding motive power and passenger rolling stock. Tyler noted that the WC&ER possessed *only two engines, one of which is disabled, and no passenger carriages!* It appeared that the Egremont company intended to purchase an additional locomotive, and to lease carriages from the W&FJR, but bearing in mind his previous comments about WC&ER-W&FJR relationships, Tyler rejected this arrangement, recommending that the WC&ER acquire its own passenger rolling stock.

As a result, opening to passenger traffic was refused, pending a further inspection, which Tyler carried out the following year, on 29 June 1857. He noted that two key objections had been resolved, the first being the WC&ER's acquisition of *an extra engine, and three passenger carriages and a break* [sic] *van fitted with 'Newall's Break'.* He secondly approved of the more satisfactory working agreements with the W&FJR for exchange of traffic at Corkickle. On this basis, Tyler authorised the opening of the WC&ER to passenger services, although he also made additional recommendations.

The first was that the Corkickle-Moor Row section should be doubled as soon as possible. The second was that the electric telegraph should also link these two locations, presumably to link up with the telegraph system installed on the W&FJR around 1854. Somewhat curiously, it appears that the electric telegraph was laid through Whitehaven Tunnel when it opened in 1852, but was not operational for long, Lord Lonsdale announcing, at the W&FJR's 1853 Annual Meeting, that *the Telegraphic Wire through the tunnel ... has again failed ... It should be allowed to remain out of action, as ...* [this] *expensive item ... can very well be done without.*

The WC&ER opened for passenger traffic on 1 July 1857, the same year as the company gained Parliamentary authority to increase its share capital by £25,000, together with loans to complete the railway. Bearing in mind Tyler's reasons for refusing the planned 1856 opening, the initial locomotive fleet is likely to have consisted of two 0-6-0 saddle tanks, built in 1855 by Robert Stephenson & Co. These were numbered 1 and 2, and named *Ennerdale* and *Carlisle* respectively. In all probability, the third locomotive needed to comply with Tyler's requirements was an 0-6-0 side tank, also built in 1855 but by Messrs R & W Hawthorn, which carried the number 3 and the name *Victoria*. The fleet was augmented in 1858 by an additional 0-6-0ST, numbered 4 and named *Keekle*, constructed locally by Fletcher, Jennings & Co., who had taken over the Lowca Engineering Works from Tulk & Ley the previous year.

The opening of the WC&ER, first to freight, then to passenger, traffic, created significant new revenue for the W&FJR, but the level of W&FJR tariffs to the new company was soon causing problems for the latter. These tariffs had been set, by the 1854 Act, at 8½d (3.54p) per ton between Mirehouse Junction and Corkickle Exchange Sidings, Whitehaven Harbour, or Bransty station (via the tunnel), and at 4d (1.67p) for empty workings. An 1856 Working Agreement between the two companies confirmed tariffs at these levels for ten years.

Passenger services began in 1857, with three daily return workings between Egremont and Frizington, and Whitehaven (Bransty). In all probability, this meant that Whitehaven departures contained Egremont and Frizington coaches, with the train dividing at Moor Row. Interestingly, the 1857 timetable suggests that the coaches were stabled overnight at Frizington and Egremont, probably to avoid incurring additional W&FJR storage charges. On weekdays, the last departure from Corkickle was at 5-55 pm, but on Saturdays, when Whitehaven Market was held, there was an additional train from Bransty at 8-00 pm, arriving at Egremont at 8-30 pm and Frizington at 8-45 pm. It is likely that the WC&ER considered that Egremont, being the larger town, merited more coaches than Frizington, as, on 29 June 1857, the company agreed to hire a composite coach for working the Frizington branch. This would have allowed First, Second, and Third Class passengers to be accommodated within one vehicle.

Initially, all trains ran through the tunnel and reversed into Bransty station, but within a month, the W&FJR had imposed a 'tunnel charge' of 1s (5p) per train on these workings. This was for the *expense of a special engine* through the tunnel, presumably as a pilot locomotive. Vigorous objections from the WC&ER resulted in a proposed reduction to 6d (2.5p), but the Egremont company refused this compromise, and began to use Corkickle station as its Whitehaven terminus in order to avoid these charges. However, this must have been a gradual process, as the January 1858 timetable showed that the 8-40 am from Egremont ran through to Bransty, returning from there at 10-10 am for Egremont. The same timetable showed that the Saturday Market train had been re-timed to leave Bransty later, at 8-30 pm.

On 6 May 1859, the WC&ER Directors decided to terminate the morning workings to and from Egremont at Corkickle *for the month of June.* It was presumably on this date that all WC&ER passenger trains ceased to use Whitehaven Tunnel.

It seems that these disagreements over tunnel charges led to the construction of an extremely short and separate WC&ER platform at Corkickle, to keep the company's terminating passenger trains clear of the W&FJR's single line. The platform must have been built relatively quickly, as the Minutes of a WC&ER Directors' meeting, on 6 August 1858, stated that *application* [will] *be made to the W&FJR Co., to make a narrow wooden extension ... to the* [WC&ER] *platform at Corkickle station.* The W&FJR agreed to this request at a Board meeting on 14 September. A further reference to this separate platform came in WC&ER Minutes on 14 July 1859, stating that *the Whitehaven & Furness directors could not see their way to alter the mode in which* [WC&ER] *passengers have to cross the line at Corkickle.* This was in response to the Egremont company's correspondence with the W&FJR, pointing out what was presumably the lack of a designated foot crossing at Corkickle. The platform was extended again the following year, the W&FJR Board agreeing to lengthen it to accommodate two additional coaches, on 5 November 1860.

This platform was situated 200 feet south of the W&FJR's platform, and the track layout allowed WC&ER trains to run round. The platform would have had a relatively short life, and would certainly have been rendered redundant when WC&ER passenger trains resumed running to Bransty in January 1863. It is not shown on the 1865 OS 25 inch map. A Furness Railway plan from around 1877 appears to show an uncompleted new siding on the site of the former WC&ER platform, opposite the south end of Corkickle's existing platform and the W&FJR siding to the west of that company's running line.

Despite these arguments over tariffs, however, business was booming for the WC&ER, Joy noting that *completion of the line had an immediate and dramatic effect, ushering in a new era of industrialisation and enabling West Cumberland to take full advantage of its unique concentration of iron ore, coal, limestone, and sand.* At the August 1857 shareholders' meeting, the company's directors reported that iron ore traffic had shown a 97% year-on-year growth and other freight a staggering 195%. Between 1855 and 1860, output of the West Cumberland iron-ore field increased from 201,000 tons per annum to nearly half a million, and the WC&ER played a major role in this expansion of production, facilitating the opening of new ironworks in the area. It is hardly surprising that, by the beginning of 1861, the WC&ER was paying the W&FJR £2,000 per month in tolls and traffic charges. In August 1857, production started at Harrington Ironworks, ore reaching the furnaces over WC&ER and Whitehaven Junction Railway metals, and finished goods being despatched southwards via the WJR, the W&FJR, the Furness Railway, and the newly-opened

The bleak Cumberland landscape at Rowrah, 600 ft. above sea level, on 7 May 1966. Class 4MT 2-6-0 No. 43006 stands on the last remaining stub of the C&WJR's branch from Distington, closed in 1939, which had been retained as a headshunt for Rowrah Hall Quarry. The WC&ER's Marron extension (by this time cut back to Rowrah) can be seen passing beneath.

(Peter Robinson ref. 052c21)

Ulverstone & Lancaster Railway. Similarly, the opening of the Oldside ironworks at Workington, adjacent to the WJR, was facilitated by the opening of the WC&ER, once again allowing owners to erect furnaces at some distance from the ore-fields; here, the furnaces commenced operations towards the end of 1859, under the management of James Smith, who had previously held a similar position at Cleator Moor ironworks.

While the population of Whitehaven stagnated (its 1861 population of 14,064 representing a decline over the 1851 figure), the population of the ore-field towns grew. Cleator Moor was once described by Norman Nicholson, the Cumberland poet, as *a strange town which sprang into prosperity out of the bare rock, and now stands with the dead bones of that prosperity lying all around it.* Nevertheless, this planned town, a unique social monument to the age of mining, saw its population more than double, from 1,779 in 1851 to nearly 4,000 in 1861. By 1871, the town had a population of more than 7,000.

By 1860, the WC&ER was returning dividends of 7% per annum for the half-year, one of the country's best-performing railways, but this also had a knock-on effect for the Whitehaven & Furness Junction Railway, with the tariffs for using the Mirehouse Junction-Corkickle/Bransty section contributing to a 30% increase in receipts and allowing dividends to rise from nothing in 1856 to 4% per annum for the second half of 1860.

Extensive sections of single line, especially the W&FJR section through Whitehaven tunnel, were, however, imposing constraints on operational expansion of WC&ER traffic, and the Whitehaven, Cleator & Egremont Act of 7 June 1861 was the first stage in removing the bottleneck, authorising the company to *extend their Railway from Frizington to Lamplugh,* [and] *to widen and enlarge their present* Railway. The Lamplugh extension, running through Rowrah and taking the WC&ER to nearly 600 feet above sea level, was opened to mineral traffic in November 1862 and to passenger traffic (as far as Rowrah) on 1 February 1864, with the existing Mirehouse Junction-Moor Row section doubled from the same date. The BoT Inspector's report, dated 28 December 1863, referred to Mirehouse Junction signalbox and *the junction box at the goods branch* (obviously Preston Street Junction), inferring that these boxes were commissioned around this date. It was clear from the report that signalling was rudimentary, the Inspector commenting that *it would be desirable to connect the points and the signals, so that the signals cannot be lowered until the points are properly set.*

Additional powers were obtained, on 18 June 1863, to extend the line another 6½ miles to a triangular junction, at Marron, on the Cockermouth and Workington Railway just north of Bridgefoot, thus providing the WC&ER with a route into Workington, and its associated blast furnaces, independent from the W&FJR line and its constraints. The Marron extension was opened for mineral traffic on 15 January 1866 and for passengers on 2 April the same year. Two years earlier, double track had been extended from Moor Row to Frizington, although it was not until 1873 that doubling of the whole route through to Marron Junction was completed. Joy closed this chapter in the company's development by commenting that: *Today it seems scarcely credible that a railway through this remote country ... required double track, but ... traffic volumes were enormous ... Parkside* [mine], *near Frizington station produced 150,000 tons of ore in 1874.*

Dividends for both the Whitehaven, Cleator & Egremont and the Whitehaven & Furness Junction companies continued to be first-rate, the former declaring 10% in the first half of 1865 and the latter 8%. Both northern and southern outlets of the WC&ER continued to handle heavy mineral traffic, and even at the Corkickle end, where relations with the W&FJR remained difficult, more than 400 ore wagons were transferred each day to the Preston Street branch from where they made their way through the Market Place and onto the Sugar Tongue.

However, consolidation of the network of railway companies serving Whitehaven was on its way, and this was to be the most marked feature of the following decade.

Corkickle exchange sidings on 13 September 1963. Class 4F 0-6-0 No. 44505 pulls out of Corkickle No. 3 siding and prepares to join the Up Main at Corkickle No. 1 (the former Mirehouse Junction) with a mineral working for Moor Row.
(CRA Photo Library ref. PE-A926)

The single-platform Corkickle Station, as rebuilt by the Furness Railway, and looking towards the southern portal of Whitehaven Tunnel, from where Type 2 Co-Bo No. D5715 is emerging with the 5-7 pm Workington-Carnforth on 13 September 1963. Note the Furness Railway patterned ironwork supporting the typical glazed canopy, and an example of the company's squirrel-pattern seats beneath the station nameboard. Prior to 1866, the running line through the station was the sole property of the Whitehaven & Furness Junction Railway, while the long siding on the right was the joint property of the W&FJR and the Whitehaven, Cleator & Egremont Railway.
(CRA Photo Library ref. PE-A928)

Consolidation of the Railways:
Its Effect on Whitehaven

8

THE PROBLEMS involved in exchanging traffic at Corkickle with the Whitehaven & Furness Junction Railway have been well-described in the previous chapter. In the second half of 1862, all WC&ER passenger trains were still terminating at, and starting from, Corkickle. With poor connections into W&FJR services here, many passengers preferred to walk to and from Bransty – a reversion to the pre-1852 situation, prior to the tunnel's opening – although even at this station, facilities for passengers were far from acceptable.

However, the population of West Cumberland served by the WC&ER was increasing, due to the continuing expansion of the iron industry, and it was clear that the use of Corkickle as the WC&ER's passenger terminus could not be sustained indefinitely. On 18 September 1862, WC&ER Board member and iron mine proprietor Samuel Lindow informed the Board that he would support acceptance of the W&FJR's proposed 6d (2½ p) charge for the haulage of the Cleator passenger trains through Whitehaven Tunnel. Negotiations were obviously successful, especially for the WC&ER, as the W&FJR agreed to waive the 6d locomotive charge if the Bransty arrival and departure times were approved by the latter company. As a result, Whitehaven newspapers reported that all WC&ER passenger trains recommenced running to and from Bransty from January 1863, continuing the custom of reversing into, and out of, the WJR platforms there.

In practice, it would appear that WC&ER arrival and departure times at Bransty were amicably integrated with W&FJR schedules. Although records of the January 1863 timetable remain to be discovered, the public timetable for 3 January 1865 showed W&FJR arrivals at 9-15 am, 1-15 pm and 7-11 pm, with WC&ER arrivals at 9-50 am, 2-20 pm, and 5-15 pm. The agreement was not legally concluded until 1 January 1865, when it formed part of a new Whitehaven and Furness Junction Railway Act, including a 6d charge for use of a 'Special Engine' through the tunnel. It is likely that this charge would only have been invoked in the event of a late-running Cleator train or a non-timetabled working.

Working relationships between the three Whitehaven railway companies, however, were still not totally amicable. A W&FJR Board Minute in June 1863 recorded that *the alterations at Preston Street* [station] *which they had agreed to make for the joint use* [of the W&FJR and the WJR] *having been completed ... the Board now call upon the WJR Board to carry out their part of the agreement by covering Bransty station with a roof, which is so much needed to protect the carriages and passengers from ... the weather*. This squabbling continued into the following year, the Whitehaven Junction board noting, on 8 July 1864, that *the W&FJR were determined to have the present arrangements for the use of* [Bransty and Preston Street] *abandoned, and a new agreement ... entered into*.

In addition to its problems with its northern neighbour, the W&FJR's problems with the WC&ER continued to escalate. Congestion at the Corkickle exchange sidings was an increasing problem, as more mineral workings reversed onto the W&FJR en route to the furnaces at Barrow, where the Haematite Iron & Steel Company was well on its way to becoming the world's largest Bessemer plant. In 1864, the WC&ER proposed extending its line south from Egremont to a junction with the W&FJR north of Sellafield, utilising the natural routeway of the Ehen Valley, as a means of avoiding the Corkickle bottleneck. The W&FJR, alarmed at the potential loss of revenue from the ore traffic, countered by reviving James Dees' 1851 scheme for an Egremont-Nethertown line, although this would have involved heavier earthworks for the three-mile route.

It was possibly the cost of this line, plus continuing squabbling between the parties, which convinced the W&FJR that an agreement between the two concerns was desirable, as a result of which the W&FJR proposed reducing its mineral tolls, as well as increasing payments to the WC&ER for 'own haulage' over the Mirehouse-Corkickle line from £23 to £700 per annum (apparently, the tolls fixed in 1854 included an element for the provision of W&FJR motive power). The proposal of 10 October 1864 saw these tolls reduced from 8½ d (3.3p) to 6½ d (2.7p) per ton going north over W&FJR metals, and from 8½ d to 3d (1.3p) for traffic heading south from Corkickle. The W&FJR now agreed to abandon its plans for the Egremont-Nethertown line, in return for which the WC&ER agreed not to promote any railway in the district between Ravenglass and Workington. Additionally, the WC&ER undertook not to oppose the W&FJR's plans for a Duddon Estuary crossing, the Bill for which had been deposited in September 1864. As a result, a 25-year Agreement on these proposals was signed by both companies on 14 November 1864, with formal agreement incorporated in Schedules A and B of the 1865 Whitehaven and Furness Junction Railway Act.

Railway politics over the Duddon Crossing were soon to upset this new-found harmony, however, when the Furness Railway lost out to the Whitehaven & Furness Junction in the battle to cross the estuary, the latter's scheme being approved on 29 June 1865. This left the FR with no alternative but to purchase the W&FJR, which it did on 1 July 1866, and the Furness main line now extended all the way from Carnforth to Bransty. The terms of purchase, guaranteeing W&FJR shareholders 8% on Ordinary shares, reflected the Whitehaven company's current prosperity.

The WC&ER now reopened negotiations over the proposed Egremont-Sellafield link with its future neighbour, the board meeting James Ramsden (the FR's General Manager) on 9 October 1865. Ramsden suggested that this line, running along the Ehen Valley, should be jointly owned, as a result of which the five-mile route was authorised on 28 June 1866. The Act established the Cleator & Furness Railway Committee for its joint operation, this body consisting of three W&FJR (or its successor) and three WC&ER Directors.

Construction of the line presented few problems, and the C&FR, with an intermediate station at Beckermet, was inspected by Colonel Hutchinson on 14 May 1869. Opening was refused, on the grounds that station facilities were incomplete, and the line was not opened until 1 August 1869 (after a re-inspection on 28 May), all trains being worked by the WC&ER under an arrangement with the Furness.

Consolidation south of Whitehaven was also mirrored northwards from the town. In the summer of 1865, realising that it had to purchase the W&FJR, the Furness board was advised that, if they had any ambitions of reaching Scotland, the W&FJR was useless without the Whitehaven Junction Railway and that purchase of both companies was essential. However, it was the London & North Western Railway which now saw its chance, and took it without hesitation, absorbing both the Whitehaven Junction Railway and the Cockermouth & Workington Railway on 16 July 1866, the latter giving the Euston company access to West Cumberland via the Cockermouth, Keswick & Penrith Railway. The LNWR clearly thought it had made an excellent purchase: in later years, Sir Richard Moon, the financially-astute LNWR Chairman, noted that it was the best bargain the company had ever made.

43

Chapter Eight

With the FR absorption of the W&FJR and the joint operation of the Cleator & Furness, improved relationships between the FR and the WC&ER appeared to ease operational problems at Corkickle and through Whitehaven tunnel. Slack operating, however, was the cause of the August 1866 accident in the tunnel, the root cause of which lay in the still-inoperative electric telegraph between Corkickle and Bransty.

Because of this, a 'Pilotman' was responsible for conducting all engines through the tunnel (the commonly-held notion, that all trains through the tunnel had to be led by a pilot locomotive, is incorrect). The Furness Railway's 'Rules and Regulations' for 1874 contains an interesting section on 'Regulations For Trains Passing Through Whitehaven Tunnel', and this is likely to have been applied for several years previously. Special Regulation 327 stated that *a Pilotman will conduct all engines through the tunnel and no engine is ... to enter the tunnel except on the order of the Pilot after he has seen the proper signals exchanged on the Block Telegraph*. The Pilotman's role as train despatcher was confirmed in Regulation 334: *When the Pilot has sent an engine through the tunnel, intending to follow on the next engine, he must not proceed* [on that engine] *until the all clear signal has been received from the other end*. The following Regulation noted that the Pilot *may at any time make use of the jobbing engine to facilitate this work*, which confirms that a 'tunnel engine' was available to transfer the Pilot through the tunnel as workings required.

By itself, this was a totally safe practice, but it appears that the Pilotman, at Corkickle and responsible for authorising trains to enter the tunnel, was (because of the inoperative telegraph) permitted to let a second train enter the bore in the same direction after a fifteen-minute interval, provided that this did not conflict with a timetabled southbound working. On 10 May 1866, at around 9-00 am, a Maryport-bound mineral train entered the tunnel, as directed by the Pilotman, but the couplings parted, leaving three wagons and the guard's van underground on the single line. Under the 'fifteen minute' rule, the Corkickle pilotman allowed the 8-49 am Broughton-in-Furness to Bransty passenger train, headed by the Joint Committee's 2-2-2WT No. 4 *Oberon* hauling five vehicles, to enter the tunnel, where it collided with the stranded vehicles at 10 mph. 30 to 40 passengers suffered varying degrees of injury, but the driver was badly injured through scalding, and the fireman, who was probably riding on the buffer beam to sand the damp rails, was killed outright. Damage to the passenger locomotive was described as *end frame ... broken and chimney damaged*. The driver, Thomas Shippin, was later commended for having quickly reversed his train out of the tunnel into Corkickle station. The Pilotman, Richard Johnson, who had long experience of working the tunnel, and the Corkickle station master were suspended from duty.

South of Whitehaven, the expansionist tendencies of the London & North Western Railway continued, the company now having the Whitehaven, Cleator & Egremont firmly within its sights. Initial overtures were rejected, with A B Steward, the Cleator company's Chairman, declaring another 10% dividend at the 1867 Annual General Meeting and noting sarcastically that *the mighty* [LNWR] *considered that its shareholders did well when they got 5½%*.

It was events in 1873 which marked the beginning of the end for the WC&ER as an independent company. The LNWR was not well-regarded in West Cumberland (one local paper describing the company's main characteristics in the county as: *Unpunctuality, defective management, high fares, exorbitant rates for traffic, scarcity of rolling stock, and second-class passengers treated as so much rubbish*, and the WC&ER felt that this unpopularity, coupled with its virtual monopoly of rail-borne mineral traffic within its region, would allow it to push through swingeing rate increases. In 1873, under the new chairmanship of Henry Jefferson, the WC&ER decided to increase its rates by 7% for iron ore and by an even larger 11% for coal and coke.

This was the last straw for local industrialists, and in the following year, several local ironmasters proposed a scheme for an independent railway from Cleator Moor to Workington, thereby avoiding the metals of the WC&ER and the FR between Cleator Moor and Bransty. Supported by the third Earl of Lonsdale and H F Curwen, a Provisional Committee was formed on 9 October 1875 to establish the best route for the new line, which of necessity had to run inland from the coastal route. The planned route diverged from the WC&ER just south of Cleator Moor station, and climbed steeply to a summit 460 feet above sea-level near Moresby Parks before descending at 1 in 70 through Distington and Workington to a junction with the LNWR at Siddick. The distance from the proposed junction at Cleator Moor through to Siddick was 11 miles 20 chains.

Despite considerable opposition, most notably from the WC&ER, the Cleator & Workington Junction Railway was incorporated on 27 June 1876, with a capital of £150,000. A further Act, on 28 June 1877, empowered the Furness Railway to work the system, and another, in July 1879, authorised the Barrow company to buy C&WJR shares up to a value of £25,000 and to have the option to purchase the latter company if the C&WJR board decided to sell the line.

Coach Road level crossing, on the Corkickle-Preston Street goods branch, looking north on 31 July 1967. The crossing is fully signalled, with the nearest signal being of Furness Railway origin.

(CRA Photo Library ref. PE-AA70)

The construction contract for the C&WJR was awarded to Messrs R Ward & Co. (later Ward, Ross & Liddelow), who encountered problems with the amount of material which needed to be removed to create the lengthy cutting just south of Moresby Parks station. The contractor decided that an additional locomotive was required to work on this site, moving it from Whitehaven in the most extraordinary manner, as described in a December 1981 historical article in 'The Whitehaven News'. The author described how, in May 1878, the locomotive was initially moved by rail to Preston Street yard, before travelling under its own steam to Coach Road level crossing. At this point, the Furness Railway track was slewed sideways, to make an end-on connection with a short length of track laid on the highway! The locomotive then steamed onto this temporary track, ran for a short distance, and then halted. The section of line behind the locomotive was then detached, hauled forward by a team of horses, and then attached to the section of line in front of the locomotive. The locomotive moved forward once more, and the process was repeated, until the site at Walkmill was reached the following day. It must have been an amazing site to see this locomotive travelling up the steep street through Hensingham!

The line was officially opened for freight traffic on 4 August 1879, although passenger traffic between Moor Row and Workington (Central) was not inaugurated until 1 October 1879, being extended to Siddick Junction the following year. Passenger services were always sparse, the August 1887 'Bradshaw' recording only four weekday workings each way between Moor Row and Siddick, and took second place to the heavy mineral traffic over the line. Oliver Wood noted that the C&WJR brought Durham coke to the furnaces at Cleator Moor and Distington from Siddick or Workington, and distributed their pig iron, as well as carrying all the output of Moresby Colliery and the coal from Broughton Moor.

For most of its existence, the C&WJR paid a dividend, though it was never as profitable as the Whitehaven, Cleator and Egremont had been, and remained independent right up to the Grouping, the final Annual General Meeting being held on 8 February 1923, when a dividend of 3% was declared. The final Shareholders' Register showed that 95% of the company's Ordinary shares were held by the United Steel Companies (owners of the Workington Iron & Steel Co.). The Board had been made up increasingly of USC nominees in preceding years, but the majority of directors remained men whose names were well-known in the ore-mining and iron-making industries of West Cumberland. The C&WJR remained an ironmasters' line until the end.

The WC&ER's partial response to the planned Cleator Moor-Workington line was the so-called Gilgarran branch, although this was only one line in a much larger scheme. An Act of 2 August 1875 authorised the construction of *a branch railway (two miles six furlongs and 182 yards in length) commencing by a junction (with the WC&ER) ... at or near to the Ullock station ... and terminating west of the village of Gilgarran ...* [near] *a coal-pit of the Gilgarran Coal Company called No. 2 pit.* On 27 June 1876, the same day as the C&WJR was authorised, the WC&ER obtained additional Parliamentary powers to extend the Gilgarran line to Distington and then down to Parton, to join the former Whitehaven Junction Railway. The Distington-Parton section involved a severe descent, averaging 1 in 53 over the 2½ miles down to the coast.

It is worth summarising the WC&ER's extensive plans for opposing the proposals of the C&WJR. As a defensive measure, the WC&ER projected a total of six lines, four of which replicated those proposed by the C&WJR. Two were to serve the Derwent and Moss Bay works, and one was to run parallel with the WJR to make a junction south of Workington. These lines were to commence at Distington, and, as the WC&ER had access to Distington by 1876, there would be no need for the direct line from Cleator Moor Junction to Distington as proposed by the C&WJR. In the event, only three of the six proposed lines were authorised. One, the Mowbray branch, was built from a junction off the Lamplugh extension east of Frizington to serve mines on the outskirts. The second had been promoted as the Moss Bay Extension, running from the Gilgarran Branch to make a junction near Moss Bay with two other lines proposed but not authorised, and with a spur off to join the WJR line. It was intended to run this line through Distington and High Harrington, but in the event it was only approved as far as Distington, becoming known as the Gilgarran Extension Railway. The third line, the Whitehaven Branch, was an extension to the already authorised Gilgarran Branch and truncated Gilgarran Extension, and linked Distington to the WJR main line at Parton.

It should be mentioned here that the 1875 Act also authorised the acquisition of land at Mirehouse for the construction of a new station and sidings, to alleviate the congestion at Corkickle. Purchase was agreed with John Postlethwaite, who owned the Hollins estate, but construction did not proceed, being overtaken by the LNWR's later purchase of the WC&ER in 1877.

The WC&ER must have been aware of plans for the opening of blast furnaces at Distington, although, according to Lancaster and Wattleworth, it was not until 1878 that a partnership of several ironmasters from the Kilmarnock area formed the Distington Hematite Iron Company on land leased from H F Curwen. However, by the time the 6¼ miles between Ullock and Parton opened,

The Whitehaven branch (Distington-Parton) of the WC&ER. On 26 April 1966, Class 4MT 2-6-0 No. 43036 propels its coal train up the 1 in 53 from Parton. The coal originated from Solway Colliery, near Workington, and was destined for the washery at Lowca (Harrington No. 10 pit).

(Peter Robinson ref. 051a36)

on 2 May 1879 (the permanent way appears already to have been laid by July 1878), Distington's three blast furnaces had already been in operation for three months. Joy records that the Ullock-Distington line passed through the ironworks yard, thus providing a direct link for iron ore and limestone from the Rowrah area and enabling pig-iron to be despatched to Whitehaven Harbour via Parton (and the former WJR). However, Joy is probably incorrect as to the line's course through the ironworks, as the Joint Committee, on 18 July 1878, authorised the expenditure of £4,500 on an ironworks siding, running on the south side of the Gilgarran branch. The branch was opened on 24 January 1880. The 1914 edition of the Railway Clearing House's Junction Diagrams shows this branch to have been 37 chains long.

The Gilgarran branch (together with the Extension railway and the Whitehaven branch) remained freight-only for all of its life, apart from a short period between 1 June 1881 and 8 December 1883, and again (on Thursdays and Saturdays only) between 2 November 1913 and 1 September 1914, when a passenger service operated between Whitehaven Bransty, Parton and Distington. It is likely that these services terminated at, and started from, the otherwise-unused LNWR & FR Joint Line platforms at the latter station. During the first period of passenger services, traffic was sparse: on 30 October 1883, the Joint Committee noted that passenger revenue was no more than £10 per annum, and that services would be discontinued from 1 January 1884. The earlier actual closure date indicates that the Joint Committee saw no inconvenience to passengers.

Despite the benefits from coal and iron traffic which would have accrued to the WC&ER through the opening of the Gilgarran branch, the start of construction works on the C&WJR in 1877 only served to amplify the worries of the Egremont company about the impact of the interloper. The London & North Western, sensing this anxiety and determined to add further strategic mileage to its West Cumberland network, offered to take over the WC&ER by guaranteeing shareholders a perpetual 10% dividend. This was accepted, and vesting took place on 1 July 1877, under an Act of 28 June.

Prior to this acquisition, the general relationship between the LNWR and the Furness Railway in West Cumberland appears to have been benign. Evidence for this comes from the Duke of Devonshire (the FR Chairman), who wrote in May 1865 that *the London & North Western ... appear to be disposed to act fairly towards us*. However, James Ramsden, the FR's Managing Director, was becoming extremely unhappy about the takeover negotiations between the LNWR and the WC&ER, and its implications for Furness activities in West Cumberland. Having been authorised to work the Cleator & Workington Junction line in June 1877, Ramsden was keen to exploit the C&WJR's 1876 proposals to build a new line from Cleator Moor to a point south of Egremont, on the Cleator & Furness Joint line. Not only would this have eliminated the Moor Row reversal for C&WJR traffic, but it would also have bypassed imminent LNWR territory.

The WC&ER responded immediately by incorporating plans for their own Moor Row avoiding line, with direct access to the C&WJR, and these were incorporated in the June 1877 Act authorising the LNWR takeover.

All this territorial skirmishing quickly came to an end. Early in 1878, an agreement was reached between the three parties – the FR, the LNWR, and the WC&ER – that the FR and the LNWR should jointly acquire the WC&ER, each party owning 50%, and this was legalised under the Whitehaven, Cleator & Egremont Vesting Act of 17 June 1878, following which the WC&ER was controlled by the London and North Western & Furness Joint Committee. At the first meeting of the committee, held on 27 June 1878, it was agreed that plans for a new line avoiding Moor Row would be abandoned.

The railway was thereafter generally known in West Cumberland as 'the Joint Line'. Although this small Cumbrian company, with only 36¾ route miles, had seen its share capital increase from the authorised £100,000 in 1854 to well over £700,000 by 1878, the Joint Line accounts were to remain in deficit throughout the committee's existence, as the 10% guaranteed dividend was never met by the net profit.

After 1878, the general pattern of operations over the Joint Line was that the LNWR handled most passenger trains, many services now being extended to operate to and from Workington via both Whitehaven and Marron. Services, however, were generally sparse: in 1887, departures from Whitehaven Bransty at 6-35 am, 9-50 am, 1-10 pm, 4-40 pm and 8-30 pm ran to Rowrah, but only the 9-50 and 4-40 workings were extended to Marron Junction. In the reverse direction, the 8-05 am and 7-35 pm departures from Marron Junction ran through to Bransty and there were additional departures from Rowrah at 10-45 am, 2-00 pm and 4-14 pm.

These workings also conveyed portions for the better-served Egremont line, which were attached and detached at Moor Row. The same 1887 timetable showed eight workings from Whitehaven to Egremont, with seven in the reverse direction (plus two which terminated at Moor Row); three trains continued to Sellafield, while four started from this Cumbrian junction.

Joy also added that the LNWR was responsible for goods and mineral traffic north of Rowrah, while the FR generally worked south of the latter junction station, although, within a decade, the sphere of LNWR operation appeared to extend southwards. For example, the October 1888 Working Timetable of the LNWR's West Cumberland Division shows an LNWR freight working, probably originating from Workington, which left Corkickle at 9-10 am and ran to Frizington (via Moor Row), where arrival was at 10-00 am. Penetrating even further south, the LNWR scheduled a mineral train from Moor Row at 10-30 am to Sellafield, where arrival was at 11-00 am. In contrast, FR mineral traffic by this date was confined to the Sellafield-Egremont-Moor Row-Whitehaven section.

By 1878, the day of the small main-line company in the Whitehaven area was over, the FR and the LNWR entirely dominating affairs. It was no coincidence that this was also a period when the Lowther family's grip on Whitehaven's industries and railways was beginning to slacken. The railway-promoting 2nd Earl of Lonsdale was succeeded, in March 1872, by Henry, the 3rd Earl, who showed little interest in mining, the port, or in railways. The sickly 4th Earl, who succeeded to the title in August 1876, only paid one visit to Whitehaven, and died in 1882, at the early age of twenty-seven.

In the town and port, however, together with their immediate environs, interesting developments were still taking place.

Consolidation of the Railways and its Effect

Bransty station on 6 June 1999, with Class 20s Nos. 20 310 and 20 314 heading the 7C22 Carlisle Kingmoor-Sellafield nuclear flask train. The train crew have removed the single-line token for the St Bees section from the facility on Platform 2.

(Dave McAlone ref. P14)

Redness Point, north of Whitehaven, on 7 February 1996. After two days of heavy snowfall and closure of the line, the snowplough arrives from Carlisle with 31 275 and 31 142 in charge.

(Dave McAlone ref. P20)

The northern portal of Whitehaven Tunnel. On 24 April 1992, Class 60 No.60 072 *Cairn Toul* emerges into daylight with return Padiham-Workington coal empties. The train is signalled through Platform 3, Platform 2 being temporarily out of use because of gauging issues with the newly-introduced single-car Class 153 diesel units.

(Dave McAlone ref. U32)

47

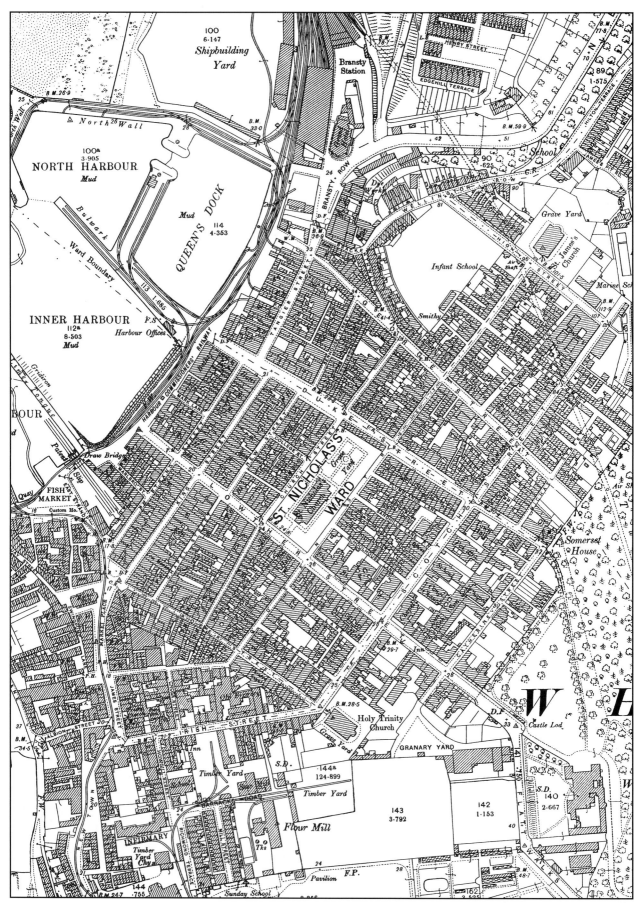

On this map can be seen part of the Harbour Commissioners' Railway, between the Bulwark and the Fish Market, completed in 1877. Note the swing bridge over the Patent Slip, which was constructed by Fletcher, Jennings & Co. The map erroneously describes this as a 'Draw Bridge'. The Harbour Commissioners' engine shed can be seen at the end of the pier between the North Harbour and the Queen's Dock. The tramway which ran from Preston Street goods station along Barracks Road can be seen at the bottom of the map.
(Reproduced from the 1899 25 inch Ordnance Survey Map sheet 67.10, Cumbria Record Office, Whitehaven, with the kind permission of the Ordnance Survey)

Industrial Railways:
The Harbour

9

THE 1865 ORDNANCE SURVEY (25 inch to 1 mile) map shows quite clearly that there was no rail connection between the Whitehaven Junction Railway's line from Bransty which ran onto the Bulwark of the North Harbour, and the Whitehaven & Furness Junction tramway from Preston Street, which served the Customhouse Quay and a short section of the Old (or Sugar) Tongue. Additionally, the W&FJR line had not been extended westwards, in the direction of the West Strand and the Howgill Staithe.

In 1871, however, the Whitehaven Dock and Railways Act empowered the Town and Harbour Trustees to build a wet dock *partly in the present North Harbour, partly in the shipbuilding yard ... of the Whitehaven Shipbuilding Co. Ltd, and partly in lands situated between the present North Harbour and Tangier Street.*

This was not the first attempt to develop a wet dock, as in 1854, the engineer James Rendel was invited to put forward plans for such a facility. Rendel's plans were ambitious, proposing a massive wall from Redness Point to the North Pier, and incorporating new railway lines onto an improved Bulwark. The Trustees baulked at the cost of both this scheme (nearly £100,000) and a cheaper scheme to construct two wooden jetties in the North Harbour, one of which would have been rail-connected.

A few years later, however, the rail element of the scheme was resurrected, with plans for a single wooden jetty in the North Harbour, running parallel to and 100 feet south-west of the North Wall. Work began on the jetty in March 1860. It had three railway lines, and the work was completed in June 1862. Scott-Hindson noted that *the WJR supplied the pointwork for the railway connections, and the WC&ER paid for the iron spouts used in discharging ... ore into the ships.* Additionally, the 'Ulverston Mirror' on 9 February 1861 noted that: *Last week, the experiment of conveying by locomotive the iron ore wagons from Bransty station to the Bulwark was tried,* [using] *a small engine belonging to the Cleator Haematite Iron Co.* [sic]*. The trial commenced by the engine bringing through the tunnel from Corkickle to Bransty, 15 loaded wagons.*

These two references raise the strong possibility that the bulk of the ore traffic originating from the WC&ER was routed via the tunnel and a Bransty reversal from 1861/2 date onwards,

with the W&FJR's Preston Street tramway seeing a corresponding decline in traffic levels: certainly, after the October 1864 agreement on reduced mineral traffic tolls between the W&FJR and the WC&ER, this would seem to have been the most rapid and cost-effective route between mine and port. The jetty had a relatively short life, being demolished sometime before the opening of the Queen's Dock in 1876.

The Trustees recognised the need to incorporate a connection between the WJR and W&FJR harbour networks, and this was incorporated into the 1871 scheme. From the north-east, the WJR lines made an end-on connection with the new railway (known as the 'Harbour Commissioners' Railway'), which ran south-west over land reclaimed from the mudflats of the Inner Harbour. The filling necessary to form this embankment (which had a minimum width of 50 feet) was obtained from neighbouring excavations for the dock walls. This section, along what was now a new sea wall, was around 200 yards long, and incorporated three parallel lines, together with new north-west to south-west and north-west to north-east connections from the Bulwark side of the new dock; the former was constructed specifically to handle ore traffic travelling via Preston Street tramway.

The line became single to cross a swing-bridge over the 'patent slip'. This was needed to allow the slipway to continue in operation. The 'patent slip' was itself an iron railway, on top of which was an oak frame upon which ships were placed, drawn up, repaired, and lowered back again. The railway consisted of three rails, 20 ft. apart, and was around 250 yards long. The winding apparatus of the slip comprised two cranked axles fitted with toothed wheels, the gearing of which allowed a vessel of 200 tons to be hauled out of the harbour by a team of 30 men. The swing bridge, built by Fletcher, Jennings and Co., was a substantial structure, the main girders being 62 feet long and 13 feet 3 inches apart from centre to centre; the total weight of the bridge and turntable, including 30 tons of balance weights, was 70 tons. A few yards beyond the swing-bridge, a curving connection gave access to the now-realigned W&FJR along the Customhouse Quay, where a further short connection allowed direct access from the Preston Street tramway towards the West Strand. Now running north-west, the final section of the new Harbour Commissioners' Railway ran for around 250 yards along the West Strand, as far as the first coal hurry.

On 22 April 1966, a train of 21-ton BR hopper wagons behind an ex-Workington Iron & Steel Co. 0-4-0ST (RSH No. 7049 of 1942) and en route for coking at the WISCo complex, heads for the exchange sidings at Bransty. The two men to the right of the locomotive are following the path of the Preston Street tramway towards the Customs House. The Marchon phosphate rock silo can be seen above the wagon.

(Peter Robinson ref. 050d13)

Chapter Nine

The Queen's Dock, in a photograph probably dating from the 1920s. An empty Whitehaven Colliery Co. Ltd. wagon stands on the site of the Harbour section of the Parton Waggonway. Behind the wagon is a rail-mounted hand-operated light crane. On the pier running towards the dock gates can be seen the single road Harbour Commissioners' engine shed.

(Sankey ref. D410)

All land required for this scheme was owned by Lord Lonsdale. Following the death of the second Earl, in 1872, negotiations continued with his agents, the necessary land eventually being acquired for £10,516.

Work on the new dock began in 1872, but construction took a number of years, the dock not opening until 22 November 1876, when it was named the Queen's Dock in honour of Queen Victoria. Four years later, the dock had to be closed, settlement around the entrance causing the dock gates to fail, and the dock was not reopened until 1882. It appears to have been undersized from the start, and was unable to deal with large vessels.

The railway works authorised under the 1871 Act were completed in 1877. In 1876, a further Act was passed which allowed the Board of Trustees to borrow more money and to levy tolls on the almost-completed Harbour network, which was now beginning to see reduced levels of ore shipments for two reasons. The first was that Cumberland haematite ore output had almost peaked (at 1,725,438 tons in 1882). The second was that local iron and steel industries continued to require virtually the total local ore output (just over 1,000,000 tons of pig iron was produced in 1882). By 1896, ore shipments out of Whitehaven had ceased completely. To supplement local ore production, Spanish ore was imported from around 1870 onwards, but although 3,000,000 tons were brought into West Cumberland between 1880 and 1890, only 83,000 tons were handled through Whitehaven, again reflecting the limited size of its harbour facilities when compared to Workington and Maryport

It is likely that the administration of the rail-traffic toll system was the responsibility of the Inspector of Cargoes, whose main task was to collect all harbour dues. Towards the end of the 19th century (probably coinciding with the 1871 Act), the holder of this position acquired the additional title of Traffic Manager, to supervise traffic on the harbour lines.

Coal traffic, however, was not to be neglected. Output from the Whitehaven coalfield continued to climb despite operational difficulties in working the pits, rising from 255,505 tons in 1866 to 281,968 tons ten years later, and reaching over 400,000 tons in the mid-1880s. By now, all production was concentrated on eight pits: William, James and Henry pits in the Whingill Colliery, and Wellington, Croft, Duke, Saltom and Kells pits on the Howgill side. It was probably this concentration of production in the Howgill Colliery which lay behind the Trustees' decision, in the late 1870s, to extend the Harbour Commissioners' Railway beneath the hurries on the West Strand and on to the West Pier. This extension opened to traffic in June 1880.

An atmospheric photograph of the West Strand hurries, probably taken not long after the extension of the Harbour Commissioners' line to the West Pier in June 1880. A chauldron wagon can be seen on the third bridge, in the distance. The coal merchant, seen on the left, has collected his load from one of the staithe's storage magazines.

(Peter Robinson Collection ref. 194c12)

Industrial Railways: The Harbour

The houses of Kells, on the Howgill side, stand 250 feet above the Harbour, as a very clean 0-4-0ST Carr (Hudswell Clarke No. 1812 of 1948) heads for the West Strand, alongside the Inner Harbour, with internal-user coal empties on 2 September 1967. The ruined building in the left-centre is the fan house of Duke Pit, which still survives today.

(Peter Robinson ref. 084a33)

There remained, however, the problem of a rail connection between the Howgill Colliery and the West Strand area, which was becoming an increasingly urgent requirement to handle rail-borne traffic. This was discussed in great detail at a lengthy and acrimonious Trustees' meeting on 4 January 1881, under the subject heading 'The South Harbour Connection for the Coal Traffic', much of which concerned land ownership around the site of the lime-kiln at the base of the former Whaite Field Quarry incline. John Musgrave (a local solicitor, who had been Chairman of the Town and Harbour Trustees during the 1870s) observed that the original plans, for a steep and sharply curved connection from Wellington Pit, joined the West Strand line in a south-easterly direction, allowing direct working from the pit and the adjacent staithes towards the Queen's Dock. The plans displayed at the meeting, however, showed *the point of connection ... at the West Pier end*, Musgrave adding that *if a train of wagons happened to go amain and run down this incline ... they would run off the West Pier end and ... choke the harbour up with ... a thousand tons of coal.*

During the discussion, mention was made of *the projected railway from Corkickle Station to Croft Pit*, Musgrave hinting that this was possibly an option for all rail-borne coal from the Howgill side. The meeting ended with the issue of the connection being adjourned to allow the consulting engineer, Sir James Brunlees, who had worked on the Ulverstone and Lancaster Railway, to give his opinion. Brunlees replied, on 31 January, concluding that, although he had originally planned the south-easterly connection, the direct connection to the West Pier was the better option, saying: *It would be* [safer] *for a runaway to go towards the West Pier than towards the town.*

The Brunlees proposal was ratified in March 1881 by the Trustees, and the 300-yard-long line was undoubtedly built the same year. A large-scale plan of Whitehaven Harbour, dated March 1904, is interesting on two counts. Firstly, the distance between the connection's junction with the Harbour Commissioners' system and the end of the line on the West Pier was only 120 yards, indicating that this was merely a headshunt, and secondly the plan shows a short section of line on the alignment of the 1923 'new' Howgill Incline, perhaps suggesting that plans for this existed much earlier than was originally supposed.

The development of the Harbour Commissioners' system was now complete, although a further short extension had been planned. Scott-Hindson noted that: *In 1880, an attempt was made to extend the ... railway on to the Old Quay, and locomotives with vertical boilers and a short wheelbase were sought ... to negotiate the very sharp* [planned] *curve from the West Strand.* This extension appeared to have little commercial justification, although a never-constructed graving dock had been considered at this site, and the plan was eventually abandoned.

A panorama of Whitehaven Harbour, taken from a point above the site of Whitehaven Gasworks on 11 August 1972. Bransty No. 2 signalbox is in the centre foreground, controlling the approaches to Bransty station and the harbour rail network. To the left of the signalbox can be seen an out-of-action NCB locomotive, probably Hudswell Clarke Solway No. 2. The North Pier and the West Pier guard the approaches to the harbour. Just below the skyline, on the far left, the line of John Peile's 1813 Howgill Incline can be seen descending.

(Allan Beck Collection / J A Sommerfield ref. 126/20A)

Chapter Nine

Apart from the Marchon (Albright & Wilson) phosphate rock silos, little changed on the harbour railway network over the years. On a damp December afternoon in 1965, Hudswell Clarke 0-4-0ST Carr waits near the coal loader at the Queen's Dock.

(Stan Buck ref. NCB-02)

The new single-line connection between Wellington Pit and the West Strand was a vital artery in supporting the increasing rail-borne coal traffic out of the Whitehaven harbour area, as the following data shows:

Year	Whitehaven Colliery Output (Tons)	Port Shipments (Tons)	Rail Balance (Tons)
1876	281,968	130,361	151,607
1886	417,039	202,565	214,474
1896	495,657	270,725	224,932

With the development of the Cumberland iron industry, a larger proportion of the coal was retained in the area for use in the furnaces. Wood acknowledged the impact of the national rail network in the distribution of coal over a wider geographical area, and although he gave no separate figures for Whitehaven, noted that rail transport from the West Cumberland collieries accounted for 371,795 tons in 1875, rising to 808,934 tons in 1913.

Despite ever-increasing tonnages, it appeared that financial margins were slim, and it was perhaps not surprising that, in August 1888, the whole of the Whitehaven Colliery, which had been worked by the Lowthers for more than two centuries, was leased to the new Whitehaven Colliery Company. This company was controlled principally by the Bain family, led by Sir James Bain and his sons, Colonel J R Bain (who lived at Moresby Hall) and Mr J D Bain. The Bains already controlled collieries and ironworks at Harrington, and owned a fleet of steamers sailing to the Irish ports. The complex financial deal involving the Whitehaven Colliery was based on a 31-year lease, and included all pits and equipment, 72 coke ovens at Bransty, and 578 cottages. The same year saw the start of the process under which the Town & Harbour Trustees would eventually disappear, being replaced by the new Borough of Whitehaven (incorporated on 20 July 1894 and with the fifth Earl of Lonsdale as first Mayor) and a separate Board of Harbour Commissioners.

Locomotive working in the harbour area was most interesting. The minutes of the Joint Locomotive Committee of the Whitehaven & Furness Junction and the Whitehaven

With the Lime Tongue on the extreme right, NCB 0-4-0ST No. 8 (Andrew Barclay No. 1974/1931) shunts coal wagons on the Harbour Commissioners' Railway on 13 May 1971. The cars on the left include a Rover P4 110 and a Singer Vogue Mk II.

(Tom Heavyside ref. 305/1)

52

Junction Railways, dated 17 October 1862, noted that a small locomotive was required, *with wheel centres only 5 ft., to enable it to pass the curves on the Bulwarks* [sic]. The successful tenderer was Fletcher, Jennings, who delivered an outside-cylinder (10 in. x 20 in.) 0-4-0ST on 22 April 1863, at a cost of £795. The works number was 29, and the locomotive carried the name *Banshee*, although this was probably allocated after delivery.

First-hand experience of this locomotive was contained in notes by its fireman, Joseph Tyson from Cleator Moor, published in the 'Furness Railway Magazine' in October 1921. Writing about the period between 1871 and 1878, Tyson noted that ore traffic, of up to 400 side-tipping wagons per day, was discharged into vessels bound for Newport (South Wales), Amsterdam and Rotterdam. Ore was loaded simply by tipping directly into the vessels' holds, initially probably from either side of the Old (or Sugar) Tongue until completion of the Harbour Commissioners' Lines allowed access to the jetty in the North Harbour (although Tyson may also have been referring to workings to this latter jetty via the Bransty reversal).

Although Gradon stated that this locomotive was numbered 15 in the joint locomotive stock of the two railways (and later FR No. 49), Russell Wear, writing in issue 64 of 'The Industrial Locomotive', gave this as Joint Committee 16. Gradon also wrote that the Joint Committee had purchased another 0-4-0ST in 1861, from Neilson & Co., with works number 571 and joint stock number 16. Wear, however, concluded that the situation was more complicated, and that this locomotive was supplied new in 1860 to the Whitehaven Hematite Iron Co. at Cleator, from whom the Joint Committee purchased it in 1862. Wear gave its number as Joint Committee 15 (later FR No. 50) and its name as *Bob Ridley*.

From 1877 until 31 December 1882, the Furness Railway was responsible for shunting the docks network under contract to the Town & Harbour Trustees, using the Fletcher, Jennings and Neilson locomotives. From 1 January 1883, however, the contract was taken over by Joseph Moore, who then purchased *Banshee* from the FR for this purpose (another source has suggested that the locomotive was sold to local 'Engineer's Furnisher' Andrew Armor McCard, although this seems unlikely). Joint Committee 15 appears to have had a much more complex career, being sold at the same time to Richard Cousins for use in the rail-connected stone quarry at Redness Point (see Chapter 4), before being transferred back to the harbour lines in 1896. Interestingly, Wear noted that the shunting contract did not extend to traffic originating from the Whitehaven Collieries and the Lonsdale Hematite Iron Co. (both Lonsdale family companies), who provided their own locomotives, or for traffic on the FR tramway into the harbour. It looks as though little love was lost between Moore and the Lonsdale companies: within a few days of the commencement of the contract, the 'Whitehaven News' was reporting that the line was blocked with wood near Bransty, temporarily preventing a Whitehaven Ironworks locomotive from legitimately accessing the harbour lines.

It appears that this agreement between the Trustees, the Whitehaven Collieries and the Haematite Co. must have been 'in perpetuity', as locomotives from William Pit (until closure in December 1954) continued to handle coal traffic at the Harbour into National Coal Board days until the final sea-shipment of coal in January 1982. This would have involved Lonsdale's paying a toll only for the use of the Harbour network and facilities, and not for a locomotive.

Joseph Moore retained the shunting contract until the end of 1885, when it was awarded to George Nelson & Sons, presumably using *Banshee* as a transferred locomotive. This was not its last transfer, however, by any means: in 1887, Joseph Moore regained the contract, holding it until his company (and locomotive) was purchased as a going concern in March 1890 by the Whitehaven Cab & General Posting Co. The following year, the contract passed to the Lonsdale (Hematite) Iron & Steel Co. Ltd. As this company had its own locomotives, it had no further requirement for the Fletcher, Jennings engine, which was auctioned locally (possibly being used by the purchaser on contract working at Moor Row Iron Mines, although evidence is scanty).

During their contract period, the Iron & Steel Co. used its own Andrew Barclay, Sons & Co. 0-4-0STs on the harbour lines, being requested on one occasion by the Trustees *not to drive* [locomotives] *over the lines of the harbour ... at* [more than] *4 mph,* [and] *not to fire the engines on the West Strand.*

By 1896, the Lonsdale Iron & Steel Co. was in financial difficulties (being finally liquidated in 1902) and according to Wear, the contract then passed to Ramsay Bros., Founders and Engineers, of the Phoenix Foundry, Albion Street, Whitehaven. As this company did not own a locomotive, it purchased the Neilson & Co. 0-4-0ST (ex-Joint Locomotive Committee No. 15) from Richard Cousins; by this time, it had been renamed *Phoenix*. When the Ramsay Bros. contract was renewed in October 1898, *Phoenix* was sold to the Ellenborough Colliery Co., near Maryport, and there is some evidence that it survived on this site until final sale, almost certainly to the scrapman, in February 1918.

In Spring 1970 and on loan to the National Coal Board, Whitehaven Harbour Commissioners' Peckett 0-4-0ST Victoria *(Works No. 2028 and built in 1942) shunts loaded coal wagons onto the north side of the Queen's Dock. Pattinson's Beacon Mills, in the background, was acquired by Quaker Oats Ltd. in 1949.*

(Stan Buck ref. NCB-07)

Chapter Nine

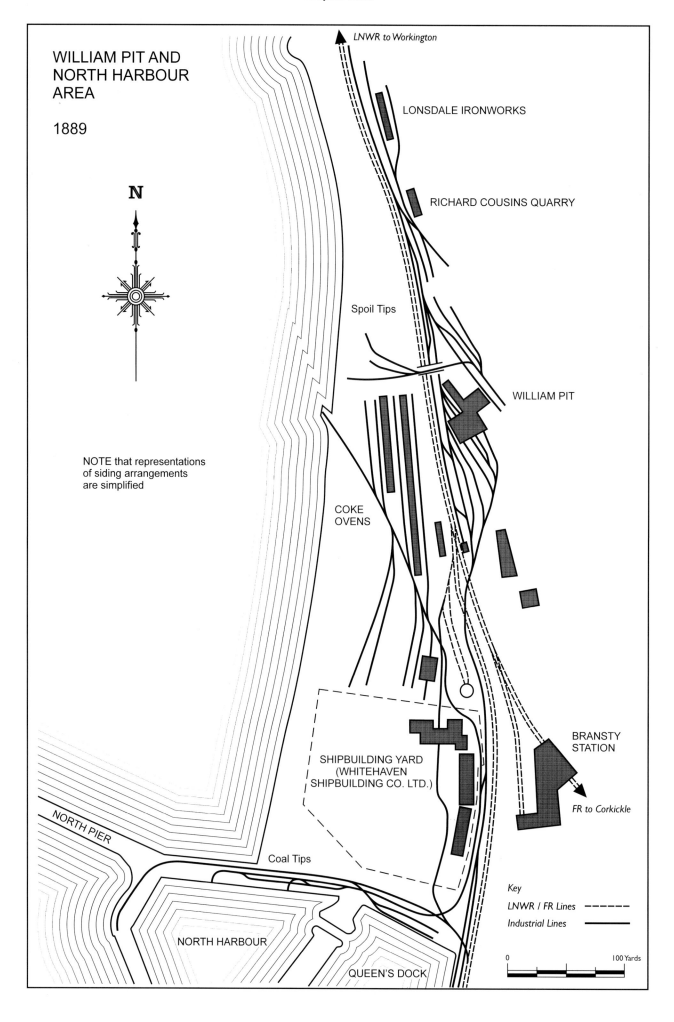

For the duration of the three-year contract, Ramsay Bros. acquired a larger locomotive, widely believed to have been a Fletcher, Jennings 0-4-0ST, although research about the origins of this engine has been inconclusive. With the expiry of the contract on 4 October 1901, the Whitehaven Harbour Commisioners decided to take over port shunting activities themselves, as the result of which Ramsay Bros. advertised their locomotive for sale in September 1901. This appears to have been unsuccessful, as on 14 October 1901 the company offered this locomotive (also named *Phoenix*) to the Commissioners, but the offer was turned down. The subsequent history of the engine is unknown, although one contributor to 'The Industrial Locomotive' speculated that it might have gone to Kirkcaldy Harbour.

After the beginning of the twentieth century, the Harbour Commissioners made very few changes to the track network within the port area. Comparison of the 1899 and 1925 25 inch to 1 mile maps shows that two of the three short sidings into premises at the rear of Tangier Street had been removed, being replaced by a siding parallel to the running lines alongside Queen's Dock, while the three-track network alongside the Inner Harbour had been enlarged to four. The third short siding survived well into British Rail days, providing a local coal merchant with the space to handle a single wagon under cover. Between 1939 and 1945, the 'patent slip' became disused, and the swing-bridge secured for rail-use only. By the late 1940s, the bridge had been dismantled and replaced with plain track, as the slip had been filled in. As the course of the Pow Beck into the South Harbour was adjacent to the slip, the opportunity was taken to embed a culvert into the filled-in area, in order to carry the waters of the beck.

The most significant change came in June 1914, when the 1881 connection from Wellington Pit, facing towards the West Pier, was replaced by the more direct south-easterly facing curve, as proposed originally by Brunlees. At around 200 yards long, it was shorter and probably steeper than the original connection, which was very likely abandoned at the same time, although its course, sandwiched between a retaining wall and the abandoned limekiln, is visible on the 1925 25 inch OS map.

The Harbour Commissioners placed an order for a new shunting locomotive with Andrew Barclay, Sons & Co. Ltd. in autumn 1901. Because of construction lead times, the company hired an engine to the Commissioners, pending delivery of the new 0-4-0ST (works number 908) to Whitehaven on 16 December 1901. This was named *King Edward VII*, Wear noting that *brass nameplates were sent along with the loco*. The engine had a long life, shunting the harbour until April 1959 when it was scrapped, being replaced by Peckett 0-4-0ST *Victoria* (works number 2028) built in August 1942. This locomotive had had previous associations with West Cumberland, having been delivered new to Royal Ordnance Factory Sellafield, where it worked until 1946. During periods when *King Edward* was out of action, the colliery company loaned the Commissioners a locomotive free of charge, although payment was required for the engineman's services.

By the early 1960s, *Victoria* saw little use, although it was steamed on a number of occasions in 1966 to handle timber imports through the Harbour. In 1967, it was loaned to (and later purchased by) the National Coal Board, being first used at Haig and Ladysmith Pits, and subsequently at William Pit, where it was noted on shed and in steam in May 1968 and in November 1970. As late as May 1974, steam was in action at the Harbour, NCB *Solway No. 2* (Hudswell Clarke No. 1814, built in 1948) deputising for the regular NCB Sentinel 4-wheel diesel-hydraulic which was being overhauled.

The Harbour Commissioners' locomotive was required to shunt the exchange sidings with the LNWR (at North Shore, Bransty) and, much less frequently, with the FR at East Strand. It is not known what regulations existed in pre-Grouping days to cover such workings, but the London, Midland & Scottish Railway soon moved to regularise the situation: a Whitehaven Harbour Board minute, dated 30 January 1923, noted that the LMS *has requested that the Board allow its engine drivers to be examined as to their fitness to drive. The Board agreed, subject to 24 hours' notice being given*. It seems likely that the Whitehaven Colliery Co. would have received a similar request, on account of its flat crossing at Bransty between William Pit and the harbour lines.

The Harbour Commissioners replaced *Victoria* in 1972 with a fifteen-year old Ruston & Hornsby 0-4-0 diesel-mechanical shunter, purchased from the Scottish Gas Board, which lasted until scrapping in August 1985. This appears not to have had good haulage capability, the previously-mentioned Sentinel being preferred on account of its power. In any case, the Ruston probably saw little use, as, from the mid-1950s onwards, the harbour handled little general cargo. Towards the end of rail operations at the Harbour, in September 1985, the preferred motive power was two NCB diesel-hydraulic shunters: a North British 0-4-0 and a Hunslet 0-6-0. The latter was sold to Marchon Products on 10 December 1985 (see Chapter 10).

The Harbour Commissioners' locomotives used a single-road wooden engine shed at the end of the pier extending from the Bulwark and separating the Queens' Dock from the North Harbour. In earlier days, this shed had been leased from Ramsay Bros. For at least part of the period between 1967 and 1972, when *Victoria* was on loan to the NCB, this shed was used to house a boat! At some point during its existence, the Commissioners' locomotive was transferred temporarily to a corrugated iron shed on the North Wall, just east of Beacon Mills, but a visit to the Harbour in 1980 revealed that the wooden shed was still use for its original railway purpose.

Left: Map showing William Pit, the Lonsdale Ironworks and the northern section of Whitehaven Harbour, as at 1889.
(Based on an original map by Roger Hateley and Russell Wear)

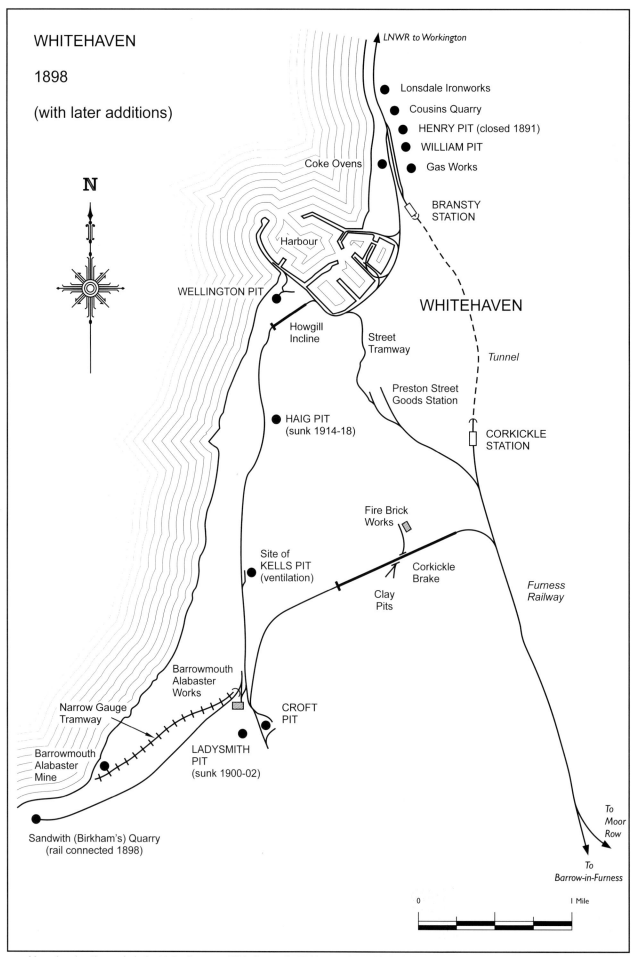

Map showing the main industrial railways at Whitehaven in 1898, together with their links to the Furness and the London & North Western Railways.
(Based on an original map by Roger Hateley and Russell Wear)

Industrial Railways:
The Inclines and Other Lines

10

THE W&FJR TRAMWAY, between Preston Street goods yard and Customhouse Quay and the Old Tongue, is unlikely to have seen much iron-ore traffic after the opening of the new jetty in June 1862, with its direct access for locomotive-hauled traffic via Bransty.

The tramway could not be used on Market Days between 7-00 am and 3-00 pm, and additionally could only be used by horse-drawn traffic, thus limiting its usefulness for rapid freight handling. Despite a widely-held belief that locomotives occasionally worked over the tramway, this is unlikely to have been the case: in February 1886, in response to a complaint about a Furness Railway engine being used on the tramway opposite the Old Tongue, the Harbour Trustees' Secretary replied that it was *not a Furness engine, because they never do run down there: it must have been Lord Lonsdale's Colliery locomotive or the engine of the harbour haulage contractors*.

However, this does suggest that the tramway was still in use by this date. The Whitehaven Dock and Railway Act of 1871 provided for the short west-facing connection between the tramway and the Harbour Trustees' line to the West Strand, although it was difficult to see any clear rationale behind this, particularly with the decline in iron-ore shipments through the harbour from the mid-1870s until total cessation in 1896. Scott-Hindson notes that this connection remained unbuilt in 1888, although it is shown on the 1899 25 inch OS map.

It is not clear when traffic over the tramway finally ceased, Daniel Hay writing that it was lifted *some time after 1918, but it had not been used for a long time before that*. OS maps show that it was still down in 1923. At a meeting of the Harbour Commissioners on 17 December 1924, it was agreed that they would *take over maintenance rights from the LMS in respect of the track on the Sugar Tongue and the East Strand as far as Nicholson's Lane*, suggesting that the new railway company saw no future in commercial use of the tramway.

A lesser-known tramway was also built towards the end of the 19th century, leaving Furness Railway property on the east side of Preston Street goods station. This line was around 350 yards long, and threw off sidings to a timber yard west of Richmond Terrace, to another timber yard between Barracks Road (along which the line ran) and Irish Street, to a flour mill south of Barracks Road, and finally to a third timber yard at the end of this road. By 1925, the timber yards had all closed, and the line terminated in the western section of Catherine Street (the renamed Barracks Road) outside the flour mill, which had now become a carpet factory. The final closure and lifting dates for this obscure line remain to be discovered.

The 3 ft. 10 in. (possibly 4 ft.) gauge Parton Waggonway has already been mentioned in Chapter 4. There is no clear record of the date of its conversion to standard gauge, but the most likely is the period between October 1870, when the Lonsdale Hematite Iron Company was formed, and August 1872, when the first furnace was commissioned. It was certainly not earlier, as an intriguing detailed map, drawn up for Lord Lonsdale's use in 1860, clearly shows mixed-gauge track within the confines of William Pit, the single mixed-gauge line through the weighing machine immediately splitting to run south to join the Whitehaven & Furness Junction Railway (standard gauge) and south-west across the Whitehaven Junction line (narrower gauge). Until conversion to standard gauge, the waggonway continued to be horse-worked. The whole of the Lonsdale Hematite Iron Company's land, acquired from the Earl of Lonsdale by Kilmarnock ironmasters, extended from the northern end of

Photographed (probably in the 1930s) from a vantage point high above Preston Street, the extensive layout of the freight depot can be clearly seen. Close examination of the photograph suggests that five tracks had crossed Coach Road at an earlier stage. The long siding serving installations behind St Begh's RC Church can be seen curving away sharply in the middle of the photograph. The low bell-tower of Christ Church can be seen bottom right.
(Sankey ref. E68)

57

Chapter Ten

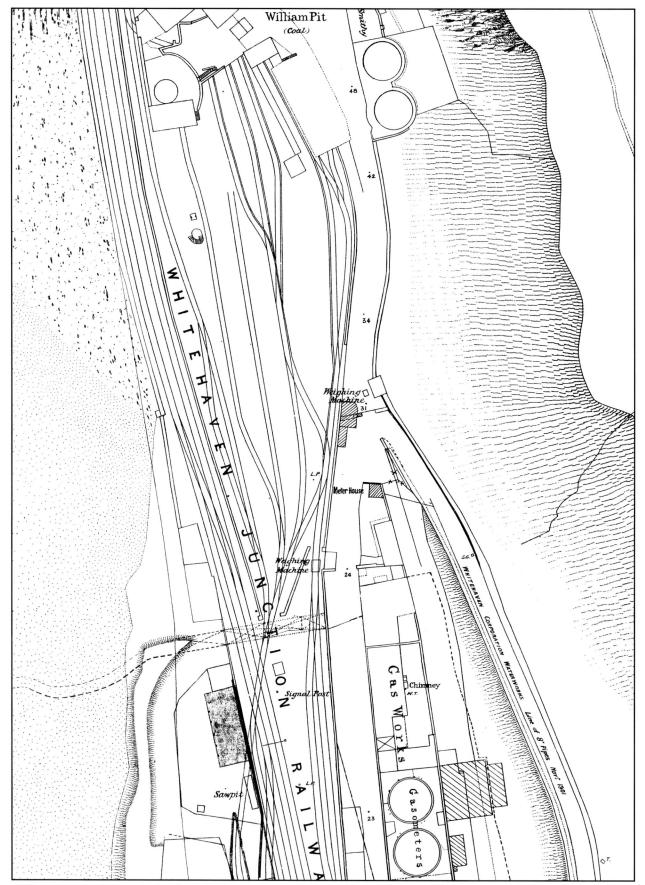

This 1860 map, drawn up for Lord Lonsdale, clearly shows mixed-gauge track within the William Pit complex. Three such lines can be clearly seen emerging from a building (probably the coal screens and dry grading plant) at the top, while a single mixed-gauge line runs through the weighing machine. The standard-gauge track joined the WFJR, while the narrower-gauge lines merged to cross the WJR on the level. (From a plan in the Cumbria Record Office, Whitehaven, ref. 67.2.8)

Industrial Railways: The Inclines and Other Lines

William Pit round Redness Point almost to the site of Parton Pit, along the narrow strip of land between the Whitehaven Junction line (now the LNWR) and the cliffs. Lancaster and Wattleworth stated that *the works site was widened by cutting into the cliff-like rock to the east of the railway, and a brick-making plant was erected at the north end.*

The former single-track Parton Waggonway now became at least double for most of its length. The tunnel north of Redness Point was undoubtedly removed as part of the cliff removal process, the 1899 OS map showing a four-track layout on its site and running alongside the LNWR main line. A south-facing connection at the brickworks site gave access to a double-track dead-end siding, about 350 yards long, which climbed to a higher level between the cliff face and the ironworks. As this ran above the blast furnaces, this was probably used for transporting limestone used as a flux in the process.

At Parton itself, coal traffic was still handled, but the site was now a coal depot, the adjoining Parton Pit shaft having been abandoned, although coal from the Countess band was still being brought to the surface elsewhere. South of the ironworks, this industrial line made trailing and facing connections into the LNWR route, and a trailing connection to the FR line just a few yards from the latter's junction with the LNWR, close to William Pit.

The Lonsdale Hematite Iron Company started operations in August 1872, on a site adjacent to Bransty station. By July 1873, the company had three furnaces in operation, but ran into problems in 1876 through a general reduction in the price paid for pig iron. It was reconstituted in 1883 as the Lonsdale Hematite Iron & Steel Company Ltd., but again ran into difficulties towards the end of the 19th century, was liquidated in 1902 and finally wound up in 1904. By 1925, the ironworks site had been cleared and the track layout

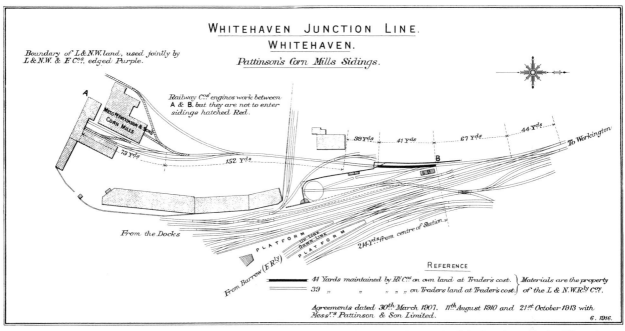

Although dated June 1916, this LNWR map of the Bransty area still refers to the line north of the junction with the FR as the 'Whitehaven Junction Line'. Note the LNWR's responsibility for maintaining 80 yards of the connection into Pattinson's corn mills, and the restrictions on loco movements within the mills complex. (Cumbria Record Office, Whitehaven)

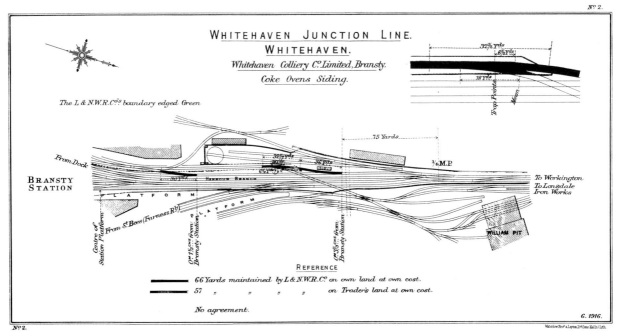

The independent metals of the Parton Waggonway are clearly visible as they cross the former WJR north of Bransty station. The map shows an LNWR-maintained connection, allowing freight trains from this Lonsdale-owned line to directly access the LNWR line to Parton and Workington. Note the minor layout differences with the previous map, particularly around the turntable, suggesting that this map is based on an earlier plan. (Cumbria Record Office, Whitehaven)

severely rationalised, leaving just a long single line along the route of the former waggonway to serve the two-road coal depot at Parton.

Perhaps the most significant 19th century railway development in Whitehaven, however, came on the Howgill side. Mention has already been made of reference to the projected railway from Corkickle station to the Croft Pit, at the Harbour Trustees' meeting in January 1881. This was undoubtedly the brainchild of the Earl of Lonsdale, who had several reasons for wanting an alternative outlet for coal traffic from the pits of the Howgill Colliery. In the first instance, the Howgill Brake (incline) was still orientated to sea-borne traffic loading from the West Strand hurries, and the proposed new connection offered only a tortuous link to the national network. Secondly, Lonsdale was at the mercy of the Harbour Trustees when it came to the level of tolls for working his wagons over the harbour network, and he would have known that construction of an alternative outlet would place him in an advantageous position in future negotiations with the Trustees. The Furness Railway, aware of potential increased coal traffic volumes through Whitehaven Tunnel, was determined to support Lonsdale's plans. The Board Minutes of the FR show that Lonsdale approached the FR Directors, requesting that rail access to Croft Pit should be improved, and that subsequently, on 6 July 1881, the Board agreed to build a 'branch' from Corkickle to Croft Pit, at a cost of £5000, which Lonsdale would repay in annual £1000 instalments.

Construction must have been relatively rapid as the Corkickle Brake is recorded as being opened in the same year. The brake was 525 yards long, with a gradient ranging from 1 in 5.2 to 1 in 6.6, and was designed for a maximum descending load of 72 tons and an upwards load of 60 tons. A passing loop at the half-way point could accommodate four wagons. The brake was single-track from its base to the mid-way passing loop, while the upper section to the brake top was laid with three rails. At the base of the incline, a level section of track, about 400 yards long, connected the brake with the Up and Down goods lines of the Furness Railway, the junction facing towards St Bees.

The incline had a number of other names, including the Kells or Marchon or Monkwray Brake. Many local people referred to it simply 'The Brake', this term being in common use in Whitehaven to describe a rope-worked rail incline.

Between 1900 and 1902, the Whitehaven Colliery Co. sank the new Ladysmith Pit to a depth of 1,090 ft. alongside Croft Pit, which was then abandoned in 1903 (although performing a new role as an air-shaft). Croft Pit had been in continuous production since 1774. In 1904, it was recorded that the brake was 'modernised' to cope with increased traffic from Ladysmith, although, as the incline was now an asset of the Whitehaven Colliery Co. and not the FR, the former would have been responsible for the capital expenditure. It appears that the Whitehaven Colliery Co. later wished to replace the brake with a conventional siding, this being shown on a plan drawn up for the company on 25 October 1915 and possibly coinciding with the erection of the Ladysmith Pit coke ovens, but there is no evidence that this plan ever got beyond the design stage.

The Corkickle Brake was originally operated by a steam winding engine, powered by Cochrane boilers, at the brake top, near the present Lakeland Avenue, and this existed until early 1955, although out of use for many years. For the first thirty years of its life, the brake appears to have handled coal traffic only, but the erection of sixty-nine coke ovens at Ladysmith Pit around 1915 brought coke traffic down the brake, together with by-products destined for the steelworks at Workington and Barrow. Officially, the incline was open for traffic between 6-00 am and midnight, but during periods of heavy traffic, it was not uncommon for the incline to operate until 4-00 am. Ladysmith provided the locomotive for shunting the top of the brake: Russell Wear, in his article 'The Corkickle Brake' (published in 'The Industrial Railway Record' in 1987), noted that, after 1913, this was usually an Andrew Barclay 0-4-0 *Whitehaven No. 1* (Works No. 1331).

The deteriorating financial position of the Whitehaven Colliery Co. resulted in the closure of the Ladysmith complex in December 1931, and the brake was abandoned for nearly a quarter of a century. (The Ladysmith washing plant remained open, however, to serve the new Haig Pit, which was opened in stages between August 1914 and March 1918.) The line between the washing plant and the brake top saw some use for the storage of wagons.

The Corkickle Brake is unlikely to have re-opened, had it not been for the establishment of Marchon Products Ltd. in premises at Hensingham in late 1940. Initially manufacturing firelighters, Marchon then began to supply raw materials for detergent manufacture, the company moving to Kells in 1943, where they occupied the site of the now-abandoned Ladysmith coke ovens. By 1951, the company employed nearly 600 people. One component of detergent manufacture was sulphuric acid, manufactured from the mineral anhydrite, and Marchon discovered that the factory lay directly above one of the largest sources of anhydrite in the country. A new company, Solway Chemicals Ltd., was formed in 1951 to sink the new mine and to manufacture sulphuric acid. Eventually cement production was added to this manufacturing base. By 1955, 1500 people worked on the Kells site, and Marchon Products became one of the UK's main detergent manufacturers. In November 1955, both Marchon Products Ltd. and Solway

Ladysmith Washery on 28 August 1973, looking south. Hunslet Engineering 0-6-0ST Repulse *(Works No. 3698/1950) shunts loaded wagons in the washery sidings. On the left can be seen buildings and a chimney on the neighbouring Marchon Products (Albright & Wilson) site. The single line on the extreme left leads to the head of the Corkickle Brake. Marchon Products metals could be accessed via two connections from the Ladysmith site.*

(Tom Heavyside ref. 74/29)

Industrial Railways: The Inclines and Other Lines

Chemicals Ltd. were taken over by the much larger chemical corporation Albright & Wilson Ltd., although the old names were officially retained for many years.

In the early 1950s, Marchon began to use the National Coal Board's Howgill Brake, which had been re-aligned in 1923 to give direct access to the Harbour Commissioners' network on West Strand, for despatch of products from the Kells site. From the West Strand, an NCB locomotive from William Pit handled the traffic through the Harbour and into the exchange sidings at Bransty. This caused serious operational problems, as the Marchon vehicles had to be diagrammed into the heavy washery traffic to and from Ladysmith, and from Haig Pit to the top of the Howgill Brake.

In late 1953, in order to resolve this capacity problem, the NCB proposed that the long-disused Corkickle Brake, together with the former rail link from Ladysmith (about ¾ mile long), should be handed over to Marchon Products. Marchon would then incur the capital costs associated with reinstatement and modernisation, and would be responsible for all rail traffic to and from the brake head. Both parties agreed, and by early 1955, the reinstated brake was ready for testing. The steam winding engine was replaced by a Crompton-Parkinson 500hp electric winding engine, within a new engine house straddling the tracks at the brake head adjacent to the Lakeland Avenue level crossing (the gates of which still survived in 2007). A new footbridge here provided a bypass for pedestrians when the lines were in use. The sidings at the brake foot were shunted by British Railways locomotives, although a small stationary electric engine was used to move wagons the final few feet to the haulage cables. A control system limited wagons to 9 mph on the descent. If this speed was exceeded, electro-pneumatic points automatically diverted vehicles into a sand-drag.

On 31 March 1955, Marchon Products took delivery, via the Corkickle Brake, of a new locomotive, the company having previously relied on the NCB to provide motive power. The new locomotive was a Peckett 0-4-0ST (Works No. 2138), and apparently was a good performer, often being loaned to the NCB at Ladysmith, where it seems to have been most of the time between 1967 and 1969; it was scrapped in 1970.

Wear records that *full traffic working on the brake began in May 1955,* [and was] *a far cry ... from the two or three wagon loads of sawdust a week and the occasional tank ...*

On 6 August 1981, one of Marchon Products' Sentinel four-wheel diesel-hydraulic locomotives hauls two tank wagons across Lakeland Avenue and away from the head of the Corkickle Brake. Note the 110-yard-long run-round loop in the background.

(CRA Photo Library ref. PE81/3/4)

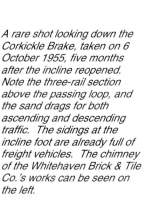

A rare shot looking down the Corkickle Brake, taken on 6 October 1955, five months after the incline reopened. Note the three-rail section above the passing loop, and the sand drags for both ascending and descending traffic. The sidings at the incline foot are already full of freight vehicles. The chimney of the Whitehaven Brick & Tile Co.'s works can be seen on the left.

(Allan Beck Collection)

Chapter Ten

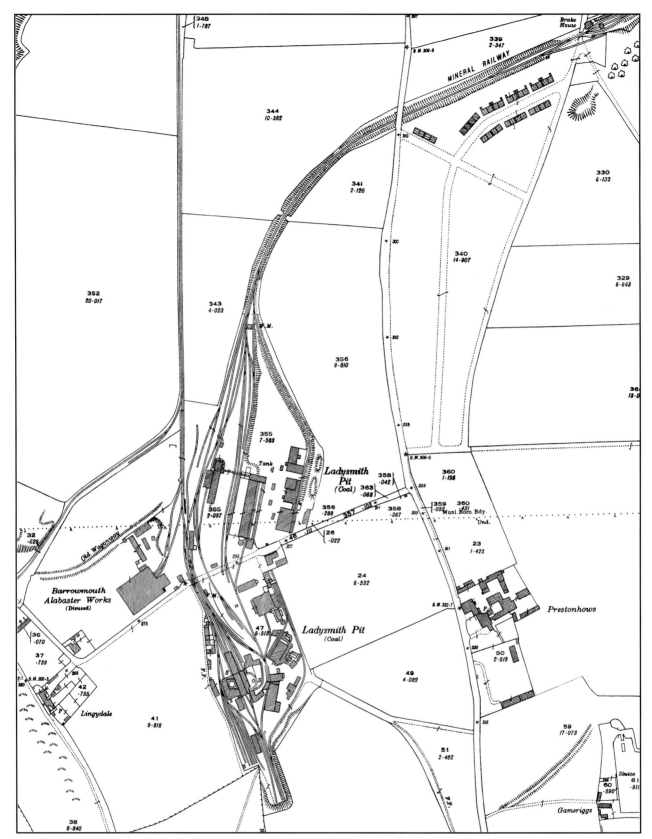

The rail network at Ladysmith Pit (opened between 1900 and 1902 to replace Croft Pit). From the top of the map, the incline up from Ravenhill runs directly into the complex, while the single line from the Corkickle Brake head curves in from the north-east. The Barrowmouth Alabaster Works had closed in 1903, but appears to have survived intact. The course of the abandoned 2 ft. 3 in. gauge waggonway down to the alabaster drifts is marked just north of the works. Its course appears to have been severed by the standard-gauge line to Sandwith Quarries, which line can be seen above the line of the waggonway.
(Reproduced from the 1925 25 inch Ordnance Survey Map sheet 67.6, Cumbria Record Office, Whitehaven, with the kind permission of the Ordnance Survey)

Industrial Railways: The Inclines and Other Lines

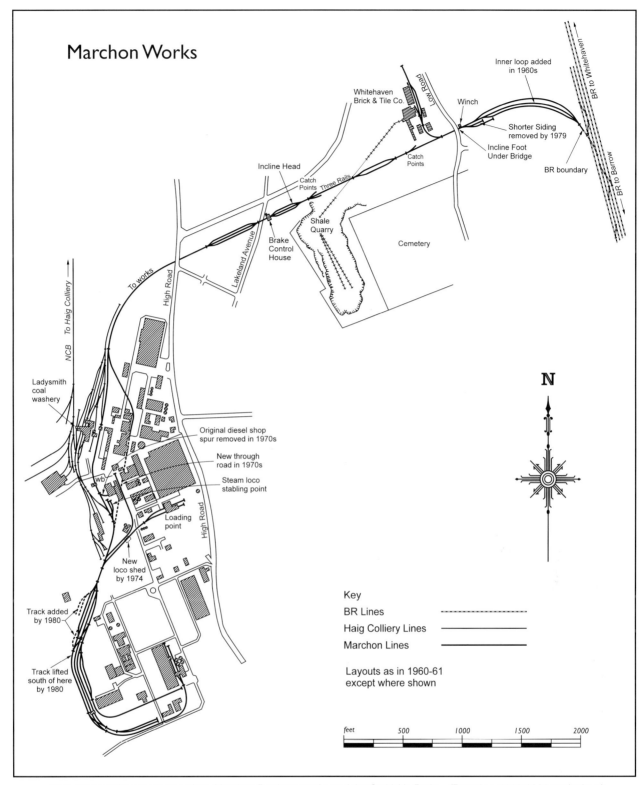

Map showing the rail layouts of the Marchon Products works and the Corkickle Brake. (Based on 1960-1961 track plans)

of tar or naphthalene which had once travelled to Marchon. The brake was soon running on a two-shift basis (between 6-00 am and 10-00 pm), with a third shift sometimes resulting in round-the-clock working. The brake could handle more than 200 wagons during the sixteen hours, representing 2000 tons of traffic daily to and from the Marchon site. The amount of traffic passing over the brake quickly became a source of friction with residents of adjoining properties, a request being made to ban the use of Lakeland Avenue level crossing on Sundays, Bank Holidays, and during the night. At a meeting of Whitehaven Town Council on 18 July 1955, it was proposed that there should be 'minimum' usage of the crossing at these times, and this was accepted by the Council.

Loaded rail wagons were held in Marchon's own internal sidings until a trainload was made up; these sidings were adjacent to the Ladysmith coal washery, just south of which lay the connection between Marchon and NCB metals. One of the company's locomotives then took four or five wagons along the single line as far as the short loop which lay south-west of the brake head, from which it was separated by the Lakeland Avenue level-crossing. After all brakes had been pinned down, the locomotive ran round its train to return to the works, leaving a shunter to release the brakes of one wagon at a time. This allowed each vehicle to run gently over the crossing and onto the brake head, where it was attached to the incline cable.

Chapter Ten

View down the Corkickle Brake from the brake engineman's control cabin, on 6 August 1981. This well illustrates the height difference of 250 ft. between the incline's head and foot, where (centre) a long rake of wagons is stabled in the sidings curving south towards Corkickle No. 1 signalbox (far right).

(CRA Photo Library ref. PE-81/3/3)

One initial problem was that the brake engineman's control cabin was not sufficiently high to give the operator an unbroken view down the incline. As a result, he had to rely on his own instruments and on bell signals from the operator at the incline foot - not a safe method of handling traffic. The problem was not, however, resolved until 1972, when a new control cabin, with all-round visibility, was built on the roof of the engine house, giving the operator a clear view down the full length of the brake.

Wear noted that good relations always existed between Marchon Products and the NCB, no problems being experienced if NCB locomotives used the Marchon system, and vice-versa. He quoted one example, in April 1959, when the NCB moved a large Robert Stephenson & Hawthorns 0-6-0ST from the North-East, to work at Ladysmith. On arrival at Bransty, the plan was to haul the locomotive up the Howgill Brake, but its chimney would then have faced north, the wrong direction for the former Croft Incline between Haig and Ladysmith. The Marchon management was quickly contacted, following which BR transferred the loco to Corkickle for haulage up the Corkickle Brake, leaving the 0-6-0 facing south after its transfer to the Ladysmith system.

By 1964, the Corkickle Brake was handling over 500,000 tons of freight per annum, a large proportion of which was sulphuric acid. The incline was working virtually at full capacity, and with further production capacity coming on stream, British Railways sought Parliamentary powers, in the 1963-4 Session, for a new three-mile-long branch from the Kells site down to a junction with the Cumbrian Coast line just north of St Bees. On 12 November 1963, local councils in the area of the proposed line were issued with the obligatory full set of deposited plans, plus a Book of Reference, indicating works required, such as land purchase and the stopping-up of footpaths. However, this line, with its ruling gradient of 1 in 63, was never built, partly because of opposition from local landowners, but also because BR would only guarantee two workings per day to and from the works, making it difficult to justify financially.

There was a curious footnote to this saga in the November 1965 edition of 'Modern Railways', which stated that *a new access line from St Bees to ... Marchon Products is under construction to supersede* [the existing line] *to the works from Corkickle station*. Despite this announcement, there is no evidence that any works were started.

The Marchon locomotive fleet continued to expand, the Peckett being joined briefly in 1958 by Avonside 0-4-0ST *Stone Cross* (Works No. 1729) on loan from the NCB and permanently by an Andrew Barclay 0-4-0ST (Works No. 2192), which Marchon purchased from the Workington Iron & Steel Co. and which arrived, via the Corkickle Brake, on 15 August 1960. Dieselisation of the system began in January 1962, with the arrival of a modern-looking four-wheel Sentinel diesel-hydraulic (Works No. 10086), joined in August 1969 by sister locomotive No. 10085, reconditioned after eight years' service at the Bass brewery in Burton-on-Trent. Ten years later, the company purchased a more powerful Rolls-Royce four-wheel locomotive (Works No. 10206), relegating the Sentinels to a standby role. These two locomotives were cut up on site early in 1986, being replaced by the Hunslet 0-6-0 diesel-hydraulic (Works No. 7017) which was surplus to NCB requirements following the closure of the Harbour rail network in 1985.

The Hunslet never turned a wheel in Marchon service. After 1981, traffic using the Corkickle Brake began to decline, and its operating times each day were reduced, the busiest period being between 08-00 and 10-00 hours. The introduction of long wheelbase wagons caused operating problems on the incline, with productivity reduced as only one wagon at a time could be handled. Additionally, BR advised Marchon about the future preferred use of bogie (as opposed to fixed wheelbase) wagons, which could not be handled on the brake.

When the Howgill Brake had finally closed early in 1972 due to a landslide, the NCB may have used the Corkickle Brake to remove eight BR wagons which had become marooned at Haig Pit, although this has not been confirmed. In the same year, a small amount of NCB traffic was diverted by the brake, one of the Marchon Sentinels handling this traffic, although this was never considered a long-term solution, due to the twin pressures of Marchon's own traffic levels at the time and the increasing problems of industrial insurance liabilities.

One safety feature not upgraded on the brake until late in its existence was catch points, the normal method of controlling runaway wagons on steeply graded lines. 'The Railway Magazine' of November 1975 recorded that: *An order has been received for the operation of ... catch points on* [the Corkickle Brake] *... The Albright & Wilson works is situated on high ground 200 feet above, and half a mile west of, British Railways' Corkickle station ... Wagons travel in rakes of three or four at about 8 mph up and down simultaneously. Three sets of catch points will divert wagons in to sand drags, should their speed exceed 8 mph. Equipment to be supplied for operation of the three catch points includes treadles, relay apparatus cases, and a mimic diagram for the haulage* [engine] *house, to show the lie of the catch points and the points at the top of the incline where the track divides.*

Industrial Railways: The Inclines and Other Lines

The foot of the Corkickle Brake on 6 August 1981. The line on the left held vehicles inbound to the Marchon site, while the two roads on the right were used to hold outbound wagons. In the background, rakes of 'merry-go-round' coal wagons can be seen in Corkickle Sidings.

(CRA Photo Library ref. PE-81/2/7)

By the mid-1980s, the Corkickle Brake's days were numbered. On 31 October 1986, the last wagons were lowered down the incline, and the Marchon site's internal rail network was closed for good. On 4 November, the Rolls-Royce and Hunslet shunters were also removed down the brake, being destined for the Derwent Railway Preservation site at Workington. The last commercially operated standard-gauge cable haulage incline in the country thus passed into history.

However, this was not quite the end for rail traffic from the Marchon (now Albright & Wilson) site. Bulk road vehicles from the Kells works now pressure-charged the PCA wagons with sodium tripolyphosphate powder in the surviving sidings at Preston Street, access being gained via the former Up line. This traffic could be handled using two sidings. Preston Street yard was normally shunted around lunchtime, empties from the previous day having been left on Corkickle No. 1's south siding. Because all run-round facilities at Preston Street had been removed, the empties had to be propelled down the branch. Loaded PCAs, destined for the Proctor & Gamble soap factory at Thurrock (Essex), were collected by the same trip working, and taken to the south siding at Corkickle No. 1 to await attachment to the evening Workington-Willesden 'Speedlink' service. This bulk powder traffic survived Speedlink's demise by being reorganised into a weekly Saturdays-Only block train from Corkickle. This ran for the final time on 2 July 1994, behind Class 31s Nos. 31 312 and 31 229, these locomotives being exchanged at Carnforth for Class 56 No. 56 049. In anticipation of a possible restoration of this traffic, a rake of PCA wagons was stored at Workington until 1996, although demolition work at Preston Street started less than eight weeks after the final departure.

Additionally, the siding adjacent to Corkickle No. 2 signalbox was still in use, handling caustic soda for the Albright & Wilson works. The caustic soda was discharged into a small store behind the box, and was then loaded into

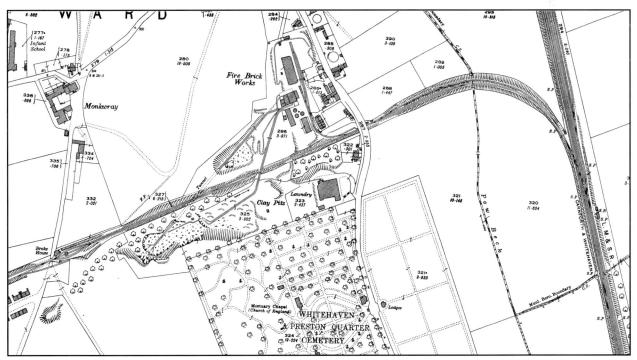

The full length of the Corkickle Brake can be seen on this map. The midway passing loop can be clearly seen, as can the segregation of tracks for ascending and descending vehicles at the brake top, where what appears to be a sand-drag for runaway vehicles was installed between 1899 and 1925. Note the brickworks' connection into the incline itself, as well as the 2 ft. 6 in. gauge internal network.
(Reproduced from the 1925 25 inch Ordnance Survey Map sheet 67.6, Cumbria Record Office, Whitehaven, with the kind permission of the Ordnance Survey)

Chapter Ten

A view, probably around 1962, taken from the Low Road bridge and looking up the Corkickle Brake. A descending empty mineral wagon, acting as a balance to ascending loaded vehicles bound for Marchon, is approaching the connection to the long siding leading into the adjacent brickworks. Note the three upright rollers, for guiding the wire rope, to the right of this siding. A single sand drag can be seen above the wagon.   (Allan Beck Collection)

who immediately floated the company on the stock market. Poor results made the company vulnerable to a takeover, which came in the shape of a bid from Rhodia, a division of the French chemical giant Rhone Poulenc. By 2000, the A&W operation was in French hands.

The following year, Rhone Poulenc sold the detergents operation to an American company, Huntsman of Salt Lake City, Utah, who announced that they would invest in the Kells site. The remainder of the industrial operation, however, closed in January 2002, when Rhodia transferred all phosphate business to France. Despite Huntsman's announcement, in 2004, that an £11 million investment would protect the employment of the remaining 160 workers, an about-turn in the late summer of that year resulted in the closure of the fatty alcohol plant, when 90 workers lost their jobs. Closure of the drier unit in 2005 reduced the workforce to a mere 20, and further redundancies left just nine employees on site. Final decommissioning and demolition of the Whitehaven plant was planned to take place by the end of 2006, although early in 2007 some abandoned plant and offices (still bearing the 'Huntsman' sign) were left standing at the Kells end of the complex. The southern area, however, had been cleared and tidied. It was a sad ending for a site which had employed over 3,000 people in the 1970s.

Returning to the Corkickle brake, the incline was joined, about fifty yards up from its foot, by a further incline, the first section of a 200-yard-long siding into the Whitehaven Brick & Tile Co.'s works. Wagons from here were lowered to the brake foot by cable, using a small stationary electric engine, but unlike the main brake, this was only a single-acting unit, meaning that the cable had to be let down first before a wagon could be drawn up.

This standard-gauge siding was not built until early last century, but the brickworks was already served by a 2 ft. 6 in. gauge line, which ran from north-east to south-west, passing beneath the Corkickle Brake to serve clay pits south of the incline. It is not known whether this 300-yard-long line was cable-hauled, but before the Great War, an additional cable-hauled narrow-gauge line was built, nearly 400 yards long, for transporting spoil to a shale pit. Because this siding was less steeply graded than the main brake and because the pit also lay south of the incline, a 100-yard-long tunnel was constructed under the brake. The standard-gauge siding was closed in the late 1960s, when the traffic was transferred to road.

Completion of Haig Pit, in March 1918, meant increased production and more pressure on the single-line curve, opened in June 1914, from Wellington Pit and running directly onto the West Strand. In any case, access to this curve from

bulk road tankers for the final leg of the journey to Kells. It is not known when this traffic ceased, but there have been unconfirmed reports of a final working from this siding in the first few weeks of 1997.

By this time A&W's Whitehaven operation was in decline, despite the expenditure of £8.5 million, in 1995, to increase phosphoric acid capacity. A&W's American parent, Tenneco Inc., sold the company to its managers,

The Howgill Incline in British Railways days, showing two descending loaded wagons about to enter the single-line tunnel under the Wellington Pit approach road. A sand-drag, to catch runaway wagons, can be seen to the right of the portal. Long lines of internal user (NCB) coal wagons line the Bulwark, the North Wall and the Old North Wall. In the background can be seen the winding gear of William Pit, closed in 1954 (left of centre) and the silos of the Beacon flour mills.

(Michael Andrews Collection ref. A182)

Haig Pit was tortuous, involving a reversal at the base of the Howgill Brake across the top of the coal hurries. In August 1920, the 'Contract Journal' noted that *the Whitehaven Colliery Co. are building a new railway to cope with the output of the new Haig Pit. The line will be ... 1½ miles long from Mirehouse to Ladysmith. After completion of this railway, the present cable system will only be used in an emergency.* Although this seems to imply a new direct Mirehouse-Ladysmith line, Wear believed that this was a mistaken reference to plans for a realigned Howgill Brake.

Documentary evidence on construction of the new Howgill Brake, which opened in 1923/4, is difficult to obtain. The double-track incline, at 440 yards long, was 150 yards longer than the old brake, and necessitated the construction of a completely new winding house, around 140 yards south of the original. Passing through a short tunnel under the road to Wellington Pit, just west of the castellated gatehouse (dating from 1843 and which still survives), the incline became a single track, curving sharply south-east to join the Harbour Commissioners' Lines opposite the Old Quay. As the new brake crossed the line of the old, at an angle of 22 degrees 70 yards below the old winding house, it is likely that this marked the end of rail wagon traffic onto the coal hurries. Communication between the brake house, at the top of the incline, and the West Strand brakeman was via a series of bells.

Other evidence for forthcoming cessation of loading coal vessels via the hurries was noted in the Minutes of the Harbour Board, dated 3 August 1922, stating that *the Harbour Commissioners discussed the proposed new loading plant and working of traffic on Dock Quay, together with alteration to the railway track.* The scheme's proposer was the Whitehaven Colliery Co., who, by September 1922, had prepared detailed plans for the site. The agreement between the Harbour Commissioners and the Colliery Co. was to run from 1 May 1923, the loading plant to be built by F Turnbull & Co. of Newcastle-upon-Tyne.

The operation of the coal loader was fairly simple. Capable of handling 400 tons per hour, it consisted of a continuous moving belt long enough to reach from beneath a coal wagon to the centre of the largest ship likely to use the facility. By default the belt was level, but at the point of the dock wall it was jointed, so that its seaward extremity could be lowered to deflect the coal into the side of the ship nearest to the dock wall and/or to lose height to avoid damage to the coal as it was loaded.

This was achieved by a system of pulleys and cables driven from motors in the control room above the conveyor, from where the controller could see into the hold of the ship. The conveyor was also pivoted vertically, so that the coal could be deflected left or right to give a wider spread to the point of delivery. However it was also necessary from time to time for the vessel itself to be winched further along the quay by the ship's crew when the loader had reached the limit of its delivery. The controller communicated with the ship's crew and the stevedores with a series of coded whistle-blasts.

At dockside level, the Colliery Co.'s locomotive positioned a rake of loaded wagons over the sump (and thence the belt), into which the coal was emptied through the bottom door of the wagon. The wagons were then winched forward, one at a time, using an electric capstan at the rail-side. A stevedore then leaned over the top of each wagon and, using a long pole, loosened any coal reluctant to make its way into the sump. After all the wagons had been emptied, the locomotive re-coupled to the south end of the train and proceeded back through the harbour towards the West Strand.

It is unclear as to when the coal loader was fully commissioned, as the installation of the electric capstan was not agreed until mid-October 1924, but on 28 October 1924, the General Purposes Committee of the Harbour Board agreed that both the existing hurries on the Dock Quay of the Queen's Dock could be dismantled, suggesting that the loader was working satisfactorily.

The Harbour Board Minutes provide no direct information about the dismantling of the West Strand hurries, but a contract was awarded, in February 1922, to *raise the quay on the West Strand*. This was followed, in April 1924, by a plan (not seen by the author) to *improve coal shipping at the South Harbour*. These minutes certainly indicated a significant amount of reconstruction work on the West Strand at around the time that the new Howgill Brake was opened. A further minute, dated 26 February 1924, stated that *debris from the tunnel of the Whitehaven Coal Co. on the south side* [of the South Harbour] *is to be carried free of toll*, and this certainly implies that all works connected with the new brake had not yet been completed.

In this period, coal exports from the port continued to decrease, as a percentage of the total Whitehaven Colliery output. In 1925, only 38.8% of the colliery's output was exported, declining substantially to 18.2% in 1927, although rising again to 32.8 % by 1930. The number of pits on the Howgill side was also in decline. In 1920, Ladysmith, Haig, and Wellington were all in production, but during the decade, frequent pit explosions and several lengthy strikes severely weakened the financial position of the Whitehaven Colliery Co., resulting in the closure of Ladysmith Pit in December 1931, followed by Wellington in July 1932.

An unusual view, taken on 13 November 1971, showing the point where the 1924 Howgill Brake crossed the line of the original 1813 incline. Note the sandstone retaining walls of the older incline, together with the width, which suggests that this was single track only. By this date, the William Pit site had been cleared.

(Michael Andrews Collection ref. A897)

Chapter Ten

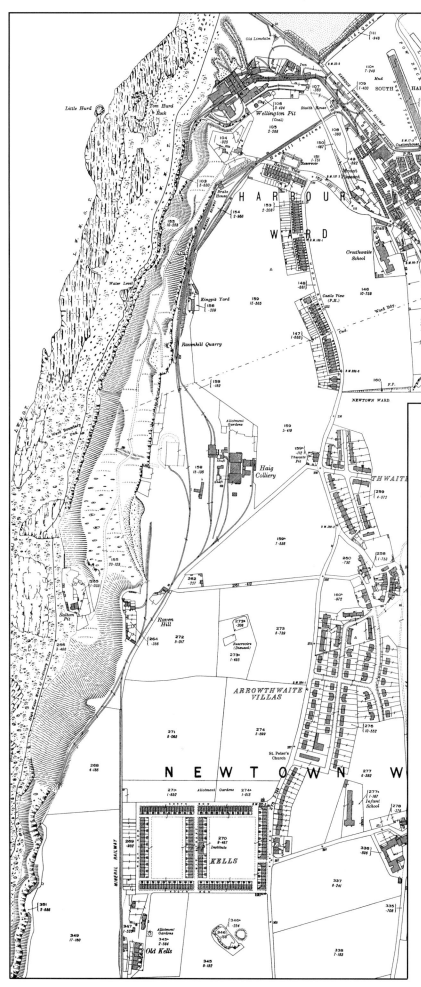

Most of the Saltom Waggonway has little changed in 150 years. This interesting map of 1925 shows the 1813 Howgill Incline still in operation, serving the West Strand hurries, but the new incline is clearly under construction, and about to sever the former as it descends to join the Harbour Commissioners' lines. On the right, the now-disused W&FJR tramway is still shown running through the town to Preston Street Goods Depot. Buildings are shown at both King Pit and Ravenhill Pit, despite closure of both pits many years earlier, and the Ravenhill site is still rail-served. Beyond Ravenhill, the incline to Croft (now Ladysmith) Pit runs due south. A passing loop at Old Kells, probably built to allow ascending and descending wagons to pass, was removed between 1899 and 1925.

(Reproduced from the 1925 25 inch Ordnance Survey Map sheet 67.6, Cumbria Record Office, Whitehaven, with the kind permission of the Ordnance Survey)

Industrial Railways: The Inclines and Other Lines

Looking up the Howgill Incline to the 1924-built winding house. A train of empty wagons, the last of which is a chauldron, has arrived at the braketop. A bell, allowing communication between the winding house and the West Strand brakeman, can be seen to the left of the door.

Michael Andrews Collection ref. A181)

For nearly fifty years, almost all coal from the Howgill side reached the harbour via the brake to the West Strand, the wagons latterly being a mix of both BR and NCB internal user vehicles. To avoid running-round at the top of the brake, locomotives always propelled the wagons out of the north end of Haig Pit yard. In January 1972, however, during a national miners' strike when traffic was suspended, a landslide affected the NCB line between the incline head and the north end of this yard. After the end of the strike, NCB engineers discovered that the trackbed on the affected section had been reduced to the width of one track, and that this too showed signs of instability. The Howgill Brake never reopened, and was officially abandoned in March 1972, the last revenue-earning traffic over the incline having been handled on 8 January that year. The section of line from the brake top to Haig Pit yard was closed completely, but internal rail traffic between Haig and Ladysmith Washery continued to use Croft Incline until the washery closed in March 1975, locomotives propelling the four- or five-wagon trains up the incline to avoid any runaways.

After the Howgill Brake closed, the NCB opened a temporary loading facility on the site of the former coke ovens just to the north of the site of William Pit, which had finally closed on 31 December 1954. Rail wagons were loaded here from lorries bringing down coal from Haig Pit and Ladysmith Washery.

Despite the continuing decline in output from Haig Pit, down from 417,371 tons in 1947 to 212,495 tons in 1977/8, the NCB continued to invest in facilities there, nearly £3.9 million being spent in the eight years up to March 1978. Most of this expenditure was accounted for when a new coal

A remarkable photograph of the Queen's Dock, looking south-east towards the town and showing the electric coal loader (centre). As the loader had been commissioned late in 1924 and in view of its begrimed state, this dates the photograph to around 1926 or 1927. Note the London, Brighton & South Coast Railway 10-ton open goods Class A wagon (numbered SR24533) in the foreground, a long way from its home territory. Its contents are not recorded.   *(Sankey ref. D415)*

Chapter Ten

The electric coal loading plant at Dock Quay, Queen's Dock, in September 1970. The retracted loading belt can be seen to the left of the structure, with a loaded wagon to the right. The steps and walkway, by means of which the stevedore could see into each wagon, can be seen to the right of the lighting post.

(Terry Powell)

On 30 August 1974, Giesl-ejector fitted Hunslet Engineering 0-6-0ST Repulse (Works No. 3698/1950) begins to propel its loaded train out of Haig Pit Yard and up Croft Incline to Ladysmith Washery. Six months later, the washery closed, and in 1976 the locomotive was preserved on the Lakeside & Haverthwaite Railway as LHR No. 11. *(Tom Heavyside ref. 116/13A)*

Haig Pit, the last colliery in the Cumberland coalfield, ceased production in May 1984 after a working life of 66 years. This view, taken on 13 November 1971, is dominated by the winding gear and adjacent winding house. (Michael Andrews Collection ref. A896)

preparation plant and washery was opened at Haig Pit in December 1976, and a conveyor built to carry the coal from the pit to a loading hopper at the South Harbour, utilizing the former NCB route, including the Howgill Brake.

This arrangement did not last long. Most of the coal was destined for power stations, mainly Fiddlers Ferry near Widnes, and was discharged into 'merry-go-round' (mgr) wagons. A local observer noted the relatively complex process for dispatching these workings, beginning with the marshalling of the trains on the Harbour departure road by one of the NCB diesel-hydraulic shunters. When a complete mgr train had been assembled, a Class 47 locomotive was attached at the Workington end before drawing the wagons forward onto the Down Main at Bransty No. 2 box, clear of the points. The locomotive was then well forward of the Bransty No. 2 Advanced Starter signal. The locomotive would now be detached from the train and run forward light engine for almost a mile and a quarter to Parton, where it would cross over to the Up Main for the run back to Bransty and into Platform 1. The Class 47 then reversed back onto its train, coupled up, and finally departed southbound through Platform 2 and into the tunnel, en route to Corkickle sidings where it would be held awaiting its booked path over the Furness line.

Some coal was loaded into the Manx-based Ramsey Steamship Co.'s vessels at the Queen's Dock, for export to Ireland, using the coal loader, but this traffic ceased in January 1982, following which the mgr export traffic was re-routed to Workington Dock. Coal production at Haig Colliery stopped in May 1984, following which all remaining pit-head coal stocks were gradually cleared down to the harbour, the last rail-borne coal traffic being moved out in September 1985. The Whitehaven Harbour rail network had closed for good. The NCB made an attempt to discover new coal reserves which could be worked economically, but these plans were effectively killed off by the bitter dispute between the NCB and the National Union of Mineworkers, which started in 1984 and was not resolved until the following year. Wear noted that *the* [Haig] *shafts were sealed on 31 March 1986,* [and] *the last colliery in the Cumberland coalfield had closed.*

Finally, mention should be made of two little-known waggonways serving mineral workings near Croft Pit. The first served the Barrowmouth Alabaster Works, which lay 150 yards north-east of Croft Pit, near the head of the Croft Incline. Alabaster had been extracted from a quarry on lands belonging to the Charities of St Bees School since 1794, but on 2 February 1887, Messrs John Robinson of Knothill, Carlisle, took over the lease, building an inclined railway of 2 ft. 3 in. gauge down to the Barrowmouth drifts which lay almost on the shoreline, controlled by a steam-operated winding house. Alabaster was a soft gypsum used in the manufacture of ornamental plasterwork such as cornices, and would have been in demand in the late Victorian era.

A standard-gauge south-facing connection from the head of the Croft Incline ran into the processing plant, from where bagged alabaster could be dispatched either via the then-new Corkickle Brake or via the Howgill Brake to the harbour. In general, the alabaster-extraction operation was not a success, and the workings closed in June 1903, although the 1925 25 inch OS map shows that the abandoned processing plant and its standard-gauge connections were still extant.

The second, and equally short-lived, line served Sandwith Quarries, to the south of Croft Pit. Commercial working of these Lonsdale-owned quarries began in 1850, managed by Richard Cousins, who later also managed the Redness Point Quarry. However, a standard-gauge line into the quarries was not built until 1898 (the year when the St Bees Head Red Freestone Quarries Co. took over the enterprise), the first working down the line being handled by Andrew Barclay 0-4-0ST *Charlton* (Works No. 109). The quarries were connected to the 'main-line' system by a branch off the Whitehaven Colliery Co.'s system at Croft Pit, and when the Andrew Barclay was under repair, a locomotive was supplied by the colliery company, the latter insisting that its own crew manned the locomotive. It appears that the quarry rail system was 'portable' in nature, lines being moved from face to face as reserves were worked out. The Sandwith Quarries Company went into liquidation in March 1918, although the quarries had not been worked for several years, and *Charlton* was cut up on site.

In LMS days, former Midland Railway 4-4-0 No. 353 stands in Platform 2 at Bransty with a northbound inspection saloon of LNWR origin. Platform 1 can be seen between the glazed awnings and the roof of the saloon, while the island platform 3/4 can be seen on the right. By this date, Platform 3 (previously goods-only) had been re-signalled for use by passenger workings as well.
(CRA Photo Library ref. PA0904)

The Furness Railway's Paley & Austin-designed main building at Bransty awaits demolition on 6 August 1981. The white board above the BR Bedford van shows the demolition contractor to be T Hannon of Workington. Note that, by this date, Bransty station carried the name 'Whitehaven', while Corkickle's name remained unchanged.
(CRA Photo Library ref. PE-81/3/5)

The Main Lines:
From Consolidation into the Twentieth Century

11

THE WHITEHAVEN Junction Railway had obtained an Act, on 2 June 1865, authorizing the enlargement of Bransty station. The Act defined the enlarged station's limits as *commencing at the point of junction with the Whitehaven & Furness Junction Railways and terminating on the north side of the Bransty Archway*, in effect extending the station southwards by just over 100 yards. After the Furness Railway took over the W&FJR in 1866, a new Act for an expanded station was obtained on 13 July 1868, this Act also authorizing the through platforms on the former W&FJR between the northern portal of Whitehaven Tunnel and the physical junction with the former WJR at Bransty. It is clear that the FR must have been responsible for promoting this Act, as a later plan, showing the completed station, clearly indicates that the LNWR owned only the relatively small area of Platform 1, plus the adjoining trackwork. The plan shows that the remainder of the station area (Platform 2 and its associated buildings, the later Platforms 3 and 4, and Bransty No. 1 signalbox) belonged to the Furness company, as did all of the through trackwork right up to the junction with LNWR metals just to the north of Bransty No. 2 box, the latter being LNWR-owned.

On 11 February 1870, the Furness Railway's Engineer was instructed to prepare plans for the new Bransty station, but it does not appear to have been a high priority for the railway company, the FR Board authorising the expenditure more than two years later, on 19 February 1872. The contract was eventually awarded to Messrs Vernon Cropper of Liverpool on 20 March 1873, at a value of £7,579. Interestingly, the FR minutes make no mention either of a 'joint' station, or of cost-sharing between the FR and the LNWR, presumably because by far the greater part of the site was FR-owned.

The architects for the new station, initially only a single-storey structure, were the Lancaster practice of Paley & Austin. Work was not completed until 24 December 1874, when the tiresome reversal to and from the terminal platforms at Bransty for passenger trains using the tunnel was eliminated. Because of the short distance between the tunnel portal and the junction at Bransty, the new station was some distance north of the WJR's original structure. The LNWR bay became Platform 1, with the reversible single FR line becoming Platform 2. It is likely that the Furness Railway signalbox at Bransty (later Bransty No. 1) was built around this time, controlling the junction between the short double-track section from LNWR metals and the single line through the tunnel. No date for the opening of this box has been found, although the structure is shown on the 1899 25 inch OS map.

In February 1881, Paley & Austin drew up plans for adding a second storey to the original single storey structure, these additions being completed in 1885. However, the later island platform, on the east side of the FR line and to the south of William Pit, was not added until 1902, Platform 3 being a reversible goods road and Platform 4 serving Joint Line trains (both to Workington, via Moor Row and Marron Junction, and to Sellafield, via Egremont). The contract for building this platform was awarded to the Barrow firm of W Gradwell & Co. Ltd. Platform 3 was signalled for passenger use around 1920. This island platform appears to have been planned for a number of years prior to 1902, as the 1899 25 inch OS map clearly shows the space between running lines where this structure would later be built. A subway connected the main platform with this island platform. The track layout immediately to the north of Platform 4 allowed the locomotive of an arriving Joint Line working to run round its stock, without having to pass over LNWR metals.

The reversing movement mentioned above was not without its dangers. On 23 December 1874, the day before reversing was discontinued, the Furness Railway's 3-30 pm Whitehaven-Carnforth working, after having set back from the London & North Western's terminal platform to a point near William Pit, was derailed as it crossed the points onto the Furness line, throwing two carriages and a van onto their side and injuring two people. It is interesting that 'The Whitehaven News', in reporting this incident, noted that it occurred beside *the platform intended for WC&ER trains* (with no mention of the Furness Railway).

An under-researched area in the history of Whitehaven's railways has been the extent of 'joint' operations between the LNWR and the FR in the Whitehaven area. A written statement, dated 29 March 1917, jointly prepared by FR and LNWR

The crossover (foreground) controlled by Corkickle No. 1 signalbox (formerly Mirehouse Junction) marked the approximate southern limit of LNWR running powers over the W&FJR section of the Furness Railway. Type 2 (later Class 28) Co-Bo D5709 approaches Corkickle with the Workington portion of the 6-40 am W33 from London Euston, which made no fewer than 36 stops between the capital and Bransty, where arrival was at 4-31 pm. Note that three coaches are of LMS design.

(CRA Photo Library ref. PE-A924)

73

Chapter Eleven

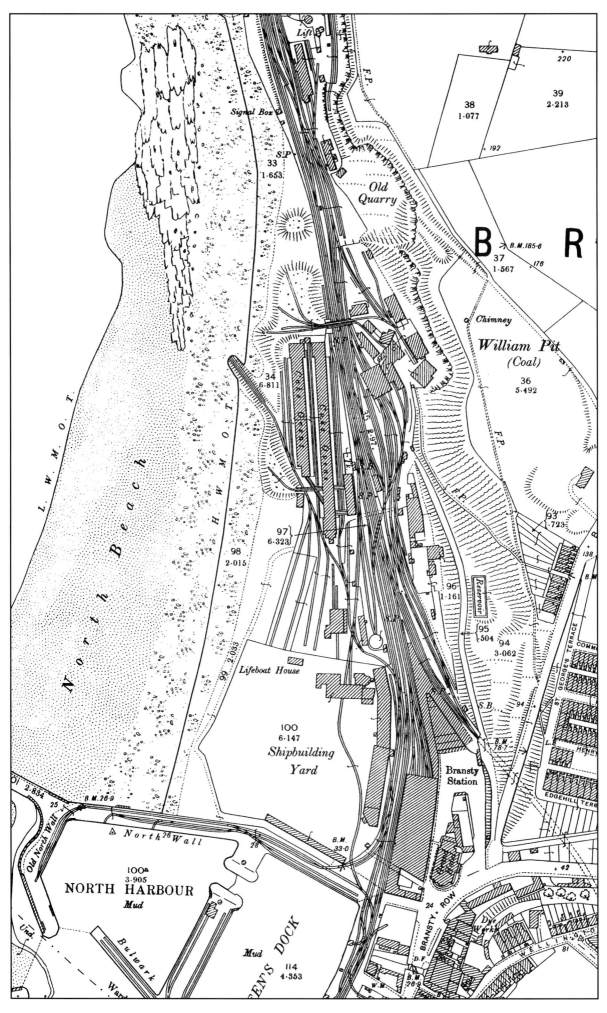

From Consolidation into the Twentieth Century

In 1939, an unidentified LMS 0-6-0 locomotive (possibly ex-Lancashire & Yorkshire Railway No. 12091) leaves the narrow confines of Whitehaven Tunnel and runs into Platform 2 at Bransty. As the loco is not displaying a headcode, it is likely to be returning on a trip working from Corkickle or Preston Street. Note the cramped location of Bransty No. 1 signalbox, and the 5 mph restriction through the tunnel, which was to continue until 1958.

(Norman Collection ref. N433)

solicitors and covering the two companies' respective liabilities in respect of Corkickle Station maintenance, contains interesting historical information about running powers. The 1866 Act, under which the LNWR purchased the Whitehaven Junction Railway, gave the LNWR running powers over the Whitehaven & Furness Junction Railway in order to access Preston Street Goods Station. The southern limit of these powers was defined as a point in Corkickle Sidings *22 yards south of Mirehouse Junction Signal Box*, presumably the limit of a headshunt from which LNWR freight workings could reverse down the branch. The Act of the same year, under which the FR purchased the W&FJR, gave the former company running powers over the WJR *between the Bransty Station of that railway ... (including the said Bransty station) and the North Harbour of Whitehaven, together with the station sidings, roads, watering places, booking offices, warehouses, platforms,* [and] *works*.

By 1869, there was certainly an understanding between the FR and the LNWR on the division of responsibilities at Whitehaven. In a memorandum for the 'Special Committee', dated 24 September, it was made clear that the Bransty Station Master was an LNWR appointment, responsible for all passenger activities there, and, additionally, Bransty No. 1 signalbox would come under his control. Preston Street was managed by the FR's Goods Agent there, who additionally controlled Corkickle Sidings and the Tunnel Pilot. The memo intriguingly referred to the future appointment of a 'Joint Manager' at Whitehaven, a senior position presumably controlling both sites, and with a suggestion that this position would rotate between the two railway companies.

Further evidence supporting the existence of some form of operating agreement between the two companies came in 1876, when William Cawkwell, an LNWR director, was giving evidence against the Cleator & Workington Junction Bill. In a comment on railway operations at Whitehaven, Cawkwell stated that Bransty and Preston Street *are thrown together and worked as a joint station, our goods traffic going to Preston Street and their passenger traffic going to Bransty station. We each pay half the expenses, but there is in reality no payment as between the two Companies*.

Left - This map of 1899 well shows the complexity of Whitehaven's rail network north of the tunnel. Note the space for the island platform opposite Platform 2 - the new platform was not added until 1902. The Parton waggonway, having been converted to standard-gauge for almost 30 years, now has more connections into the local industrial rail network. The rail-served shipbuilding site closed in 1901, with the Beacon flour mills occupying the southern portion after 1907. (Reproduced from the 1899 25 inch Ordnance Survey Map sheet 67.10, Cumbria Record Office, Whitehaven, with the kind permission of the Ordnance Survey)

Distortion in the red sandstone and brick lining of Whitehaven Tunnel was evident as early as 1874, and the tunnel was closed to passenger traffic the following year, although it is not clear for how long. The 'Ulverston Mirror' of 20 March 1875 noted that *the tunnel*[had] *been condemned by a Board of Trade Inspector ... A section of the wall of the tunnel, about 90 feet in length, has bulged in, owing ... to the action of water which has oozed into the clay bed ... It is not expected that the work will be completed much within three months*. Apparently, mineral trains were still allowed through, hauled by *small locomotives (with cut-down chimneys)*. Joy noted that, in the WC&ER Working Timetable for 1 May 1875, all trains terminated at Corkickle once more, an indication that the tunnel was still closed, although Joy believed (probably wrongly) that this was due to a re-escalation of the 'tunnel charges' dispute between the FR and the Egremont company.

One rapid development arising from the Furness Railway's 1866 purchase of the W&FJR was the introduction, in 1867, of a Royal Mail service between Whitehaven, Ulverston, and Carnforth. By 1869 some sorting was being carried out on this train, the Furness Railway having purchased an ex-LNWR 2nd class passenger coach for this purpose. In March 1875, the FR introduced, on behalf of the GPO, the Whitehaven Sorting Tender (rail carriage), which now had its own cancellation stamp inscribed 'Whitehaven S.T.' Once again, the Furness company turned to the LNWR for stock, this time purchasing a purpose-built GPO Sorting Van. The Up tender normally left Whitehaven around 5-45 pm, connecting at Carnforth into a London-bound Travelling Post Office (TPO) from Scotland, while the Down tender arrived in Whitehaven at 6-45 am. In 1887, the FR built its own GPO Sorting Van (FR 1) and a new 'Late Fee' facility was introduced, allowing the public to post a letter in a box on the 7-30 pm departure from Whitehaven for a small additional fee, and this late post was transferred to the Sorting Tender at Carnforth. By 1899, the tender itself incorporated a 'Late Fee' box, and took up the 7-30 pm departure from Whitehaven, coupled to passenger stock. In 1891, the service became known as the 'Carnforth & Whitehaven TPO', and in 1903 was equipped with a new sorting carriage (FR 2), built at Barrow Works by the FR. This vehicle continued in service until withdrawal sometime after the 1923 Grouping.

In the early 1870s, Preston Street Goods Depot handled all traffic in-bound from Ireland and the Isle of Man for destinations served by the Furness Railway and the WC&ER. This was still handled via the street tramway from the Old (or Sugar) Tongue. Joseph Tyson, writing in 'The Furness Railway Magazine' in October 1921, noted that *it was quite a common thing to have to run two or three trains onto Corkickle Bank* [the incline up from Mirehouse Junction towards Moor

75

Chapter Eleven

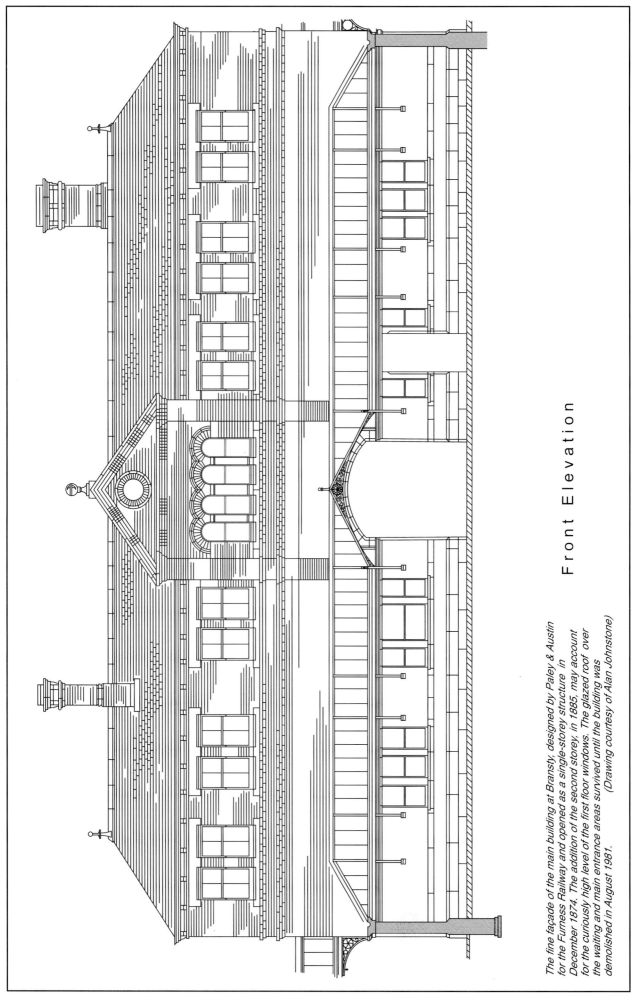

Front Elevation

The fine façade of the main building at Bransty, designed by Paley & Austin for the Furness Railway and opened as a single-storey structure in December 1874. The addition of the second storey, in 1885, may account for the curiously high level of the first floor windows. The glazed roof over the waiting and main entrance areas survived until the building was demolished in August 1981. (Drawing courtesy of Alan Johnstone)

Row] *before beginning to shunt Preston Street Yard in the mornings. This was before the Barrow Docks were made: when they were completed, it made a great deal less work at [Whitehaven].* This suggests that Irish and Manx traffic through Whitehaven began to decline after 1873, the year in which the Buccleuch Dock was opened at Barrow. The reference to Corkickle Bank also suggests that the Preston Street Yard shunting locomotive could be called on, as required, to bank heavy freight trains up the 1 in 52 incline from Mirehouse Junction to Moor Row. The LNWR also had running powers for 'merchandise traffic' between Bransty, Mirehouse Junction, Corkickle Sidings, and Preston Street Goods Depot, although such running powers did not extend into the FR's Corkickle Engine Shed.

The Furness Railways (note the plural) timetable of 1 July 1882, issued one month after the opening of the new Barrow Central station, showed six workings in each direction between Bransty and Carnforth, the average journey time being a little over three hours, although the Up Mail, leaving Bransty at 7-30 pm, took only 2 hours 20 minutes for the 74$\frac{1}{2}$ miles. South of St Bees, this train stopped only at Millom, Askam, Barrow Central, Dalton, Ulverston and Grange. In the Down direction, the Mail took 2 hours 40 minutes, leaving Carnforth at 4-40 am, and running fast to Barrow; north of the industrial town, calls were made at Foxfield, Millom, Bootle, Drigg, Sellafield, St Bees and Corkickle. Connections were made at Sellafield in both directions with the 'Joint Line' serving Egremont and Moor Row, with three into Up workings and no fewer than five into Down trains.

By August 1887, little had changed on the Furness line, although one Down working, the 9-20 am arrival at Bransty, started from Ulverston, and the Up Mail had had Sellafield and Seascale stops inserted at the cost of only an additional two minutes' running time. However, the 11-00 am from Leeds now contained a through coach to Bransty, arriving at 4-20 pm.

Traffic on the London & North Western line from Maryport was heavier, with nine trains northbound along the coast each day, and eight southbound, taking around 35 minutes for the 12$\frac{1}{4}$ mile journey. One curious northbound working was the 11-10 am arrival at Maryport, which left Bransty in two portions, an all-stations at 10-25 and a non-stop (to Workington) at 10-40, the two portions being combined at Workington. The reason for this split working is unclear, as the connection from the South arrived in the Furness platforms at Bransty at 9-20 am. Workings over the former Whitehaven Junction line were further enhanced by LNWR workings from Penrith, over the former Cockermouth, Keswick & Penrith route, providing an additional four southbound workings between Workington and Whitehaven.

Services over the former Whitehaven, Cleator, and Egremont system are described in Chapter 8, although mention should also be made of the 1-10 pm departure from Bransty which, on Mondays only, was extended from Rowrah to Cockermouth (arriving at 2-35 pm), using Marron East Junction Curve. The return working, leaving Cockermouth at 3-30 pm, reached Bransty at 4-55 pm.

Freight workings around this period can be analysed from studying the working timetables of the various companies. The LNWR (West Cumberland Division) WTT for October 1888 showed seven fast/express mineral, three fast/express goods, and one mixed goods-and-mineral workings running north from Whitehaven towards Maryport. The goods workings originated from Preston Street Goods Depot, but most of the mineral workings ran through from the 'Joint Line'. For example, the 11-45 am ex-Corkickle originated from Gillfoot Junction (just over $\frac{1}{2}$ mile north of Egremont station) at 10-25 am, while the 1-50 pm departure started from Frizington at 1-00 pm. Most of the mineral workings terminated at Maryport Ironworks, with goods services running to Maryport and beyond. Perhaps surprisingly, the 1888 WTT showed no overnight freight or mineral workings, the first daily departure (from Preston Street) being a Maryport fast goods at 8-00 am, and the final departure a Workington fast mineral at 5-50 pm.

In the reverse direction, southbound to Whitehaven, much of the traffic was mineral empties, although an interesting working was a Mondays-only express cattle train which left Cockermouth at 3-20 pm, arriving in Preston Street Goods at 4-45 pm; the same working had a conditional path for the remainder of the week, leaving Cockermouth at 4-05 pm and arriving in Preston Street at 5-25 pm. This service may also have conveyed passenger vehicles (possibly for the accompanying cattle drovers), as the WTT shows a stop at Parton for 'ticket collection' purposes.

Southbound from Whitehaven, the 1888 LNWR WTT indicated eleven freight departures over the former Whitehaven, Cleator & Egremont system: eight LNW workings and three Furness Railway diagrams. All LNW workings were booked to pass Bransty, indicating that these were mainly return mineral empties originating north of Whitehaven; their destinations included Frizington, Gillfoot Junction, and the Crossfield mine near Moor Row. One working, the 7-15 am from Bransty, was classified as a goods working to Cleator Moor. The three southbound Furness Railway workings were also classified as 'mineral', all departing from Corkickle sidings and running to Egremont, the Pallaflat mines accessed via Woodend, and Moor Row.

A Class 108/2 DMU leaves Whitehaven's now-shortened and decrepit Platform1 with the 11-05 working to Carlisle on 21 July 1979. The corner portion of the station building above the subway shelter (left) shows the height of the original single-storey structure of 1874, before the second storey additions completed by 1885. Note the wooden steps on the low platform, to give easier access to passenger stock. On the extreme right, the harbour lines curve sharply away alongside a surviving section of wall from the seven-road carriage shed.

(Tom Heavyside ref. 501/19A)

Chapter Eleven

The Furness Railway's triple-shed goods depot at Preston Street, photographed in the early 1970s. Most of the rail vehicles are fitted box vans, but to the right of the nearest shed, two CovHops are discharging their contents into a fleet of road tankers to be taken up to the Marchon Products plant at Kells. The isolated white wooden gate at the site entrance is the point where the W&FJR's Harbour Tramway emerged from railway property.

(Allan Beck Collection)

On the Furness Railway main line, the WTT indicated freight departures for the south at 7-30 am, 12-40 pm and 4-25 pm from Preston Street, with Down arrivals at 11-15 am, 2-30 pm, 3-20 pm and 9-00 pm. Despite its opening less than ten years previously, the former WC&ER Gilgarran branch was already virtually moribund. The 4¼ miles between Ullock Junction and Distington Ironworks saw only one out-and-back daily working from Ullock, and there was no traffic from Wythemoor Pit, closed in 1886 due to incompetent management. The three-mile section from Parton to Distington fared little better, with a morning out-and-back mineral working between Parton and Bain & Co.'s No. 4 Pit, and a return working to and from the ironworks.

With the November 1885 introduction of Tyer's Train Tablet instruments on the Bransty No. 1-Corkickle Preston Street Junction section (through the tunnel), replacing the electric telegraph, the role of Tunnel Pilotman had come to an end. As a result, the 1888 WTT reflected actual scheduled movements through the tunnel on a daily basis, shown in a specific 'Whitehaven Tunnel' section. In the Up direction, the first movement was an LNWR mineral working, leaving Bransty at 5-35 am, and the last an FR light engine at 9-30 pm; in total, there were 35 train movements in this direction. Down movements started with an FR light engine at 6-30 am, ending with an LNWR light engine at 9-20 pm, and there were also 35 train movements. It is probable that at least some 'light engine' movements represented paths for trip workings between Preston Street Goods and the Harbour Commissioners' lines at Bransty. The 1899 WTT was more specific on these trip workings, showing four daily return movements worked by the 'Furness Tunnel Engine'. Passenger trains were allowed between three and four minutes for the passage of the ¾ mile-long bore, while freight workings were allowed five minutes.

This 1888 timetable probably reflected the zenith of railway activities in the Whitehaven area. Perfection of the Gilchrist Thomas process of steel making (which was not haematite-dependent), coupled with the importation of cheaper Spanish ores, meant that West Cumberland's heyday was short lived. As Joy wrote, *a gradual decline from the late 1880s was coupled with virtual cessation of railway expansion*. Main line passenger services, however, remained virtually unaltered, the Furness still scheduling six Up and six Down workings between Carnforth and Whitehaven in the April 1910 timetable, with three of these conveying through carriages to and from London (Euston) and London (St Pancras). As an example, the 10-10 am departure from Euston arrived at Lancaster (Castle) at 4-06 pm, and with some smart running, came into Bransty at 6-50 pm. The 2-00 pm departure from the capital was even faster,

with a Bransty arrival time of 9-55 pm. Some Carnforth-Whitehaven services conveyed vehicles from both the LNWR and the MR, the Summer 1901 timetable showing that the 4-25 pm working included coaches from the 10-30 am ex-St Pancras and the 11-30 am ex-Euston.

On the London & North Western section between Bransty and Maryport, the number of daily services in April 1910 had actually increased since 1887, with ten Up and nine Down workings. By this date, however, through services between the West Coast route and Whitehaven via the CK&PR had virtually ceased, with only one working, the 5-15 pm arrival at Bransty, being advertised as including through carriages from Carlisle.

For the LNW and Furness Joint Line, services on the northern section had also improved, with four through workings daily from Bransty to Workington (LNWR) via Marron Junction, and three in the reverse direction. In addition, there were two Up and two Down workings from Bransty to Rowrah. The Whitehaven-Workington service via this route was of interest in that one of the workings, the 9-40 am from Bransty, was combined at Camerton with the 9-30 am from Penrith. It was no longer possible to do this at Marron Junction station, following its closure on 1 July 1897. The 9-40 am from Bransty included a through Cockermouth portion, and the 3-35 pm from Cockermouth included Whitehaven coaches. As Marron East Junction curve had closed on 1 October 1902, combining of portions was probably also carried out at Camerton.

April 1910 Whitehaven to Egremont services were also unchanged since 1887, with eight workings between Bransty and Egremont, and seven in the reverse direction. A definite improvement, however, was that five of these daily workings were extended to and from Sellafield.

The same 1910 timetable revealed an unusual, though somewhat poignant, working south from Bransty. Output of Cumberland haematite iron by this period was more than 20% down on its 1889 level of 1,594,000 tons, leading many miners to look for work in South Africa, Australia and Canada. As a result, a through working for Southampton Docks left Bransty each Friday to take these emigrants south, the coach being serviced at Barrow in the afternoon before being sent north to Whitehaven to be attached to the Up Mail, leaving Bransty at 7-30 pm. After arriving at Carnforth at 9-52 pm, the coach was worked forward to Leeds, to be attached to the Edinburgh/Glasgow-Bristol overnight train (the 'Scotch Express') leaving Leeds at 12-05am. On arrival at Cheltenham, this through working was transferred rapidly to the 4-50 am 'Ocean Boat Express' of the Midland & South Western Junction Railway, reaching the Southampton Docks terminus at 8-21 am via this now-closed route across the

Cotswolds. The summer of the following year, 1911, saw a further improvement in Furness main line services to and from Euston. It was now the 11-25 am departure from the capital which carried the through Whitehaven portion, arriving at Bransty 7³/₄ hours later at 7-10 pm.

An interesting development in 1913 was the re-introduction of passenger workings between Whitehaven and Distington via Parton, a previous short-lived service having operated between 1881 and 1883. With the consolidation of seven iron and steel works into the Workington Iron & Steel Co. in 1909, and the subsequent expansion of Lowca Pit to include a coking plant, an increasing number of miners required transport to the mine. The revived service, operated as a 'Joint Line' working but with LNWR locomotives, ran from 2 November 1913 until 1 September 1914, when the outbreak of the Great War appeared to result in suspension of the workings. It was not clear where the miners disembarked for Lowca, although possibly there was an unofficial stopping place. Services to and from Bransty recommenced on 11 January 1915, although only as far as the new Parton Halt (also known as Lowca Pit) on the Gilgarran branch, situated 100 yards from the junction with the coast line. There were three workings daily to and from the halt, coinciding with shift changeovers. It seems as though the status of these workings changed from 'public timetable' to 'workmen only' at some point, the July-September 1916 WTT for the Joint Line advertising these as 'passenger', while the LNWR West Cumberland WTT in the following April described them as 'workmen's'. The July 1922 edition of 'Bradshaw' does not show these workings at all (probably because they were not available to the public), although the October 1922 WTT indicates four workings in each direction. This service was finally withdrawn on 1 April 1929.

The Summer 1913 timetables appeared to show passenger workings at their zenith between Whitehaven and the rest of the country. Through coaches for Euston, via the Furness Railway, were carried on the 6-40 am, 8-10 am, 11-30 am and 2-45 pm departures, with departures from the capital at 12-05 am, 10-10 am, 11-25 am and 2-00 pm, and there were also through workings to and from Liverpool, Manchester, and Leeds. Most surprising of all was a through coach from Cambridge, which left the university city at 9-42 am, and was attached at Bletchley to the 10-10 am from Euston, giving a Whitehaven arrival time of 6-30 pm. This had been running for at least three years, having first been noted in the Summer 1910 timetables, but did not survive the Great War, although the coach was shown in the Summer 1914 timetables, with a Cambridge departure at 9-16 am. There was no Up equivalent of this service.

The Great War brought increased traffic volumes to all routes radiating from Whitehaven, although this was not without its attendant problems. The Barrow-Whitehaven-Workington section in particular was in intensive use, carrying imported iron ore from Barrow Docks to the West Cumberland iron and steel works, while West Cumberland coal was moved down to Barrow under the Coal Transportation Scheme. Gradon referred to the so-called 'Jellicoe Specials', additional workings over the Furness, LNW, and Maryport & Carlisle sections of the West Cumberland line, which he described as *LNWR 0-6-0 'Cauliflowers'* [working trains of] *50-odd wagons*. These coal trains were commissioned by the Admiralty, originated in South Wales collieries, and were destined for Grangemouth in Scotland, for transhipment into supply ships for Scapa Flow. While apparently diagrammed via the Cumbrian Coast to free up paths on the main line via Shap, it now seems likely that only a relatively small number of 'Jellicoes' was routed this way. The LNWR Special Traffic Notices throughout 1916, and the WTT for April 1917, make no mention of these workings, but these specials are likely to have operated on an 'ad hoc' basis, coordinated between Crewe Timings Office, Carnforth Control, and the Furness and Maryport & Carlisle operating departments. Firm evidence that 'Jellicoes' were routed via Whitehaven came with an LNWR Special Traffic Notice for 9 June 1918, covering four trains of coal empties between Brayton Junction, Workington and Saltney Junction at Chester, from where the Great Western Railway would have worked the trains back to their origination point at Pontypool Road.

Increased traffic levels during the Great War were causing congestion at Preston Street Junction, where former W&FJR and WC&ER metals converged just before the single-track tunnel. To increase capacity and operating flexibility, a new connection between the double-track WC&ER route and the single-track W&FJR line was constructed 905 yards south of Mirehouse Junction, just before the Egremont line began to climb away to the south-east, and a new signalbox erected at this point. Named Corkickle No. 1, it was not opened until 9 March 1919. Mirehouse Junction was now called Corkickle No. 2 with Preston Street Junction becoming Corkickle No. 3. As a result, the former W&FJR line between Corkickle No. 1 and No. 3 boxes (a distance of 1455 yards) became a permissive block goods line, with all passenger services using the double-track 'Joint Line' between the two boxes, a manoeuvre which often confused unwary Barrow passengers into thinking that their train was being routed towards Moor Row and Egremont!

The war meant that some services were worked by 'foreign' motive power, in the interests of better resource utilisation. The 1917 WTT showed that the 11-40 am goods

Against a glorious backdrop of the Cumberland mountains around Ennerdale Water, Class 4MT Fairburn 2-6-4T No. 42236 comes off the Egremont line past Moor Row No. 1 box with a short pick-up freight destined for Whitehaven. Moor Row No. 2 can be seen in the distance. As the date is June 1966, demolition work on the right may be linked to the final withdrawal of the workmen's service to Sellafield the previous September.

(Peter Robinson ref. 055c18)

Chapter Eleven

On 5 June 1968, Type 1 (later Class 17) Bo-Bo D8528 brings a loaded coal train from the United Steel Companies Ltd.'s No. 4 Pit down the final surviving section of the steeply-graded Gilgarran branch, and runs alongside the Whitehaven-Workington main line, towards Parton box. The section of line on which the train is standing survived until relatively recently as a Civil Engineer's siding.

(CRA Photo Library ref. PE-AA359)

from Barrow was worked by a Furness Railway locomotive and crew beyond Whitehaven as far as Workington, and then by a Maryport & Carlisle locomotive and crew on to Maryport: the return working from Workington for the FR locomotive was at 3-55 pm. Towards the end of the war, M&CR locomotives were also working between Maryport and Whitehaven, as the 7-05 pm Bransty-Carnforth was booked for an M&CR 0-4-2 locomotive between Whitehaven and Millom. This allowed the M&CR locomotive to return north with the 7-00 pm from Carnforth, arriving back at Bransty at 9-43 pm. An LNWR Weekly Notice issued in 1918 showed that, on 1 October, four 'as required' return freight workings (possibly for iron ore) were operated between Workington and Barrow, two being booked for LNWR motive power throughout and the others for FR locomotives. By 1919, rolling stock also began to work onto 'foreign' metals, two FR six-wheel coaches being attached to an LNWR set to work the 9-30 am Workington-Whitehaven and the 1-20 pm return. On Mondays, two M&CR third-class vehicles were attached to LNWR six-wheelers on the 7-35 am Whitehaven-Carlisle. LNWR and M&CR locomotives were now diagrammed to work services between Whitehaven and Carlisle throughout, without locomotive changes.

This 1917 wartime timetable showed that Carnforth-Whitehaven passenger services had been reduced to five each way, from the six of previous years. The LNWR and Furness Joint Line had now been singled over the 7¾ miles between Rowrah No. 1 signalbox and Bridgefoot (with crossing loops at Lamplugh and Ullock Junction). Passenger services on this line were also reduced: three trains ran between Bransty and Workington (LNWR), but only one in the reverse direction, although the 3-20 pm from Cockermouth ran through to Whitehaven after reversal at Marron Junction. Only two freights in each direction covered the whole of this once-busy line as far as Marron.

Services between Whitehaven and Workington were little changed from pre-war days, with ten northbound and nine southbound workings. On the Egremont branch of the Joint Line, the situation was the same, with eight Up and eight Down passenger workings between Moor Row and Egremont, although fewer ran through to Sellafield, and not all originated and terminated at Bransty. Three Up and three Down Egremont services ran to and from a station at Beckermet Mines, opened on 15 January 1912 and closed around the time of the 1923 Grouping. The mine itself was served daily by two LNWR mineral workings, both of which ran through to Workington, via Whitehaven, with iron ore.

Compared with 1888, April 1917 freight services over the Parton-Distington section of the Gilgarran branch had vastly improved, with three workings in each direction between Whitehaven, Parton and Distington Ironworks, the traffic being mainly pig iron destined for Whitehaven Harbour. There were also three workings between Parton and the Workington Iron & Steel Co.'s No. 4 Pit. There was no change, however, to the service between Ullock Junction and Distington, an FR through working from Cleator Moor arriving at Distington Ironworks at 10.05 a.m., and returning at 11.20 a.m. The return working dealt with traffic from Wythemoor Colliery, where production had resumed in 1904. Gradon wrote that the Ullock Junction-Distington Ironworks section had closed by the end of 1917 with the final closure of the colliery, although Joy gives an official closure date of 14 February 1929. Little traffic is likely to have traversed the route in these final twelve years.

With the dramatic decline in the pig iron traffic after hostilities ceased in 1918, the Parton-Distington section only saw regular usage over the 1 mile 242 yards between Parton Junction and No. 4 Pit, with a mixture of workmen's traffic to Parton Halt and coal workings.

The passenger timetables for July 1922, the last summer schedules before the 1923 Grouping, when all Whitehaven area main lines became part of the new London, Midland, & Scottish Railway, make interesting reading. On the Furness line, there were eight workings each way between Whitehaven and Carnforth. The 6-55 am departure from Carnforth arrived in Whitehaven at 10-00 am, from where it continued to Carlisle, while the 3-00 pm Up working from Bransty was a through working from Carlisle (1-30 pm departure). Through coaches from Euston arrived in Whitehaven at 4-55 pm, 6-10 pm and 9-43 pm. In the reverse direction, Euston portions left Bransty at 6-35 am, 11-35 am and 1-55 pm, with a fastest journey time of 7 hours 55 minutes. As in previous years, several Up and Down workings carried Leeds, Liverpool, and Manchester portions.

As a portent of things to come, the only 1922 FR Sunday service using Bransty was the 10-10 am to Carnforth, all other arrivals and departures being scheduled to use Corkickle. This was to allow the Civil Engineers access to Whitehaven Tunnel for routine maintenance, a situation which was to change drastically in 1935, when the decision was taken to reline the bore completely.

North of Whitehaven, on LNWR and M&CR metals, all services now operated through to Carlisle, although the service was slow, with some trains taking around two hours for the 40¼ mile journey. Frequency was also slightly reduced compared to previous years, with eight northbound and nine southbound workings over the route. On the northern section of the LNW and Furness Joint Line, passenger services between Bransty and Workington (LNW), via Marron Junction, had reached an all-time low. Northbound, only two trains ran

80

Class 47 No. 47 332 approaches Bransty on 29 December 1994 at the head of a short southbound tank train destined for Sellafield. The site of William Pit lies to the right, while the background is dominated by the 258-ft.-high outcrop at Redness Point.

(CRA Photo Library ref. HUG 547)

the full distance, one of which, the 4-15 pm from Bransty, maintained a connection into a Cockermouth service at Camerton. Southbound, two workings ran between Workington and Bransty, augmented by a working which left Cockermouth at 3-25 pm and which reversed at Marron Junction to gain the 'Joint Line'. A rather unbalanced service of two Up and four Down through trains continued to operate between Bransty and Rowrah.

The Moor Row-Egremont service continued to see improvements, with ten Up and eight Down workings each day, most of these originating and terminating at Bransty. Six of the Up services terminated at Sellafield, while five Down workings originated there.

Freight traffic over the FR to and from Whitehaven had declined since the end of the Great War. By 1922, there was only one 'express goods' working to and from Carnforth, the Down train running via the Barrow Avoiding Line (Dalton Junction to Park South) to Corkickle Sidings in three hours, with only one stop for water at Millom. The Up train included traffic from the Allerdale coke ovens, near Clifton in the Derwent Valley, to Millom ironworks. Gradon also noted that there were two additional 'fast goods trips' to and from Barrow, with a return daily pick-up goods from Whitehaven to Millom.

On 1 January 1923, the Furness, London & North Western, Cleator & Workington Junction, and Maryport & Carlisle Railways all became part of the new London Midland & Scottish Railway. Henceforward, all main lines from Whitehaven would be served by the same company. The era of the independent lines was over. As Joy wrote, *never again* [would] *brightly-painted steam locomotives haul long trains of iron ore and coal over ... one of the most fascinating railway complexes in Britain.*

Stanier Class 4MT 2-6-4T No. 42429 awaits departure from Platform 1 at Bransty on 5 September 1954, with the 11-00am departure for Carlisle. The running-in board on the left was designed to give the train crew a clear indication of the station they were entering.

(CRA Photo Library ref. DEN 132)

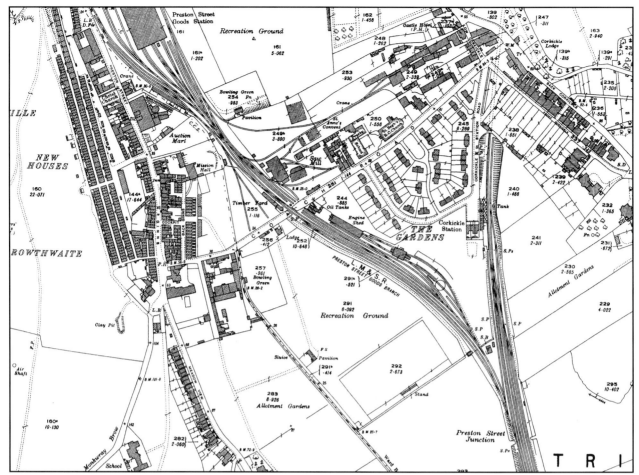

The Preston Street branch from Corkickle can be seen on this map. The FR's 1898 engine shed, coaling shed, and turntable are visible between Coach Road level crossing and Preston Street Junction. Another of Whitehaven's 'long sidings' served a saw-mill and associated timber yard to the rear of St Begh's Church.

(Reproduced from the 1899 25 inch Ordnance Survey Map sheet 67.10, Cumbria Record Office, Whitehaven, with the kind permission of the Ordnance Survey)

The staff of Preston Street Goods Depot around 1946. Back Row: Harry Bryan 4th from left, John Mann next to crane jib, Mr. Charters 2nd from right. Middle Row: John Bragg, Bill Lofthouse and Albert Rickerby immediate left, Mr. Williamson 5th from left, Joe Rickerby 7th from left. Front Row Standing: John Fawcett on left, Mr. Little 5th from left, Reggie Monkhouse 9th from left, Mr. Crawford 10th from left, Joe Walker on extreme right, Jim Birkett, Joe Williams and Mr. Mawson 2nd, 3rd and 5th from right respectively. The lady is Myra Simpson.

(Collection Mrs. Eva Green)

The Main Lines:
From Grouping to Nationalisation and Beyond

12

THE FIRST FEW years of the London Midland & Scottish regime in the Whitehaven area were relatively uneventful, although Joy noted that one effect was the rapid diversion of iron ore traffic, originating in the Cleator area, away from the former Cleator & Workington Junction line and through Whitehaven instead. Withdrawal of the workmen's service between Bransty and Parton Halt (also known as Lowca Pit) on 1 April 1929 was not considered a major closure, nor was the total withdrawal of services between Bain's No. 4 Pit siding and Distington Junction, on the same section of line, on 2 May 1932. (The surviving 1 mile 242 yard section between the coastal main line and the Lowca pits had a relatively long life, not closing until 23 May 1973, when Lowca Washery was closed.) Through traffic between Distington and Parton must have been virtually non-existent after production at Distington Ironworks ceased in early 1922.

Mention should be made here of Whitehaven's two little-known engine sheds, both of which closed in the early years of the Grouping. The Whitehaven & Furness Junction Railway constructed a shed at Preston Street almost certainly around the time that this line opened in July 1850. The site of this depot was about 50 yards south of the passenger station, and on the east side of the layout. With the advent of closer relationships between the W&FJR and the Whitehaven Junction Railway, culminating in the establishment of the Joint Locomotive Committee in January 1854, the two companies agreed to use the Preston Street shed to accommodate the combined locomotive stock. In consequence, the depot was enlarged to two roads, with a new coal stage and two water tanks, probably around the time that Preston Street became the goods depot for both companies on 3 December 1855.

Little has been written about this depot in the following 40 years. However, in the early 1880s, after the setting-up of the North Western & Furness Joint Committee, discussions were under way concerning joint developments at Bransty Station. At a Committee meeting held on 17 November 1881, it was minuted that *Stileman & Worthington* [Consulting Engineer to the FR and LNWR Lancaster District Engineer respectively] *value the loco shed at Preston Street, taken from the FR, at £1300. To be added to the cost of the Joint Station*.

By 1898, the Furness Railway had erected a new two-road engine shed, around 75 yards south-east of Coach Road level crossing, on the north-east side of the layout, the old shed then being demolished. The shed could only be accessed through a covered coaling shed, built between the main shed and the junction with the Furness line. The 1899 25 inch OS map shows that both roads ran through the coaling shed into the engine shed, but an existing undated plan shows only the southernmost road running through the coaling shed, the other ending at buffer stops within the shed, the second through road being obviously created shortly after the coaling shed was built. Described as being of *recognisably massive Furness style*, the sandstone engine shed, now known as 'Corkickle', was 170 ft. long. The 42 ft. diameter turntable was situated on one of the coaling shed lines, on the Preston Street Junction side.

In 1916, the shed's allocation numbered only nine locomotives, although this had risen to twelve after the Great War. However, the shed could have seen a much larger allocation had a proposal made by William Pettigrew, the FR's Locomotive Superintendent, been put into effect. In January 1915, Pettigrew proposed extending Corkickle engine shed and incorporating Moor Row's servicing and fitting facilities into the new structure, at a total cost of £11,050. However, the proposal was deferred by the FR Board. Pettigrew re-submitted the proposal the following year, presumably with more detail, as the extended shed would have been large enough to accommodate forty locomotives. The cost had risen to £35,000 – presumably the reason why the Board deferred the proposal *for further consideration after the War*. It does not appear that the proposal was ever put forward again.

Corkickle shed provided the previously-mentioned 'Tunnel Engine', the diagram of which now also included a local passenger turn to Millom and a short goods working to St Bees. Closure of Corkickle shed came on 4 January 1932, when recession in West Cumberland was beginning to bite, although as late as 1949 British Railways were using the building for carriage cleaning and painting.

By contrast, information on Bransty engine shed is very meagre. The opening of the Harrington-Bransty section of the Whitehaven Junction Railway in 1847 presumably meant some kind of servicing facility at Whitehaven. In their book 'LMS Engine Sheds – Volume 1', Chris Hawkins and George Reeve note that repairs were made to the Bransty facility in 1862 at a cost of £130, although it is unclear why, as all locomotives under the control of the Joint Locomotive Committee were shedded at Preston Street during this period. Examination of the 1865 25 inch OS map shows a turntable on the site of the tapered point of the later buildings between Platforms 1 and 2, linked into the Down W&FJR line via a trailing connection. A siding about 15 yards long led off the turntable, but there is no evidence of any building on this site. However, about 50 yards north of the Bransty terminal building, the OS map shows a building served by a single line, and sandwiched between the WJR's station sidings and the harbour lines. This was the company's shed, a curious affair around 300 ft. long, where locomotives were stabled on a lengthy single line which continued as covered carriage accommodation. This dual-purpose building is likely to have been in existence since the completion of the WJR in 1847, the 'Whitehaven Herald' of 30 October 1852 stating that *a new railway station* [probably in connection with the opening of Whitehaven Tunnel] *is to be built at Bransty ... on a site ... occupied by the wooden carriage shed of the WJR and opposite the present station*. This scheme was not carried out, the ground-plan of the 1874 rebuilding occupying a somewhat different position. It appears that the locomotive-stabling capacity of this shed was expanded in 1864, as a WJR Minute noted that *the urinals at the end of the Engine Shed* [should] *be removed to make room for three engines*!

Despite these modifications to the shed, they appear to have provided few new facilities, as, at the time of the dissolution of the Joint Locomotive Committee, the shed appeared incapable of handling even small repairs. At a meeting of the LNWR's Locomotive & Engineering Committee on 23 October 1866, it was noted that, following the closure of the Preston Street facility to ex-WJR stock on 30 November, *light repairs of* [former WJR] *stock and of the Cockermouth & Workington stock will ... be done in the Company's shops at Cockermouth*. This referred to the CWR's two-road locomotive shed there. Erected in 1847, its role as a repair shop is likely to have been limited after 1867, when LNWR-designed locomotives began to appear on the CWR and WJR sections. In any case, the LNWR was already making some minor investments at Bransty, the same Committee meeting reporting that a Mr Harrison had *executed additional steam shed accommodation* there, at

83

Chapter Twelve

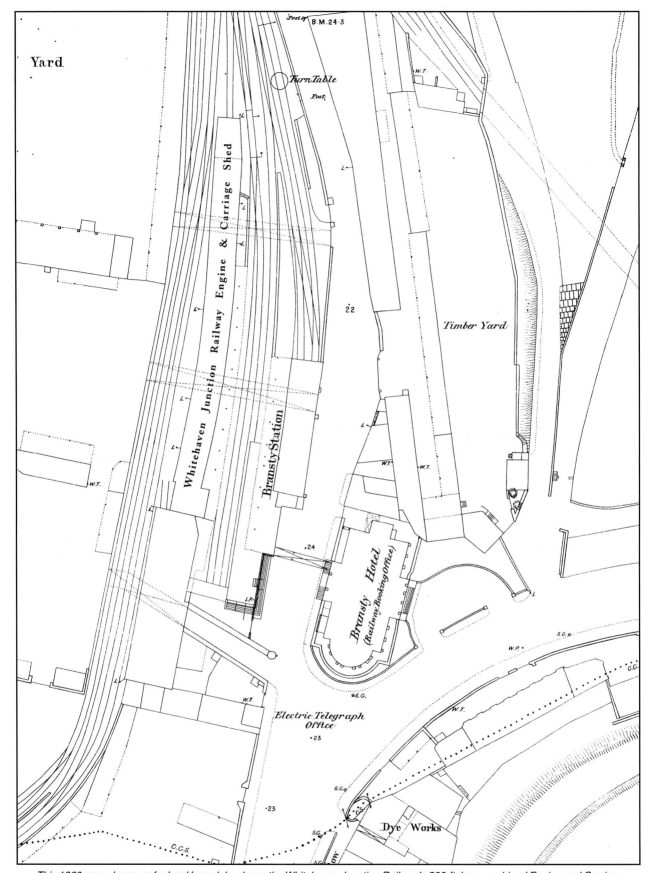

This 1860 map, drawn up for Lord Lonsdale, shows the Whitehaven Junction Railway's 300-ft. long combined Engine and Carriage Shed at Bransty. It is believed that carriages were accommodated in the southernmost section of this structure. The 1874 rebuilding of Bransty station involved relocation of the turntable about 100 yards to the north-west.
(From a plan in the Cumbria Record Office, Whitehaven, ref. 67.2.13)

a cost of £130. It is possible that this accommodation was actually the same proposal as the WJR's 1864 plans, and that the latter had never been carried out, since one of Mr Harrison's building works was *to remove and rebuild water closets for men*.

Hawkins and Reeve noted the 1866 division of the locomotives controlled by the Joint Committee, pointing out that the WJR locos (or rather their Crewe successors) were ultimately accommodated in a separate shed at Bransty. The land reclamations of 1872 westwards to the North Beach meant that more space was available for railway expansion, while the rebuilding of Bransty station in 1874 forced relocation of the turntable to a new position almost opposite, and to the west of, the tapered point of Platforms 1 and 2. A building adjacent to the turntable and 90 ft. long is shown on the 1899 25 inch OS map, but is not shown as rail-connected at this date, although the tenuous possibility remains of rail connection (and of use as an engine shed) in previous years. The 1925 map shows the building to have been demolished, and Hawkins and Reeve recorded that the shed had closed the previous year.

Evidence of the existence of a shed post-Bransty station rebuilding comes first from LNWR records, which note that Whitehaven (together with Tebay) was made a sub-depot to Carlisle in January 1876. Later, a North Western & Furness Joint Committee minute dated 17 February 1880 recorded that *the Engine shed* [at Bransty] *is to be removed to Preston Street goods station*. This may not have been carried out immediately, as a further minute of the Joint Committee, dated 18 January 1882 and covering station works at Bransty, noted that *an old engine shed and workshops had to be removed to make way for the new works*. This is clear evidence that the original WJR shed (or part of it) still survived at Bransty as late as 1882. Its transfer to Preston Street (if it took place) may have been intended to enlarge the existing Furness shed there, as an alternative to the new shed which was eventually built.

More recently, a plan has been found, dated January 1880, showing the seven-road carriage shed at the south end of Platform 1. This noted that one road was to be converted into an engine shed, 222 ft. long by 21 ft. wide, and that coaling facilities would be included. The plan was marked 'Agreed by Sir James Ramsden and Mr Cawkwell, March 1880', and endorsed 'Mr Worthington to proceed, 3 May 1880'. This strongly suggests that this new engine shed freed-up the original WJR structure at Bransty for eventual transfer. William Cawkwell was an LNWR director and former General Manager.

By the 1920s, the coal industry at Whitehaven was in decline. At the end of the Great War, William, Wellington, Haig and Ladysmith Pits were still in production, but the financial position of the Whitehaven Colliery Co. continued to deteriorate, and Ladysmith Pit closed in December 1931, followed by Wellington in July 1932: closure of the latter marked the end of John Peile's greatest achievement, after a production life of nearly a century. Several haematite iron ore mines in the district, such as Dalzell's at Moor Row, also closed between 1919 and 1925.

Against this background of high unemployment (more than 50% in Whitehaven) and economic depression, and as the LMS was a major shareholder in Thomas Tilling Ltd, into which the local bus company, Cumberland Motor Services, had already been absorbed, major rail closures were inevitable. On 13 April 1931 came withdrawal of passenger services over the former Cleator & Workington Junction Railway between Moor Row and Siddick Junction, and also over the former LNWR & FR Joint Line between Moor Row and Marron Junction. At a stroke, 25¼ miles of West Cumberland lines had lost their passenger services. Joy notes that *both routes became 'ghost railways', carrying ... [only] small amounts of coal and limestone*.

Probably because of this reduction in traffic, there was a further re-organisation of signalboxes in the Corkickle area. On 29 January 1933, Corkickle No. 1 (which had only opened in 1919) was closed, with No. 2, the former Mirehouse Junction, becoming the new No. 1 and No. 3, Preston Street, becoming the new No. 2. Both of these boxes were rebuilt again (to a modern flat-roof standard LMR design) in the British Railways era, No. 1 in April 1958 and No. 2 the following year. North of Bransty, there was little rationalisation, although Lonsdale Ironworks box, 437 yards north of Bransty No. 2, was closed on 20 October 1935, having been open only on an 'as required' basis for many years. Originally controlling connections from the ironworks site into both Up and Down Main lines, it was replaced by a ground frame, named 'Whitehaven William Pit', which merely controlled a siding into the Down Main.

Withdrawal of passenger services, on 7 January 1935, over the 10½ miles of the former Joint Line from Corkickle to Sellafield via Moor Row and Egremont coincided with the designation of West Cumberland (under the Special Areas Act of 1934) as a 'distressed area', where 13,000 people were now out of work. Worse was to come: in October 1935, the Whitehaven Colliery Co., now trading as Priestman (Whitehaven) Collieries Ltd., closed the last operational pits, probably because of excessive capital expenditure rather than local economic circumstances, throwing nearly 2000 miners out of work. For over a year, the pits were

In early LMS days, ex-LNWR 6 ft. 6 in. 'Jumbo' 2-4-0 (possibly 5069) pulls out of Platform 2 at Bransty with a northbound express of ex-LNWR stock. The driving wheels of the locomotive are on the flat crossing of the Parton waggonway, which had been converted to standard-gauge between 1870 and 1872. A Midland Railway clerestory coach, probably destined for Leeds, can just be seen in Platform 3 (left).

(Norman Collection N1030)

Chapter Twelve

A rare photograph, taken around 1965, showing the tipping of colliery waste onto the beach opposite the site of William Pit, with 0-4-0ST Askham Hall *heading a rake of NCB wagons. The bicycles, prams, and sacks belong to members of the public gathering coal and anxious not to be photographed.*

(Collection William Bragg)

idle while strenuous efforts, backed by the newly-formed Cumberland Development Council, were made to reopen the colliery. In 1937, the colliery was taken over by the Cumberland Coal Co. (Whitehaven) Ltd., in which the main shareholder was the Coltness Iron Co., and production recommenced in March 1937.

With the approaching end of the Second World War, a number of schemes were put forward to reconstruct the economic base of West Cumberland, in order to guarantee a sounder economic future. One such scheme, supported by the Cumberland Economic Council and assisted by O M Roskill Consultants, was drawn up towards the end of 1944, and recommended the establishment of suitable new industries for the area. The main ones were the production of crucible steel and engineering edge tools, manufacture of tissue paper, rayon staple fibre production, and meat and vegetable canning. The report on the scheme also recommended the establishment of a small chemical industry to provide materials for local major industries already established or proposed, citing the rayon industry's requirements for sulphuric acid and carbon disulphide.

Roskill considered that existing industries such as coal mining, coke manufacture, and iron ore mining could be expanded, but recognised that modern methods of production would require less labour, calculating that the post-war output of the whole West Cumberland coalfield could increase by 10-15% with 20% fewer miners and surface staff. The new industries, however, would not only absorb these employees, but would create sufficient new jobs to reduce significantly unemployment levels. Despite much post-war government support, however, these ambitious plans never achieved the long-term intended results.

While services over the secondary routes were being withdrawn in the 1930s, there was better news concerning the future of the troublesome Whitehaven Tunnel. Routine repairs had been carried out between 1922 and 1931, and in 1932 more extensive work was carried out to eliminate some of the more dangerous distortions. It soon became clear that the tunnel needed to be relined throughout, and this was approved in 1935 by the LMS's Chief Civil Engineer. One proposal was to close the tunnel completely while repairs were carried out, which would probably have involved extensive diversionary use of the former C&WJR line, but the final decision was to close the bore for a complete possession only for five hours per night. It was known from the start that this decision would prolong the reconstruction period, which was further extended when the outbreak of the Second World War brought all work to a halt.

Corkickle No.1 signalbox (formerly Mirehouse Junction), of Furness Railway design, seen here in 1955 prior to its 1958 rebuilding. The Furness line Up working is approaching the connection between the Up Main and No.1 Through Siding (to the left of the train). Note the signalman returning to the box, having given the token for the single line to St Bees (converted later to Tokenless Block).

(Michael Andrews Collection ref. C217)

Work on the tunnel did not restart until 1948, when a 5mph speed limit was imposed for all traffic. Around 10-00 pm each evening, after cessation of normal traffic, the engineering train was propelled into the bore from the Bransty end, so that work could begin for the night. On Sundays, the engineers had possession of the tunnel for most of the day. By January 1950, the roof section under the New Road had been completed, and the District Civil Engineer authorised the immediate reinstatement of all weekend services, having assessed that completion of the task could be handled through week-night possessions only. The mammoth reconstruction task was not finally concluded until 1958, a commemorative plaque celebrating this achievement being unveiled at the Corkickle portal on 29 June 1958. The opportunity to open out this portal was taken during the construction work, resulting in an 11-yard-reduction in tunnel length.

The July 1938 timetable, with another war only one year away, was perhaps the best-ever over the Furness section, with no fewer than thirteen workings between Carnforth and Whitehaven. Through portions originated in several cities: three from Euston, two from Manchester, and one each from Leeds and Liverpool. Two workings were of particular interest: the 12-12 pm departure from Carnforth terminated at Corkickle instead of Bransty, while the Whitehaven portion of the 12-00 pm ex-Euston continued to Maryport, terminating at 8-17 pm. The southbound service was curiously unbalanced, with only eight workings between Whitehaven and Carnforth: the 2-05 pm to Manchester conveyed through coaches from Maryport, while the 4-23 pm was a through working from Workington (Main) to Morecambe Promenade.

On the former Whitehaven Junction and Maryport & Carlisle sections, the service was also relatively frequent, and consisted almost totally of through workings between Whitehaven and Carlisle, 13 northbound and 12 southbound. Most trains stopped at all stations and were generally slow, although the limited-stop 6-45 pm departure from Bransty ran the 40¼ miles to the Border City in 1 hour 23 minutes.

Shortly after the outbreak of the Second World War, a workmen's service was reintroduced over the former Joint Line between Rowrah, Moor Row, Egremont, Sellafield and Drigg, calling at all intermediate stations. It was extremely short-lived, commencing on 11 March 1940 and being withdrawn again on 8 April the same year. As work on the Royal Ordnance Factory at Drigg had started in January 1939 and was completed in February 1941, it is likely that this service operated to bring in labour to speed up construction at a critical phase, especially as the plant was designed to produce the high explosive TNT used in naval shells and other armaments.

At the end of the Second World War, a greater future was planned for Sellafield. Norman Nicholson wrote that *the factory is soon to become an atomic power plant, drawing its labour force from the half-derelict area around Egremont and Frizington*. No doubt this lay behind the LMS's decision to re-introduce a passenger service between Bransty, Moor Row, Egremont and Sellafield on 6 May 1946, but the service quickly fell victim to the post-war fuel crisis, as a result of which the service was 'temporarily suspended' on 16 June 1947. (As late as August 1949, Bradshaw still showed this service as 'temporarily suspended'.) This marked the end of publicly-timetabled services over the Joint Line, but it was not the end for other types of passenger working. The 1956 completion of the world's first full-scale nuclear power station at Calder Hall, controlled by the UK Atomic Energy Authority and built adjacent to the site of the former Sellafield Royal Ordnance Factory opened in May 1943, once again demanded a large labour force. This resulted in the reinstatement of a workmen's service, in 1953, between Moor Row and Sellafield, calling at Woodend, Egremont and Beckermet. As Sellafield was already served by Whitehaven services via St Bees, there was no requirement for the Joint Line service to start from, or terminate at, Bransty. British Railways withdrew this service as late as 6 September 1965, at the same time stating that, with the appearance of the first diesel multiple-units on Whitehaven-Barrow services, reintroduction of a full Whitehaven-Moor Row-Sellafield DMU-worked public service was under consideration.

This is likely to have been linked to a proposal, made several years earlier, on 27 February 1956, when Whitehaven Town Council requested the British Transport Commission to provide 'a new railway halt' at Mirehouse, to serve the adjacent Mirehouse council housing estate. The precise site is a matter of conjecture, but the most logical site would have been on the double-track Joint Line, with access from the Daisy Road viaduct which crossed both lines. Unfortunately, the local Member of Parliament suggested that the scheme should be deferred, writing on 24 September 1956 that the matter should be raised again when British Railways introduced DMUs on Barrow services. Despite local discussions concerning this stopping-place in 1964/1965, in connection with the new DMU-worked Barrow service, plans for Mirehouse Halt were never taken any further.

Between the end of the Second World War and the final service withdrawal, the southern Joint Line towns also enjoyed a good service of advertised excursions, particularly during the summer months, when trains ran to Morecambe, Blackpool, and other holiday destinations.

Even this was not quite the end for passenger services over the Joint Line, a daily return working for the pupils of Wyndham School operating between Seascale and Egremont from September 1964 (although this appears to have been watered down from an original proposal to route a Barrow-Whitehaven working via Egremont for this purpose).

A rare photograph of Whitehaven William Pit Ground Frame, opened on 20 October 1935 as a replacement for the signalbox at Lonsdale Ironworks, the surviving remains of which can be seen on the left. The single line along the route of the Parton Waggonway can just be glimpsed through the gate. The sandstone building in the centre was either the ironworks offices or the Manager's house.

(CRA Photo Library ref. PA0912)

Chapter Twelve

A rare shot, taken on 5 June 1968, of the empty stock of the Seascale-Egremont school train, seen here passing Parton southbound from Workington. The diesel units are the so-called 'Derby Lightweights'. The LNWR-design Parton Signalbox, built in 1879, can be seen to the left of the trailing unit.

(CRA Photo Library ref. PE-AA363)

This seems to have been a most interesting working, leaving Seascale for Egremont at 08-10, and returning from Egremont at 16-08 as a combined school and workmen's train to Barrow. Initially, the northbound service was worked by an Ivatt Class 2MT 2-6-0, but these locomotives had difficulty handling 8-coach trains and were soon replaced by Class 4MT 2-6-0s. The southbound working was normally a Class 5MT 4-6-0 working. By April 1966, 'Derby Lightweight' diesel multiple-units had taken over on this duty. This service was withdrawn on 11 December 1969

A month later, the Beckermet Mines junction to Sellafield section was taken out of use, and a valuable inland diversionary route south of Whitehaven was lost.

After the Second World War, the mining industry in Whitehaven suffered a further blow on 15 August 1947, when 104 miners died in an explosion at William Pit. The mine remained out of production until 1948. Production resumed at 55,000-75,000 tons per annum, but finally ceased on 31 December 1954, when the workings ran into a solid rock fault. This meant that further rail freight traffic was lost.

Despite Nationalisation on 1 January 1948, when the LMS became part of the new British Railways (and Whitehaven came under the control of BR's London Midland Region), the initial timetables showed many services to be unchanged from pre-war. In the September 1957-June 1958 timetable, there were nine through workings between Carnforth and Whitehaven, with the first departure being the northbound 'Mail', leaving Carnforth at 4-28 am, conveying through carriages from Euston. The next departure, at 5-40 am, conveyed a Sleeping Car, which had left London at 11-25 pm the previous evening, and which reached Corkickle at 8-48 am. There the car was detached, although the other vehicles continued as far as Workington (Main). The 7-55 am Euston departure provided a daytime through working to West Cumberland out of the capital, Bransty being reached at 4-35 pm and Workington at 4-54 pm; north of Barrow, this train stopped only at Millom, Seascale, Sellafield and St Bees.

The West Cumberland sleeping car was a post-war innovation, first introduced between Euston and Barrow on 7 October 1947, and extended to Whitehaven (Corkickle) on 5 June 1950, the year before the existing fleet was augmented by a new build of what were later known as Mk 1 sleeper vehicles. It has never been fully explained why the Whitehaven car terminated at Corkickle (where it was removed and returned to Barrow for servicing), while the rest of the train continued to Bransty and Workington. The 1957/8 timetable showed that, in the Up direction, the Whitehaven sleeping car departed from Barrow at 7-41 pm, coupled to the Barrow sleepers. Whitehaven passengers could leave Bransty in day carriages at 6-46 pm and join the sleeper at Lancaster. This was a sensible arrangement, avoiding unnecessary mileage for the Whitehaven car, as well as allowing West Cumberland passengers access to their berths at a more acceptable hour. This pattern of working continued unchanged until withdrawal of the Whitehaven car, as announced in the 'North Western Evening Mail' on 12 February 1966: *When full-scale electric services start between London and the North West in mid-April, the sleeping cars that now run between Euston and Whitehaven will terminate at Barrow ... It is no secret that, at present, the cars are worked to West Cumberland by what the local railwaymen have long known as the 'second Mail' - the passenger train which leaves Preston shortly after 4 am following the postal express to Furness and West Cumberland ... It must be doubtful if Whitehaven business men use the service when returning from London, because the variety of sleeping car expresses offered between London (Euston) and Carlisle is probably a more attractive proposition.*

The 1957/8 timetable also showed that no services from Barrow and the South now ran through to Carlisle: this resulted from the introduction, on 7 February 1955, of new 'Derby Lightweight' diesel-multiple units on the coast line north of Whitehaven. This allowed a relatively intensive service to be introduced on this section, with 14 northbound and 16 southbound workings, allowing a 1 hour 11 minute schedule between Whitehaven and Carlisle. The frequency of this service meant that Whitehaven passengers for the South of England now tended to travel via Carlisle rather than Barrow.

In the Summer 1962 timetable, the number of workings between Carnforth and Whitehaven had increased to ten, but the number of originating points was beginning to decline. As well as the overnight services, trains left Euston for Whitehaven at 6-35 am (arr. Bransty 4-31 pm) and 11-35 am (arr. 8-12 pm), but only one service daily originated from Manchester Victoria, leaving at 9-50 am and taking 5 hours 19 minutes to reach the Cumbrian port; the last arrival of the day, at 11-01 pm, was a through working from Liverpool Exchange. Through carriages no longer ran from Leeds. The intensive service between Whitehaven and Carlisle, which had resulted in a dramatic increase in revenue, remained unchanged from the 1957/8 timetable.

Post-war freight traffic originating at, and routed through, Whitehaven remained healthy. Lengthy trains of 'Covhop' wagons conveyed soda ash from the ICI Works at Burn Naze

On 13 September 1963, Class 5MT 4-6-0 No. 45445 heads north along the Up & Down Permissive Goods line, past Corkickle No. 2 box, with a special working of 'Prestflo' wagons from Corkickle Sidings to Dundee.

(CRA Photo Library ref. PE-A922)

(Fleetwood) to Corkickle Sidings, for use in the Marchon plant. By 1965, this soda ash train was originating from ICI Northwich. Pilkington's Ravenhead works at St.Helens despatched a daily train of glass containers for Corkickle, again for use in Marchon, while the steelworks at Workington generated extensive outbound traffic, mostly using bogie bolster wagons. Despite the continuation of mining at Whitehaven, some inbound coal traffic (presumably for domestic purposes) remained, a 22-56 Wath (Sheffield) to Workington service operating until withdrawal in 1976. In the early 1970s, Marchon introduced a new flow of phosphoric acid between Whitehaven and Associated Chemicals at Barton-on-Humber, leaving Whitehaven at 08-23 (Tuesdays only), returning the following day as a 19-14 working to Corkickle. Withdrawn in 1980, the service was re-introduced on an 'as required' basis in 1983, but by January 1984, the working had become timetabled, leaving Corkickle on Thursdays at 17-28 and returning from Barton-on-Humber at 18-30 on Tuesdays. The service, using Immingham-allocated Class 47s, was finally discontinued on 19 March 1987.

An interesting, and little-documented, working was milk tanker traffic from Egremont's Milk Marketing Board factory, destined for Southern England. It is not clear when this traffic began, but it is likely to have commenced following the opening of the factory (which had its own shunting locomotive) in 1946. During the week, the loaded train ran from Egremont via Moor Row, where it reversed to gain C&WJR metals for the onward journey to Siddick Junction and Carlisle, avoiding any delays through Whitehaven Tunnel. On Sundays, however, the working was routed via Moor Row, Corkickle and Bransty, leaving Egremont at 4-35 pm. Motive power was provided by Workington Shed, the light engine running direct to Egremont. All empty milk tankers returned to Egremont through Whitehaven, reaching Egremont at 7-32 am as a trip working from Corkickle.

The coastal main line gained additional traffic in November 1953, when limestone from Rowrah Hall Quarry, destined for the Workington blast furnaces, was re-routed via Moor Row and Whitehaven. This resulted in the total abandonment of the former LNWR and FR Joint Line between Rowrah and Marron Junction on 3 May 1954, although this 8½ mile section was not officially closed until 6 November 1960 and the track was not lifted until 1964. Nationalisation of the iron and steel industry in 1967 saw ownership of Rowrah Hall Quarry pass to the British Steel Corporation. Closure came in 1978, the last train running on 23 March. However, track lifting did not begin for some time, the first sections being removed at Rowrah on 17 September 1980, with a second lifting operation, at Parkside, below Frizington, commencing in January 1981. Moor Row became the temporary 'railhead' for recovered track. Further traffic was lost when West Cumberland's sole surviving haematite mine, at Beckermet, closed on 3 October 1980, BR closing the line between Beckermet Mines Junction and Corkickle No. 1 completely on 1 November. Interestingly, although the track was soon lifted back to the junction at Moor Row, the $2^{3}/_{4}$ mile section between Moor Row and Corkickle remained intact, though out of use, for several more years. The reason for this was that the THORP (Thermal Oxide Reprocessing Plant) project at Sellafield anticipated using material from the quarries at Rowrah or Eskett, which could have led to the revival of this last section of the Joint Line. In the event, however, the potential traffic levels, as well as the cost of reinstating $5^{1}/_{4}$ miles of track, did not justify reopening, and the Moor Row-Corkickle section was finally lifted in 1993.

The 1960s saw the first severance of the former Cleator & Workington Junction line, the seven miles between Moor Row No. 2 and Distington, on 16 September 1963, removing the only diversionary route between Whitehaven and Workington if the Parton-Harrington coastal section was closed by landslips. Distington Joint signalbox was converted to ground-frame operation on the same date, in order to allow continued rail access to the High Duty Alloys Ltd. factory, on the former ironworks site. Occasional scrap wagons were also loaded from the former Joint Line Down platform, which was now used as a scrapyard by Hanratty's of Workington. The ground-frame itself was closed on 1 June 1964 and the Calva Junction-Distington section was abandoned completely on 26 September 1965, marking the end of the residual services which had operated over the surviving portion of the Distington-Ullock line.

Earlier in 1963 came more bad news, in the form of Dr Richard Beeching's report 'The Re-Shaping of British Railways', which proposed the withdrawal of all passenger services between Barrow and Whitehaven, as well as the workmen's trains between Sellafield and Moor Row.

This proposal was the direct opposite of the recommendations of the now-almost-forgotten Lake District Transport Enquiry, chaired by Sir Patrick Hamilton, the results of which were published in mid-1961. The recommendations on the Barrow-Whitehaven section were that the line should be retained, with two-thirds of the workings converted to diesel multiple-unit operation, and that (more controversially) the section should be singled with bi-directional passing loops, using Centralised Traffic Control (CTC) from one central signalbox. Installation costs were estimated at £600,000-£700,000, with a payback period of between 15 and 25 years.

Chapter Twelve

In September 1981, an unidentified Class 47 is about to enter Whitehaven Tunnel, with an mgr working from the Lakeland (Maryport) opencast coal site to Fiddler's Ferry power station on Merseyside. A Carlisle-bound Class 108 DMU is signalled to leave Platform 2 on a Carlisle working. The new station building is under construction, although the Platform 3/4 canopy (now without glazing) still survives.

(Peter Robinson ref. 251b27)

The enquiry commented that *this railway has an assured future,* [but] *operation as it now stands will grow ... more difficult and expensive.* The enquiry was generally satisfied with the service north of Whitehaven, noting that: *Workington and Whitehaven are the most isolated industrial towns in England, but their position has been helped greatly by the ... diesel trains, introduced in 1955.*

Closure between Barrow and Whitehaven was never implemented. By mid-1965, 'Modern Railways' was recording that the Barrow-Whitehaven section had been recommended for retention and for conversion to diesel multiple-unit operation, the first scheduled units appearing on 1 March 1965, although one daily Workington-Preston return service had been temporarily diagrammed for a DMU during the 17-day ASLEF strike in May 1955. The price of this service retention, however, was a drastic reduction in services south of Whitehaven, when a new timetable was introduced on 18 April 1966. The through Euston and Manchester services were withdrawn, and the Barrow service reduced to five DMUs each way daily. By contrast, the Whitehaven-Carlisle service remained at 16 trains daily each way, although there was no attempt to improve the 1 hour 11 minute timing. The May 1968 timetable showed little change although a number of the Barrow workings started from, or terminated at, Carlisle.

By May 1974, there had been some improvement, with six Whitehaven-Barrow services in each direction, a number of which ran as a through service between Lancaster and Carlisle, although DMUs provided inadequate passenger comfort on a journey of 120^1/$_4$ miles lasting nearly four hours. The 18-56 ex-Whitehaven continued to provide a connection at Barrow into the Euston sleeping cars (this connection also ran on Sundays), although by this time few London-bound passengers used this service. The Sunday service south of Whitehaven, a DMU running south from Workington at 18-37 to make the sleeper connection at Barrow, from where it returned north at 20-50, was finally withdrawn on 2 May 1976, and never reinstated.

The May 1980 timetable showed seven daily workings between Whitehaven and Barrow, six of which now ran to and from Carlisle. This service pattern continued throughout the decade. The May 1990 timetable, however, while maintaining seven northbound and six southbound services over the Cumbrian Coast line, contained some interesting changes, the 17-50 ex-Barrow running through to Newcastle, while the 12-13 Whitehaven-Barrow started from Newcastle at 09-10.

Dramatic reductions came the following year, in July 1991, when the Whitehaven-Barrow service was slashed to four trains each way – a worse level of service than a quarter of a century earlier. North of Whitehaven, however, the Carlisle service was maintained at 15 northbound and 17 southbound workings. Some of these workings now reached Carlisle in just over the hour, stopping only at Workington, Maryport and Wigton. Little had changed in 1992, although the timetable showed that the 13-00 ex-Sunderland was a through working to Preston via Carlisle, the Cumbrian Coast line, and Carnforth: arrival was at 19-02! In the reverse direction, Sunderland was served by the 06-15 from Barrow. By May 1993, however, the Barrow-Whitehaven service had been restored to six trains each way, although the Whitehaven-Carlisle service had reverted to all-stations.

In 1993, Railtrack was constituted as the owner of track, stations, and other infrastructure, (albeit still a Government department), leaving British Rail, as operator, to introduce an outline franchising programme. As a result, it was not surprising that the May 1994 timetable showed the Cumbrian Coast line under the 'Regional Railways North West' heading, although services remained unchanged, and continued unchanged in the summer of 1996 when operated by North West Regional Railways Ltd. (a 'semi-privatised' operation, as this was still a British Rail subsidiary). By June 1997, North West Trains (as a member of First Group Rail Division) was operating Cumbrian Coast services under franchise. The last timetable of the twentieth century showed little change from the 1966 timetable, with six Whitehaven- Barrow return services, 14 workings between Whitehaven and Carlisle, and 15 between Carlisle and the coastal town. In fairness, however, despite the sinuous nature of the southern part of the coastal route, the Whitehaven-Barrow journey time had been reduced by around twenty minutes during this period, compared with only five minutes on the service north to Carlisle. By 2004 the franchise had passed to Northern Rail (a subsidiary of Serco-Nedrail), who had once more increased the number of Whitehaven-Barrow workings to seven in each direction, while maintaining the 1999 service level on Carlisle workings. In 2007 (and with the operating company now known simply as 'Northern'), the 2004 level of services remain virtually unchanged, both north and south of Whitehaven.

One service which did not survive into the 21st century was the Cumbrian Coast Travelling Post Office, which ran in both directions between Whitehaven and Huddersfield. The Whitehaven-Huddersfield TPO, stabled during the day at Workington station, ran as empty stock as far as Whitehaven before assuming its operational duties, the Post Office sorters joining the Up working at Bransty. Normally, the train did not carry passengers, although, in the early 1970s, the Up working conveyed two coaches on Sundays only, mainly for the benefit of Ravenglass & Eskdale Railway volunteers who needed to return to Millom and Barrow. This working may have been unadvertised in its first few years of operation, but had become an advertised service by the date of the withdrawal of the Sunday evening TPO in May 1975. There were also periods post-war where two passenger coaches were added to the Down TPO at Preston, sometimes being detached at Barrow and on other occasions continuing through to Workington. Although the Down train terminated at Bransty as a TPO, the final Working Timetable, in 1991, showed that it continued as a parcels working through to Workington.

On 5 September 1985, the TPO was steam-hauled, by an ex-LMS Stanier Class 5MT No. 44767, working throughout from Workington to Huddersfield. This event marked the 150th anniversary of the introduction of TPOs on Britain's rail network, and, in addition to its usual consist, the train included three preserved passenger carriages from Steamtown Carnforth. (Although the Cumbrian Coast line is an approved route for preserved steam locomotive workings, it has seen little use for this purpose in recent years. However, Bulleid Pacific No. 34027 *Taw Valley* was noted working southbound through Whitehaven on 14 October 2000, with a return charter from Workington to Crewe, while more recently, on 24 February and 10 March 2007, Class 8P 4-6-2 No. 71000 *Duke of Gloucester* worked over the full length of the Cumbrian Coast line with a Pullman excursion from Manchester).

Up to the late 1960s, the TPO still carried an ex-LMS 57 ft. Post Office Sorting Van, but by the time that the service was withdrawn, on 28 September 1991, this vehicle had been replaced by a standard BR Mk.1 vehicle. The final Working Timetable showed the Up TPO leaving Workington at 17-53 (presumably as empty stock) and Bransty at 18-50. Interestingly, in the closing weeks of TPO operations, no mail was actually loaded at Whitehaven, Seascale, or Millom, although normal operations continued south of Barrow. The train's schedule allowed the same vehicles to be used for the Down working from Huddersfield, leaving Carnforth at 04-29 and arriving at Bransty at 06-46.

The handling of the Up working at Bransty was unusual, in that, in its later years, it was signalled from Workington direct into the bay Platform 1, to allow loading to take place without interrupting through traffic. Following the forty minutes' loading schedule, departure involved a reversal onto the Down line, after which the train moved off southwards through Platform 2.

By the early 1980s, freight workings from, to, and through Whitehaven mainly operated only to support coal traffic and the Albright & Wilson (Marchon) plant, although these were still quite numerous. The WTT for May 1982 showed that, northbound, the following services operated on most days of the week: Fiddler's Ferry-Corkickle (3 workings), Walton Old Junction (Warrington)-Workington (2), Fiddler's Ferry-Workington (1), and Northwich-Corkickle (1). A similar pattern operated southbound, augmented by the daily 'Speedlink' service to Dover Town, which left Workington at 17-14. Within the limits of the Cumbrian Coast route, a coal train left Workington three times a week, at 09-39, for Roosecote Power Station at Barrow, the empties being tripped to Barrow Yard from where they returned north at 16-00. Use of internal locomotives at this power station ceased in 1984, almost certainly as the result of the lengthy miners' strike. As these locomotives were used to move the coal wagons through the discharge point, Cumbrian coal workings into Roosecote probably ceased from the same date.

With the rundown of many heavy industry sites in Cumbria in the 1980s, new workings were introduced to carry large amounts of scrap metal to furnaces in the Sheffield area. Starting on 24 August 1984, a Tuesdays-only return working was booked to run between Workington and Tinsley (Sheffield), conveying 15 loaded vehicles from Workington and adding a further 20 at Barrow. This service operated until 15 January 1985, and was then reinstated to run between 10 July and 25 September, although it was observed still to be running on 15 October. Such was the amount of scrap metal being handled during this period that an additional Fridays-only return service operated between Barrow and Tinsley, the locomotive having to run light-engine from Workington to take up this diagram.

The October 1989 WTT reflected the final closure of the Whitehaven colliery and the much reduced traffic levels from Albright & Wilson. Northbound, only two freights passed through Bransty: the 'Speedlink' service from Willesden (London) to Workington, which called at Corkickle at 09-28 (and at Bransty to change crews), and a nuclear flask train from Sellafield to Fairlie (for the Hunterston plant on the Clyde), which passed Bransty at 20-07. Southbound services were virtually the same, the Willesden service collecting Corkickle traffic at 18-26, although an mgr coal train passed Bransty at 19-05 with a loaded train from Maryport (the rapid-loading facility on the opencast site there having opened in mid-1980) to Crewe Basford Hall, for onward tripping to Rugeley power station.

With the more powerful Class 60 diesels replacing the older Class 47s on the Rugeley workings, on 23 July 1991, the weight of the mgr trains increased by 20%, and on 18 November 1991, an additional coal working was introduced from Maryport to Padiham power station, between Accrington and Burnley. Leaving Maryport Colliery daily at 01-15, the 1,400-tonne train arrived at Padiham at 08-18, but only the return empties were routed via the Furness line and Whitehaven, the loaded train travelling via Upperby Yard Curve (Carlisle) and the West Coast Main Line. The Maryport coal traffic was relatively short-lived, however, with both the Rugeley and Padiham flows ceasing on 31 March 1993.

With the demise of the 'Speedlink' network, a Carlisle Yard-Warrington Arpley departmental service was routed via the Cumbrian Coast line, between 1994 and 1996, in order to cater for residual freight traffic, calling only at Workington for both loaded and empty steel traffic, and at Sellafield for empty nuclear flasks and associated barrier wagons. When this service was withdrawn, only Scottish and Teesside flask traffic was scheduled to pass through Bransty. The era of freight on the Cumbrian Coast south of Workington was almost over.

However, this nuclear traffic was not without interest, as the train operating company, Direct Rail Services (DRS), was one of the initial 'open access operators' under the government's Rail Privatisation plans. DRS's parent company, British Nuclear Fuels Ltd. (BNFL), saw financial benefit in this approach, as 'open access' for DRS meant a reduced level of track access charges. DRS would administer and run its own train service, leaving just the railway infrastructure in the hands of a third party, Railtrack (now Network Rail).

Initial services fell into three categories. Firstly, DRS transported imported nuclear flasks between the Ramsden Dock terminal at Barrow and Sellafield. The second flow was the short-distance movement of low-level radioactive waste from Sellafield to Drigg. Lastly, DRS transported caustic soda and nitric acid from Cheshire, for use at the Sellafield complex. All these movements operated over the portion of the Cumbrian Coast route south of Sellafield, and therefore did not pass through Whitehaven. As the DRS nuclear flask business grew, however, services were added to serve the nuclear power stations at Hunterston and Torness in Scotland, and at Seaton-on-Tees. These workings continue to run to and from Sellafield via Carlisle, Workington and Whitehaven.

Much of the original railway infrastructure around Whitehaven remained unchanged until well into British Railways days. By then, the two-storey buildings at Bransty, dating from the early 1870s and mid-1880s, had become too large for their current use and were demolished in the autumn

Chapter Twelve

An early 1960s view of Bransty, looking north from the tunnel portal, and showing a southbound freight awaiting departure behind an ex-LMS Class 4F 0-6-0. By this date, Platform 4 was no longer a through road, buffer stops having been erected at the north end. The chimney to the left of Bransty No. 1 box marked the site of the closed William Pit.

(Michael Andrews Collection ref. A183)

of 1981, being replaced early in 1982 with a much simpler modern structure, though the ticket office was still manned. The cost of the new station was £180,000, of which £10,000 was provided by Cumbria County Council.

The Furness Railway's signalbox at Bransty (by now renamed Bransty No. 1), built on a cramped site around 30 yards north of the tunnel entrance, was closed on 25 April 1965, resulting in the removal of the south-facing connections to Platform 4 (which was then taken out of use and lifted) and to the disused William Pit sidings, although the track at the latter site mostly remained in place until recovery between 1968 and 1970. The semaphore signals at the tunnel mouth were also removed, and replaced by two three-aspect colour lights as Up Starters, situated at the ends of Platforms 2 and 3. The whole layout at the station was now controlled by the LNWR-design Bransty No. 2 box, built in 1899. The track in Platform 4, together with some immediate sidings, had to be lifted to allow new straight point rodding to be installed between No. 2 box and the point at the tunnel mouth. It is likely that the flat crossing of the former Parton Waggonway was removed during this period, after a life of more than 120 years.

A long-standing signalling anomaly was corrected in 1973, in connection with Stage 9 of the commissioning of the new Carlisle power signalling centre. Up to that date, trains travelling between Carnforth and Carlisle used the Down line between the former station and Bransty; between the junction at Bransty of the former W&FJR and WJR routes and Carlisle, however, the Down line was named the Up line! This was a relic of the days when the focus of the W&FJR was towards Furness and the South, and that of the WJR towards Carlisle. A BR signalling notice stated that, from 4 June 1973, the direction of the line from Whitehaven to Carlisle would now be known as 'Down', allowing standardisation of direction descriptions over the whole Cumbrian coastal route.

Transposition of direction descriptions was a possible contributory factor in an accident at Bransty, on 27 November 1973, when the loose-coupled 07-09 Workington-Corkickle freight train was brought to a stand at the Up Home signal to await acceptance by Bransty box. After a ten-minute delay, the signal cleared and the train began to move towards the station, but almost immediately, it was run into at the rear by the two-car 07-00 Carlisle-Whitehaven diesel multiple-unit, which had been irregularly allowed into the section by the Parton Station signalman. The DMU's leading car suffered considerable damage, but fortunately the 14 passengers were unharmed, while the DMU driver and the freight train guard sustained minor injuries.

The report into the accident concluded that the Parton Station signalman wrongly allowed the Carlisle-Whitehaven DMU to enter the section of line between Parton and Bransty without first obtaining the permission of the Bransty signalman. The Inspector from the Railway Inspectorate noted that the Parton Station signalman accepted full responsibility for the accident.

At Corkickle, the three-armed gantry, acting as Down Starter for Corkickle No. 2 and Outer Home for Bransty No. 1, was replaced in 1954 by a motor-driven single upper quadrant signal, below which was a three-position matrix route indicator for the three Bransty through platforms. Bransty No. 1's Inner Home was a colour-light signal, at rail level, the position of which was indicated by a gong – useful both for drivers, in the often smoke-filled bore, and as indication, to passengers, of an approaching train.

Several years elapsed before further rationalisation took place. The last rail movement over the Harbour network having taken place in September 1985, BR scheduled major engineering works between 7 March and 13 March 1988, which involved severing connections into the Harbour and the removal of the turntable opposite the junction of the former LNWR and FR lines.

The next changes to the signalling and track at Whitehaven came over a relatively extended period between 1992 and 1993. In February 1992, 'Modern Railways' reported that 'Poorhouse Siding' had been shortened by 235 yards and buffer stops erected – this probably referred to the severance of the line between the North Siding and the foot of the Corkickle Brake. 29 March 1992 saw all connections removed between the North Siding (which paralleled the Up and Down Goods between Corkickle No. 1 and No. 2) and the Corkickle Brake, which had lain disused since the end of 1986. The Up and Down Goods line itself was slewed westwards, over a distance of 120 yards, onto the alignment of the South Siding. This removed its connection with the Furness line to St Bees, as well as creating a new headshunt for the surviving Preston Street sidings. The end result was a rationalised signalling system, the main casualty being the five-armed gantry between the Corkickle boxes. The following month, on 20 April, Platform 1 at Bransty was shortened by 20 yards.

In September 1991, the single-to-double track connection at the Bransty exit from the tunnel had been secured to serve Platform 3 only, Platform 2 being taken temporarily out of use. In October 1992, the secured connection was removed and replaced by plain track. The Civil Engineer moved south of the tunnel in December 1992, taking out the Double to Single connection to the disused Moor Row line, now officially closed, pending lifting.

92

On 21 July 1979, a Class 108/2 DMU, with vehicle M50952 leading, pulls out of Platform 3 at Bransty with the 09-45 Carlisle-Lancaster. This view shows clearly the Up Starter colour-light signals, controlled from Bransty No. 2 box (right background), which had replaced semaphores in 1965. Note that both Platforms 2 and 3 are signalled for bi-directional working. By this date, most of the glazed canopies over Platforms 1 and 2 had been removed.

(Tom Heavyside ref. Q3/23)

1993 saw significant (and inefficient) rationalisation of the Bransty layout. On 21 March, Platform 3 was taken out of use, and the single Down and Up Main slewed permanently into Platform 2, now restored to use. The connection between track in the bay Platform 1 and the adjacent siding was secured only to allow access from Platform 1 to the Down Main, effectively making the siding redundant. On 14 June, the final change to the layout was made, when the connection between the Up Main line and Platform 1 was removed, and the Down Main line between the station and the trailing crossover was renamed the 'Bay' line. This resulted in operating problems within the station limits for Whitehaven-Carlisle trains, as any working from the Border City now had to terminate in Platform 2, and if a Furness line train was due, the Carlisle unit had to reverse along the Up Main as far as the crossover opposite Bransty signalbox before pulling forward into Platform 1.

The final major changes came half a decade later, over the weekend of 15/16 February 1997. On the south side of Whitehaven tunnel, Corkickle No. 1 and No. 2 signalboxes were closed, and all signals worked from these boxes were dismantled. The former Preston Street branch was taken out of use, pending tracklifting. All points and connections were removed, the remaining three sidings paralleling the former Up and Down Main were isolated, and only the Down Main line remained in use, resulting in a new single-line section between St Bees and Bransty stations, a distance of 4½ miles. At the southern portal of the tunnel, a new motor-driven Down Home semaphore signal was erected, protected by a fixed Down Distant (this being one of the new-style 'boards' displaying a representation of a Distant signal). At Bransty, the inefficient 1993 layout was modified, with the Down Main line severed 50 yards on the Barrow side of the box and 150 yards on the Carlisle side. At these points respectively, the Platform 1 and Down Main lines were slewed to connect into the Up Main line, thereby restoring direct access to Platform 1 for trains arriving from Carlisle. This layout still exists at the time of writing, and is satisfactory for current traffic levels. The Acceptance/Direction system of tokenless working between Bransty No. 2 and Corkickle No. 2, and between Corkickle No. 1 and St Bees, was replaced by token instrument working, the token being taken from a cabinet on Platform 2 at Bransty following electronic release from the adjacent signalbox.

In association with these changes, it was planned to demolish Bransty No. 2 and to replace it by a simple 'Portakabin'-type structure on Bransty Station platform, controlling colour-light signals. Given the generally sound condition of the existing box and the capital cost involved, the plan was dropped. However, by 2008, the existing 1364-yard-long single-line section between Parton South and Parton North Junctions is likely to have been re-doubled, and Parton signalbox decommissioned, creating a new 6 mile 814 yard-long section between Bransty No. 2 and Workington Main No. 2. Again, this is dependent on approval for capital investment.

Most recently, at the end of March 2003, the semaphore signal gantry controlling the northbound exit from Platforms 1 and 2 was replaced by two new semaphore signals on individual posts. At the same time, refurbishment work was carried out on the fabric of Bransty No. 2 box, including the provision of double-glazing and a new external stairway, replacing the potentially hazardous internal one which was located alongside the interlocking mechanism (although not much of this remains in use, the frame now only retaining sixteen working levers).

Could this section of the Saltom Waggonway be revived as a tourist line? With the twin winding houses of Haig Pit in the background, Giesl-ejector-fitted Andrew Barclay 0-4-0ST King (Works No. 1448/1919) waits its next turn of duty on 30 August 1974. The appalling state of the track was typical of NCB sites at this period. (Tom Heavyside ref. 144/25)

The upper end of the projected scheme. On 24 April 1968, an Andrew Barclay 0-6-0ST propels loaded coal wagons from Haig Pit the last few yards into Ladysmith Washery. The winding engine house can be seen to the left of the locomotive.

(Stan Buck ref. NCB-11)

Whitehaven:
Into the Twenty-First Century

13

THE DAYS OF WHITEHAVEN as a town of heavy industries, serviced by a busy harbour and extensive rail network, have gone forever, and will not return. In the last two decades, however, the town and harbour have enjoyed something of a renaissance, largely due to the establishment, in Autumn 1993, of the Whitehaven Development Company. The purpose of this company was to direct the joint resources of Copeland Borough Council, West Cumbria Development Agency, and English Estates towards a harbour-focused scheme, coupled with pedestrianisation of parts of the town centre. Harbour-side work included new houses, offices, retail space, and tourist facilities such as restaurants.

In general, this appears to have been successful, and is about to be boosted (in April 2006), with a new regeneration plan, entitled 'A Sea Change for Whitehaven', commissioned by West Lakes Renaissance and Copeland Borough Council, and under the guidance of Wayne Hemingway, who has previously tackled regeneration projects in Manchester and Tyneside.

It is likely that tourism will be an essential part of this plan, in particular 'heritage' tourism connected to the port and the mining industry. The Haig Mining Museum could well benefit from these proposals, particularly as some of its ideas align closely with the tourism aspects of the Hemingway plan.

As well as renovating the second winding house at the head of Haig Pit, the museum has plans to re-lay 1$^{1}/_{2}$ miles of track linking the site of the former Ladysmith Washery and the head of the former Howgill Incline, near Harbour View. This would effectively re-create both the 1735 Saltom waggonway and the Croft Incline of 1774. From the Howgill Incline head, the route of the 1923 Howgill Brake would be used as pedestrian access to the West Strand, the short tunnel under the Wellington Pit approach road being newly opened-up specifically for this purpose.

The museum has now acquired sufficient track for this scheme, donated by railfreight operator EWS and by Corus. Direct Rail Services, the railway subsidiary of BNFL, has also presented the museum with an 0-4-0 Drewry/Barclay diesel shunting locomotive, DRS themselves having purchased this locomotive second-hand in 2001.

On the main Cumbrian Coast route through Whitehaven, little has changed in the Railtrack/Network Rail era, with the 1997 track rationalisation reducing layouts almost to 'basic' status. In August 2000, Railtrack announced improvements to Bransty, costing £45,700, part of which was to be used to demolish the unused and now-isolated Platform 3/4, and to close the redundant subway which had been heavily vandalised. Work was expected to have been completed by March 2001. Four years later, however, the platform was still intact, though devoid of any structures apart from lamp-posts bearing figure '3' plates! The subway, however, had been filled in, and made flush with the platform surfaces.

Little had changed on Platforms 1 and 2 at Bransty, where the ticket office remains manned between 07-10 hrs and 18-30 hrs Monday to Friday, 07-10 hrs to 16-25 hrs on Saturday. One local commentator wrote that it was difficult to see where all the money had been spent, adding that, with all the Network Rail equipment using the redundant land, the site *looked more like a builder's yard*. Nothing particularly complimentary can be added about tidying-up at Corkickle, although improvements to the approach road and forecourt were made in 2005. Nevertheless, Whitehaven, with its population of 26,000, must be one of the few small English towns to retain two stations into the twenty-first century. In May 2007, Network Rail announced plans to completely rebuild Bransty station, and to release adjoining land for a new bus station, construction of which would be financed by Tesco plc. This would provide Whitehaven with a modern transport interchange.

Passenger traffic volumes at Bransty continue to be healthy. Data published in 2002-3 by the Strategic Rail Authority showed that 73,808 passengers started their journey at Bransty each year, with 74,988 terminating their journey there. These figures were significantly higher than those for Workington, at 47,383 and 49,080 respectively. Corkickle passenger volumes, however, remained low, with only 4,509 departures and 4,839 arrivals each year.

Hopefully, the route through Whitehaven will continue to be marketed as one of Britain's most attractive routes, and will be used by an increasing volume of excursion traffic. On 10 December 2005, the new West Coast Railways Pullman Car train was used in a railtour, originating in Scarborough, over the whole Cumbrian Coast line between Carnforth and Carlisle, the first such working since 1993. The organizers, Green Express Railtours, hoped that this would be the first of more regular railtours over the Cumbrian Coast line, which it described as *England's most scenic rail route*.

Since then, other operators have followed suit. On 25 April 2007, a Class 47-hauled Pullman excursion, originating at Peterborough, ran northbound along the coast line, returning via the Settle & Carlisle route. Such is the current popularity of the line that a UK Railtours excursion on 15 May 2007 quickly sold out, and a second working operated on 17 May. Both trains started from Euston, running down the West Coast main line to Carlisle, before attaching a Class 67 locomotive for the trip along the coast line to Carnforth.

Whitehaven was the last place in Britain to suffer a foreign invasion when, in April 1778, Lieutenant John Paul Jones sailed in from America and stormed the small fort on the Half Moon Battery. He was not a welcome visitor. Today, however, Whitehaven would be delighted to see new 'invaders', arriving not by sea but aboard air-conditioned railtours, and enjoying the many places of interest that this ancient Cumbrian seaport has to offer.

Let the final word rest with Norman Nicholson, the best-known Cumbrian poet and writer of the late twentieth century. Writing in 1969, about a train journey between Whitehaven and Workington, he admirably summed up the atmosphere of this section of the Cumbrian coast:

> *You pass through a most spectacular region of the industrial picturesque: hollow warehouses like sacked abbeys, roofless pit buildings, deserted coke ovens, old slag heaps as overcrowded with gulls as the stacks of the Farne Islands. It is a curiously unstable landscape, and after a week of heavy rain, the cliffs begin to slither down onto the railway line in a slow, treacly waterfall, delaying the trains and the mail. Here and there you will see slabs and buttresses of new brick let into the side of the cliff to stop the slide. Elsewhere, there are darnings of primroses in the spring, with the metallic gilt of coltsfoot by the lineside, giving way to dusty, miniature rhubarb leaves in the summer when the yellow of the bird's-foot trefoil dolls up the sandstone. And on the other side of the line, the tide siphons its cindery shingle over rocks gangrenous with black and green seaweed or warted with barnacles.*

Postscript - The Cumbrian Coast Line and Whitehaven Today

by Dr Paul Salveson (Head of Community and Regional Strategies, Northern Rail)

THERE IS SOMETHING very special about the railway from Carlisle to Workington, Whitehaven and Barrow. The views from the train are never dull and in parts they are spectacular. The line has an incredibly rich history – both the Maryport and Carlisle and the Furness Railways were amongst the earliest, and longest-lasting, independent railways in the country.

The railway played a dominant role in the industrial development of West Cumberland, enabling the coal, iron and steel industries to take off as major undertakings. In turn, the towns of Whitehaven and neighbouring Workington developed as major urban industrial centres as well as ports.

Like so many other parts of the North, the communities of West Cumberland experienced severe industrial decline in the 1970s and 1980s. The importance of the railway declined, and with it the variety of traffic carried. Although major route closures were limited, the scenic Workington to Penrith route was closed between 1966 and 1972.

The Coast Line, despite serving some relatively unpopulated areas, escaped the Beeching axe. The development of British Nuclear Fuels Ltd. (BNFL) at Sellafield, and the isolation of many small rural communities, ensured its survival.

Today, the line is enjoying a modest renaissance with rising passenger numbers and a greater appreciation of its role in providing a key part of Cumbria's transport network. Commuter trains from Whitehaven into Carlisle are the busiest they have ever been and are often overcrowded. More tourists are visiting the lesser known parts of the Lakes, and the railway offers a means of accessing some beautiful unspoilt landscapes. The link with the Ravenglass and Eskdale Railway allows thousands of visitors to use sustainable transport to get to a superb little railway and an important attraction.

There are some big challenges facing the railway. Firstly, the gradual run-down of BNFL at Sellafield, and the consequent decline in numbers employed there, means that the railway will lose much of what is an important market for the line. This should be seen as an opportunity. The current timetable operated by Northern Rail is heavily constrained by the importance of the Sellafield business. It means that other markets, including commuters and tourists, are less than ideally served.

There is a good opportunity to look at the timetable along the Coast Line afresh, involving all our local stakeholders, including Cumbria County Council, the districts, user groups and local businesses. I hope the Cumbrian Railways Association will be closely involved in this process as well. As we have a limited number of trains, how can we use them to best effect?

As well as the timetable, there are opportunities to look at station improvements. This is our second biggest challenge, and partnership with the local authorities is critical. The current station facilities at Whitehaven, as well as at Workington and Maryport, are not appropriate for today's travellers. They expect good quality facilities, staff, and a welcoming, safe and accessible environment with good parking and interchange facilities. We are working with Network Rail and Cumbria County Council on schemes which will make a real difference to the bigger stations along the line.

For the smaller stations, the role of the community is crucial - our third challenge. Cumbria County Council has recently appointed a Rail Officer. His role, amongst other things, will be to develop partnerships with the local communities along the line. The approach of community rail partnerships has worked well in many parts of the country. This will include more effective marketing of the line and production of line guides and other publicity. It will also involve working with village communities to develop 'station partnerships' which make the station a welcoming gateway into the rural communities of West Cumbria.

Some excellent work has already been done, for example with St Bees School which has adopted the station. Dalston has a lively 'station friends' group, which brings tender loving care to the station. Other village communities, such as Green Road, are also involved in supporting their station. The Rail Officer, working with ourselves at Northern Rail, will be able to give more support to these groups and identify new, small-scale projects which will enhance the appearance and usage of these stations.

The fourth challenge is linking the railway with business activity. The railway is not isolated from the local economy: it is an important part of it. As the economy of West Cumbria changes and develops, the role of the railway will change. 'Sustainable development' is no longer a fringe interest – it is at the heart of strategies for regenerating areas which have experienced decline of traditional industries. Rail offers a real alternative to the car for longer-distance journeys. It should not be seen as a lifeline for Cumbria so much as a catalyst for new development, bringing people into the area as well as providing a means to access other parts of the UK.

Our fifth and final challenge is transport integration. If railways cannot be isolated from the economy, they certainly cannot be isolated from other forms of transport. In more rural areas many people want to drive to the station and leave their cars in safety. We need to ensure station car parks are both big enough and secure enough to tempt motorists to use the train for the longer part of their journey.

We also need to make sure stations are easily accessible by foot and bike. Our new Cycling Strategy lays the basis to develop safe and pleasant cycling links to and from our stations, with good cycle facilities at the station.

The railway is, by its nature, linear and hugs the coast. The lines to places like Cockermouth, Keswick, Penrith, Cleator Moor and Egremont have long gone, and I very much doubt if any will come back. Developing strong links with local bus services to these and other places offers a means of connecting communities to the rail network. We need to develop more partnerships with bus operators and the County Council to create a much more integrated transport network.

The Cumbrian Coast Line has a very positive future to look forward to. It has lots of natural advantages, not least its scenery and also its ability to offer a fast commuting link into Carlisle. It has two other great advantages which should not be under-estimated. The first one is its employees, including those of Northern Rail, Network Rail, Direct Rail Services and contractors such as ISS. They are totally dedicated to their railway. Many are enthusiasts for the railway and are members of the CRA. There really is still a very recognizable railway community in West Cumbria, and long may it survive and flourish.

The other great advantage is the support the line enjoys from the community, including the County and District Councils, and also user groups like Copeland Rail Users Group and Furness Line Action Group, station adopters and bodies like the CRA who recognize that the railway is not only of great historical importance to West Cumbria, but is also of enormous value to the communities it serves today.

Chronology of the Railways and Town of Whitehaven

Notes
a. Entries in **_bold italics_** are railway-related events.
b. Entries in ordinary type are town- and industry-related events.
c. Entries in *italics* are Lowther family-related events.

1120: William Meschin founds the Priory of St Bees.
c1120: Priory records define boundaries of township of Whitehaven.
1172: Whitehaven provides shipping to accompany Henry II to Ireland.
c1272: Reference in Priory records to coal extraction at Arrowthwaite.
1553: Sir Thomas Chaloner, Lord of the Manor of St Bees, grants rights 'for the purpose of digging coal'.
1630: *Sir John Lowther of Lowther (1581-1637) takes over the estate of St Bees and Whitehaven.*
1634: Sir Christopher Lowther (1611-1644) builds a pier at Whitehaven, to handle coal trade with Dublin.
1637: *Sir Christopher Lowther succeeds to the Whitehaven estate.*
1644: *Sir John Lowther (1642-1706) inherits the Whitehaven estate as an infant.*
1663: Sir John Lowther drives a level from the Pow Beck into the Bannock seam.
1675: Sir John Lowther buys the Whitehaven mansion known as The Flatt.
1675: First load of tobacco from Virginia landed at Whitehaven.
1683: **_Wooden 'causeway' built, linking Woodagreen Pit to the harbour._**
1685: Whitehaven becomes a Customs port, responsible for the coast between Ravenglass and Ellenfoot (later Maryport).
1695: Sir John Lowther plans the new town of Whitehaven, between the Pow Beck and The Flatt.
1706: *Sir James Lowther (1673-1755) inherits the Whitehaven estate, his elder brother Christopher having been disinherited.*
1708: Whitehaven Town and Harbour Trustees established by Act of Parliament.
1717: Sir James Lowther and John Spedding erect first steam pumping engine in Cumberland at The Ginns, using Newcomen patent.
1725: Daniel Defoe writes that Whitehaven is 'now the most eminent port of England for the shipping of coals' (after Newcastle and Sunderland).
1730: Carlisle Spedding appointed as Manager of the Whitehaven Collieries.
1730: Carlisle Spedding begins work on the world's first undersea pit at Saltom.
1735: **_Saltom waggonway completed from Ravenhill shaft to Whitehaven Harbour._**
1738: **_Parker waggonway completed to Parker Pit, on Monkwray Brow._**
1754: **_Whingill waggonway completed between Harras Moor and Bransty Row staithes._**
1755: *Sir James Lowther dies childless, bequeathing the Whitehaven estate to Sir William Lowther of Holker (1727-1756).*
1755: Carlisle Spedding dies in pit explosion.
1756: *Sir James Lowther of Maulds Meaburn (1736-1802) inherits the estate. Created the Earl of Lonsdale in 1784, but dies childless, the earldom becoming extinct.*
1762: Whitehaven's population reaches 9,063.
1766: Work starts on North Wall of the harbour.
1769: Sir James Lowther rebuilds The Flatt as Whitehaven Castle.
1774: **_Extension of Saltom waggonway to Croft Pit._**
1778: John Paul Jones storms the Half Moon Battery, from ships of the American Congressional Navy.
1791: Davy Pit installs Whitehaven's first steam-powered winding gear.
1802: *Sir William Lowther of Swillington (1758-1844) inherits the Whitehaven estate. Created the Earl of Lonsdale in 1807.*
1803: **_Opening of Bransty Arch, giving Whingill waggonway direct access to the harbour._**
1806: William Pit ships its first coal.
1811: John Peile succeeds John Bateman as Lord Lonsdale's Colliery Agent.
1813: **_Completion of rebuilding Whitehaven Colliery waggonways with iron rails._**
1813: **_Construction of Howgill Incline, linking Saltom waggonway with coal staithes at the harbour._**
1817: **_Steam locomotive trials between Croft Pit and Ravenhill Junction._**
1824: **_Whaite Field Quarry incline completed, to transport stone to New West Pier site._**
1830: New West Pier of the harbour is completed.
1836: **_Parton waggonway, linking Whitehaven Harbour to Countess Pit, is fully opened._**
1838: John Peile begins sinking the Wellington Pit.
1844: *William, 2nd Earl of Lonsdale (1776-1872), inherits the Whitehaven estate upon the death of his father.*
1845: Wellington Pit completed.
1845: **_Maryport & Carlisle Railway opened throughout._**
1847: **_Whitehaven Junction Railway fully opened, from Maryport to Whitehaven Bransty._**
1848: **_Furness Railway opens northward extension from Kirkby-in-Furness to Broughton-in-Furness._**
1850: **_Whitehaven & Furness Junction Railway fully opened from Whitehaven Preston Street to Broughton-in-Furness._**
1852: **_Whitehaven Tunnel opened by W&FJR, which now makes a junction with the WJR at Bransty._**
1854: **_W&FJR opens street tramway between Preston Street and the Customhouse Quay._**
1854: **_Formation of Joint WJR/W&FJR Committee, to operate pooled locomotive stock of both companies._**
1855: **_Joint Committee concentrates passenger facilities at Bransty and freight at Preston Street, and opens Corkickle Station._**
1855: John Peile dies at the age of 79.
1857: **_Whitehaven, Cleator & Egremont Railway opened to all traffic between Whitehaven, Egremont and Frizington._**
1866: **_WC&ER extended to Marron Junction, on Cockermouth & Workington Rly._**
1866: **_LNWR purchases the WJR and the Cockermouth & Workington Rly._**
1866: **_Furness Railway purchases the WFJR._**
1867: **_Royal Mail rail service between Whitehaven, Ulverston and Carnforth._**
1869: **_Cleator & Furness Railway Committee's line opens between Egremont and Sellafield._**
1871: **_Most likely date of conversion of Parton waggonway to standard gauge._**
1872: *Henry, 3rd Earl of Lonsdale (1818-1876), inherits the title and the Whitehaven estate from his uncle.*
1872: Lonsdale Hematite Iron & Steel Co. Ltd. commissions Whitehaven furnaces.
1874: **_Expanded Bransty station opens, with new FR platform._**
1876: *St George Henry, 4th Earl of Lonsdale (1855-1882), inherits the Whitehaven estate.*
1876: The non-tidal Queen's Dock is opened.

97

1877:	**Completion of the Harbour Commissioners' Railway, connecting the LNWR and the FR harbour networks.**	1935:	**LMS approves total re-lining of Whitehaven Tunnel.**
1878:	**LNWR and FR jointly acquire the WC&ER, now controlled through the North Western & Furness Joint Committee.**	1937:	Mining resumes, following the formation of the Cumberland Coal Company (Whitehaven) Ltd.
1879:	**Cleator & Workington Junction Railway opened to freight traffic between Cleator Moor Jct. and Siddick Jct., north of Workington, and to passengers between Cleator Moor Jct. and Workington Central.**	1940:	Marchon Products Ltd. sets up in Hensingham.
		1943:	Marchon Products Ltd. moves to Kells.
		1944:	*Lancelot Edward, 6th Earl of Lonsdale (1867-1953), inherits the title upon the death of his brother.*
1879:	Blast furnaces opened at Distington.	1947:	UK coal industry nationalised, controlled by the National Coal Board.
1879:	**WC&ER opens Gilgarran Branch between Ullock (on the Marron extension) and Parton.**	1948:	**LMS becomes part of the nationalised British Railways.**
1881:	**Construction of Corkickle Brake (incline), linking FR at Corkickle to Croft Pit.**	1949:	Beacon Mills sold to Quaker Oats Ltd.
1882:	*Hugh Cecil, 5th Earl of Lonsdale (1857-1944) inherits the title and the Whitehaven estate from his brother.*	1953:	*James Hugh William, 7th Earl of Lonsdale (1922-2006), inherits the title upon the death of his grandfather.*
1888:	Direct Lowther control of the Whitehaven Collieries ends, with their lease to the Whitehaven Colliery Co., controlled by the Bain family.	1953:	**Re-instatement of workmen's service between Moor Row and Sellafield.**
		1954:	William Pit ceases production.
1889:	Shipbuilding ceases at Whitehaven, with the closure of the Whitehaven Shipbuilding Co. Ltd.	1955:	**Diesel multiple units introduced between Carlisle and Whitehaven.**
1899:	Whitehaven's population reaches 19,370.	1955:	**Corkickle Brake re-opens, to serve Kells site of Marchon Products.**
1901:	Ship repairing ceases at Whitehaven.		
1903:	Croft Pit ceases to draw coal, being replaced by new shaft at the adjacent Ladysmith Pit.	1955:	Marchon Products Ltd. taken over by Albright & Wilson.
1907:	Beacon Mills (flour production) built on former ship repair yard site.	1958:	**Re-lining of Whitehaven Tunnel completed.**
		1963:	**Proposed new line (not built) from St Bees to Marchon Products.**
1914:	Whitehaven Colliery Co. begins sinking Haig Pit.	1965:	**Withdrawal of workmen's service between Moor Row and Sellafield.**
1918:	Haig Pit in full production.		
1923:	**FR, LNWR, C&WJR and M&CR all become part of the London Midland & Scottish Railway.**	1966:	**Through coaches from Whitehaven to London (Euston) and Manchester withdrawn.**
1924:	**Opening of new Howgill Incline, giving direct access to West Strand quay.**	1972:	**Howgill Incline closes, following landslide during miners' strike.**
1924:	Commissioning of new coal loading plant on Dock Quay of Queen's Dock.	1976:	**Sunday passenger services south of Whitehaven withdrawn.**
1929:	**Closure of Gilgarran branch between Ullock Junction and Distington Ironworks.**	1982:	Final Irish coal shipment from Queen's Dock.
		1984:	Coal production ceases at Haig Pit.
1931:	Ladysmith Pit closes, but washery remains open.	1985:	**Closure of harbour rail network, after final movement of rail-borne coal.**
1931:	**Corkickle Brake abandoned, following Ladysmith Pit closure.**		
1931:	**Withdrawal of passenger services between Moor Row and Siddick Junction and between Moor Row and Marron Junction.**	1986:	**Corkickle Brake closes, following introduction of more modern wagons.**
		1991:	**Withdrawal of Whitehaven–Huddersfield Travelling Post Office.**
1932:	Wellington Pit closes, after nearly a century in production.	1994:	**Final closure of Preston Street freight yard.**
1932:	**Closure of Gilgarran branch between Parton (Bain's No. 4 Pit) and Distington Junction.**	1997:	**Track rationalisation results in new single-track section between Bransty No. 2 and St Bees.**
1933:	Whitehaven Colliery Co. goes into liquidation, and is succeeded by Priestman (Whitehaven) Collieries Ltd.	2000:	Former Albright & Wilson (Marchon) plant sold to Rhone Poulenc.
1935:	Priestman ceases trading, and all pits in the Whitehaven Colliery are closed.	2006:	Final decommissioning and demolition of the former Marchon plant.
1935:	**Withdrawal of passenger services between Moor Row, Egremont and Sellafield.**	2006:	*Hugh Clayton, 8th Earl of Lonsdale (1949-), inherits the title upon the death of his father.*

Acknowledgements

A book covering an area as complex as Whitehaven requires the support and assistance of many people and organisations, and I should like to record my great appreciation to those listed below and to apologise in advance for any names inadvertently omitted.

First and foremost, my most hearty thanks must go to Dr Michael Andrews and to Norman Gray, who have unfailingly met all my requests for information and documentation. It has not been easy to deal with an area three hundred miles from home, and additional thanks go to Norman for his numerous visits to the Cumbria Record Office in Scotch Street, Whitehaven, on my behalf. I should also like to record my appreciation of the courtesy and patience of the staff of this Record Office in supporting my research activities.

I should also like to thank Michael Moon for his permission to use reproductions of John Howard's and John Wood's maps of Whitehaven in this publication. These useful reproductions are available from:

Michael Moon's Bookshop, 19 Lowther Street, Whitehaven, Cumbria, CA28 7AL

Michael has provided much encouragement in the writing of this publication, and readers are recommended to visit his excellent premises when in Whitehaven.

Russell Wear is a well-known author on industrial railway systems, and has provided much information on the mineral lines in and around Whitehaven. With his permission, I have made much use of his articles on the Corkickle Brake (published in *The Industrial Railway Record*, No. 111, December 1987) and on Whitehaven collieries and locomotives (published in *Cumbrian Railways*, Vol. 6, No. 7, August 1998).

Thanks are due to Tom Heavyside, the well-known Northern railway photographer, for an excellent selection of Whitehaven locations, both BR and industrial, and to Michael Andrews for allowing me to use images from the collection of the late Alan Pearsall. (The Pearsall collection is now part of the CRA Photographic Library.)

Peter Robinson has kindly provided me with photographs from his own collection, as well as extracting Whitehaven-related images from the Cumbrian Railways Association archive.

Dave McAlone, whose work has been widely published in the leading railway journals, has provided an excellent selection of modern images, as well as clarifying the final activities at Preston Street yard.

Other acknowledgements must be made to Allan Beck, for information on signalling and for providing photographs; to Albyn Austin, for allowing me to see the 1845 'Crossing Agreement' between the Whitehaven Junction Railway and the Earl of Lonsdale; to Chris Lowther, for drawing our attention to the existence of his copies of the Lowther Plans in the Record Office in Whitehaven; to Stan Buck, for his fine collection of industrial steam photographs; and to the late Wyn Anderson, for useful notes on the Carnforth & Whitehaven TPO, and to Terry Powell, for the image of the electric coal loading plant.

Finally, my thanks to J D Sankey for permission to publish a number of excellent photographs of Whitehaven from the well-known collection of Edward Sankey.

Publications of the Cumbrian Railways Association are produced by the Publications Subcommittee: Mike Peascod (Chairman), Rock Battye, Les Gilpin and Alan Johnstone.

Bibliography

Books
Allen, D & Woolstenholmes, C J: *A Pictorial Survey of London Midland Signalling* (Oxford Publishing Co., 1996, ISBN 0 86093 523 X)
Barnett, W & Winskell, C: *A Study in Conservation* (Oriel Press, 1977, ISBN 0 85362 172 1)
Brunskill, R W: *Traditional Buildings of Cumbria – the County of the Lakes* (Cassell, 2002, ISBN 0 304 35773 1)
Cole, D: *British Locomotive Builders' Works Lists – No. 1: Fletcher, Jennings* (Union Publications, 1965)
Crosland, J B: *Looking at Whitehaven* (Whitehaven Borough Council, 1971, ISBN 0 9500003 1 0)
Davies-Shiel, M & Marshall, J D: *Industrial Archaeology of the Lake Counties* (David & Charles, 1969, ISBN 7153 4695 4)
Devlin, R & Fancy, H: *The Most Dangerous Pit in the Kingdom* (Hills Books, 1997, ISBN 0 95268 142 0)
Dixon, J: *An Account of the Coal Mines near Whitehaven* (1801)
Gradon, W M: *Furness Railway: Its Rise and Development, 1846-1923* (Altrincham, 1946)
Gradon, W M: *The Track of the Ironmasters* (Altrincham, 1952)
Hawkins, C & Reeve, G: *LMS Engine Sheds, Vol 4, The Smaller English Constituents* (Wild Swan Publications, 1984, ISBN 0 906867 20 7)
Hay, D: *Whitehaven: A Short History* (Whitehaven Borough Council, 1968)
Joy, D: *A Regional History of the Railways of Great Britain: Vol XIV, The Lake Counties* (David & Charles, 1983, ISBN 0 946537 02 X)
Joy, D: *Cumbrian Coast Railways* (Dalesman, 1968)
Kelly, D: *The Red Hills* (Red Earth Publications, 1994, ISBN 0 9512946 7 9)
Lancaster, J Y & Wattleworth, D R: *The Iron and Steel Industry of West Cumberland – An Historical Survey* (British Steel Corporation, 1977, ISBN 0 950929 0 0)
Lewis, M J T: *Early Wooden Railways* (Routledge & Keegan Paul, 1970, ISBN 0 7100 7818 8)
Linton, J: *A Handbook of the Whitehaven and Furness Junction Railway* (Whittaker & Co., 1852)
Manns, E: *Carrying Coals to Dunston – Coal and the Railway* (Oakwood Press, 2000, ISBN 0 85361 560 8)
Marshall, J D: *Old Lakeland: Some Cumbrian Social History* (David & Charles, 1971, ISBN 0 7153 5432 9)
Melville, J & Hobbs, J L: *Early Railway History in Furness* (Cumberland & Westmorland Antiquarian & Archaeological Society, Tract Series XIII, 1951)
Nicholson, N: *Greater Lakeland* (Robert Hale, 1969, ISBN 0 7090 5813 6)
von Oeynhausen, C & von Dechen, H: *Railways in England, 1826 and 1827* (W Heffer & Sons, for the Newcomen Society, 1971 translation, 0 85270 048 2)
Pevsner, N: *The Buildings of England: Cumberland and Westmorland* (Penguin, 1967, ISBN 0 1407 1033 7)
Pigot & Co.: *Pigot & Co.'s National Commercial Directory for 1828-29: Cumberland, Lancashire & Westmorland* (facsimile edition, Michael Winton, Norwich, 1995, ISBN 1 898593 12 4)
Powell, T: *Staith to Conveyor* (Chilton Ironworks, 2000, ISBN 0 9523 6725 4)
Quick, M E: *Railway Passenger Stations in England, Scotland and Wales – A Chronology* (Railway & Canal Historical Society, 2002)
Robinson, P W: *Cumbria's Lost Railways* (Stenlake, 2002, ISBN 1 84033 205 0)
Rollinson, W: *A History of Cumberland & Westmorland* (Phillimore & Co., 1978, ISBN 0 85033 315 6)
Routledge, A W: *History & Guide: Whitehaven* (Tempus Publishing, 2002, ISBN 0 7524 2602 8)
Rush, R W: *The Furness Railway* (Oakwood Press, 1973)
Scott-Hindson, B: *Whitehaven Harbour* (Phillimore & Co., 1994, ISBN 0 85033 917 0)
Simmons, J: *The Maryport & Carlisle Railway* (Oakwood Press, 1947)
Thomas, D St J (intr): *Bradshaw's August 1887 Railway Guide* (David & Charles, 1968, ISBN 7153 4325 4)
Thomas, D St J (intr): *Bradshaw's April 1910 Railway Guide* (Augustus M Kelley, 1968, ISBN 7153 4246 0)
Thomas, D St J (intr): *Bradshaw's July 1922 Railway Guide* (Book Club Associates, 1985)
Thomas, D St J (intr): *Bradshaw's July 1938 Railway Guide* (David & Charles, 1969, ISBN 7153 4686 5)
Thomas, D St J: *Lake District Transport Report* (David & Charles, 1961)
Wainwright, A: *A Coast to Coast Walk – St Bees Head to Robin Hood's Bay* (Westmorland Gazette, 1973)
Wood, O: *West Cumberland Coal: 1600-1982/3* (Cumberland & Westmorland Antiquarian & Archaeological Society, 1988, ISBN 0 9500779 5 X)

Articles and Papers
Unknown: *Industrial Plan for West Cumberland* (published in *Colliery Engineer*, Dec 1944)
Unknown: *The Renaissance of the North Western (Settle Jct to Wennington services)* (published in *Traction* magazine September 2005)
Wear, R & Holmes, P: *Whitehaven Harbour* (published in *The Industrial Locomotive* Vol 6, No. 64, Industrial Locomotive Society, 1992)
Williams, J E: *Whitehaven Harbour and Dock Works* (paper presented to the Institution of Mechanical Engineers, 1878)
Winding, P: *Traffic Divisions of British Railways – No. 5 Barrow* (published in *Modern Railways*, Oct/Nov 1965, Ian Allan)

Maps
British Rail Track Diagrams 4 – London Midland Region (ed. Gerald Jacobs) (Quail Map Company, 1990, ISBN 0 900609 74 5)
British Rail Track Diagrams 4 – Midlands & North West (ed. Gerald Jacobs) (Trackmaps, 2005, ISBN 0 9549866 0 1)
National Atlas showing Canals, Navigable Rivers, Mineral Tramroads, Railways and Street Tramways, Vol. 2L Cumberland (G L Crowther, privately published, no date)
Ordnance Survey of England and Wales, 1 inch to 1 mile, Cockermouth & Whitehaven, First Edition (Sheet 101), 08/1867 (facsimile reprint, David & Charles, 1971, ISBN 0 7153 5071 4)
Ordnance Survey of England and Wales, 1 inch to 1 mile, Keswick (Sheet 82, Seventh Series), revised 1951

Timetables
London & North Western Railway Working Timetable, West Cumberland Division, 10/1888 ufn
Furness Railway Working Timetable, 01/07/1891 to 30/09/1891
London & North Western Railway Working Timetable, Lancaster and Carlisle District (West Cumberland Section), 05/1899, facsimile reprint, Dragonwheel Books, 2004, ISBN 1 870177 90 8)
London & North Western & Furness Joint Railway Working Timetable, 14/07/1916 to 30/09/1916
London & North Western Railway Working Timetable, Lancaster and Carlisle District (West Cumberland Section), 15/04/1917 ufn
British Railways (London Midland Region) Timetable, 16/09/1957 to 08/06/1958
British Railways (London Midland Region) Timetable, 12/06/1961 to 10/09/1961
British Railways (London Midland Region) Timetable, 18/06/1962 to 09/09/1962

Index

A
Arrowthwaite Pit   7, 14

B
Bannock Band   8
Barrowmouth Alabaster Works   71
Bransty Arch   22, 23, 73
Bransty Beck   7, 11, 22
Bransty Engine Shed   83, 85
Bransty Quarries   25, 30
Bransty Row Staithes   11, 21, 22
Bransty Signalboxes   73, 75, 92, 93
Bransty Station   30, 31, 33-37, 40, 41, 43, 44, 46, 49, 53, 64, 73, 75, 77-81, 83, 85, 87-93, 95

C
Cleator & Furness Railway Committee   43, 46
Cleator & Workington Junction Railway   44 - 46, 83, 85, 89
Cockermouth & Workington Railway   35, 41, 43, 83
Corkickle Brake   60, 61, 63-66, 71, 92
Corkickle Engine Shed   36, 77, 83, 85
Corkickle Station   37, 39, 40, 43-46, 51, 60, 64, 65, 75, 80, 81, 87, 88, 92, 95
Croft Pit   15, 16, 50, 51, 60, 71
Croft Waggonway and Incline   15, 16, 20, 64, 69, 71, 95

D
Dees, James   33, 35, 36, 39, 43
Duke Pit   14, 15, 20, 50

F
Furness Railway   33-37, 43-46, 53, 57, 60, 73, 75, 77-81, 83, 92

G
Gale, John   8, 10, 13
Gilgarran Branch   45, 46, 78-80
Gilpin, William   9, 10

H
Haig Pit   60, 61, 66, 67, 69, 71, 85, 95
Harbour,
   North Wall   22, 23, 25, 31, 34, 49, 55
   New West Pier   18, 20, 23, 25, 29, 50, 51, 55
   West Strand   20, 49, 50-53, 57, 60, 61, 66, 67, 69, 95
Harbour Commissioners' Railway   49-53, 55, 57, 61, 67, 78
Howgill Colliery   8, 10, 14-16, 18, 21, 50, 51, 60
Howgill Brake   16, 18, 20, 51, 60, 61, 64, 67, 69, 71, 95
Howgill Staithes   16, 18, 23, 49
Howgill Waggonway   15, 21

J
Joint Locomotive Committee (WJR and W&FJR)   30, 35-37, 52, 53, 83, 85
Jellicoe Specials   79

L
Ladysmith Pit   55, 60, 61, 63, 64, 67, 69, 85, 95
London & North Western Railway   36, 43-46, 55, 59, 73, 75, 77-80, 83, 85, 92
London Midland & Scottish Railway   55, 57, 80, 83, 85, 87, 88, 91
Lonsdale Hematite Iron Co.   57, 59
Lonsdale, Henry, 3rd Earl (1818-1876)   44, 46
Lonsdale, Hugh Cecil, 5th Earl (1857-1944)   52, 60
Lonsdale, William, 2nd Earl (1776-1872)   27, 30, 31, 33-35, 37, 39, 40, 50, 57
Lowther, Sir Christopher (1611-1644)   7, 8
Lowther, Sir James (1673-1755)   9, 10, 14
Lowther, Sir John (1642-1706)   8-10, 13
Lowther, Sir William, Earl of Lonsdale (1758-1844)   16, 29

M
Marchon Products (Albright & Wilson)   60, 61, 63-66, 89, 91
Marron Junction   41, 46, 73, 77, 78, 80, 81, 85, 89
Maryport & Carlisle Railway   29 - 31, 79, 80, 87
Market Place (Preston St) Tramway   34, 35, 39, 49, 53, 57, 75
Mirehouse Junction   39-41, 75, 77, 79, 85, 87
Moor Row   39-41, 45, 46, 73, 77, 79 - 81, 85, 87, 89, 92

N
National Coal Board (NCB)   53, 55, 61, 63, 64, 69, 71
Newcomen, Thomas   10

P
Parker Waggonway   13-15
Parton Waggonway   23, 25, 27, 31, 57, 59, 60, 92
Patent Slip   49, 55
Peile, John   16, 18, 20, 25, 29-31
Pow Beck   7, 55
Preston Street Station/Goods Depot   33-37, 39, 43, 45, 57, 65, 75, 77-79, 83, 85, 92, 93

R
Ravenhill Pit   10, 15
Ravenhill Quarry   20
Rennie, John and Sir John   18, 20, 23, 29

S
St Bees   7, 10, 33, 39, 60, 64, 71, 77, 83, 87, 88, 93
St James's Church   9, 21
Sandwith Quarries Railway   71
Saltom Pit   10, 15, 50
Saltom Waggonway   10, 14-16, 20, 21, 95
Spedding, Carlisle   9-11, 14, 15, 21-23
Spedding, John   10, 15
Stephenson, George   29-31, 33
Swainson, Taylor   16

T
Town & Harbour Trustees   9, 10, 18, 20, 29-31, 39, 49-53, 57, 60
Travelling Post Office   75, 77, 78, 88, 90, 91
Tulk & Ley/Fletcher, Jennings   29, 30, 35, 36, 40, 49, 53, 55
Tunnel Engine, Whitehaven   40, 43, 44, 75, 78, 83

U
Ulverstone & Lancaster Railway   34, 35, 41, 51

W
Wellington Pit   18, 20, 50, 51, 55, 66, 67, 85, 95
Wellington Row   7, 21, 22
West Cumberland Sleeping Car   88, 90
Whaite Field Quarry Incline   18, 20, 23, 25, 51
Whingill Waggonway   11, 21-23
Whitehaven Castle (The Flatt)   7, 9, 21, 33
Whitehaven Colliery Company   52, 55, 60, 67, 71, 85, 86
Whitehaven Tunnel   33-35, 37, 40, 41, 43, 44, 49, 60, 73, 75, 78, 80, 83, 86, 87, 92, 93
William Pit   21, 23, 25, 37, 53, 55, 57, 59, 61, 69, 85, 88, 92
Woodagreen Pit and Causeway   8, 11, 13